324.623
JOH

D0301631

The Men's Share?

UWE BRISTOL
WITHDRAWN
LIBRARY SERVICES

The Men's Share?

Masculinities, Male Support and Women's Suffrage in Britain, 1890–1920

Edited by Angela V. John and Claire Eustance

U.W.E.

− 1 JUN 1998

Library Services

London and New York

First published 1997
by Routledge
11 New Fetter Lane, London EC4P 4EE

Simultaneously published in the USA and Canada
by Routledge
29 West 35th Street, New York, NY 10001

© 1997 In selection and editorial matter Angela V. John and
Claire Eustance. Individual chapters, the contributors

Typeset in Times by
Ponting–Green Publishing Services, Chesham,
Buckinghamshire
Printed and bound in Great Britain by
T.J. International Ltd, Padstow, Cornwall

All rights reserved. No part of this book may be
reprinted or reproduced or utilized in any form or by
any electronic, mechanical, or other means, now known
or hereafter invented, including photocopying and
recording, or in any information storage or retrieval
system, without permission in writing from the
publishers.

British Library Cataloguing in Publication Data
A catalogue record for this book is available from the
British Library

Library of Congress Cataloging in Publication Data
The men's share?: masculinities, male support, and women's
    suffrage in Britain, 1890–1920 / edited by Angela V. John
    and Claire Eustance.
        p.   cm.
    Includes bibliographical references and index
        1. Women–Suffrage–Great Britain–History.   2. Men–
Great Britain–Political activity–History.
        I. John, Angela V.   II. Eustance, Claire
JN979.M45   1997
324.6'23'0941—dc20   96–41555

ISBN   0–415–14001–3 (hbk)

In memory of
SEAN MORTIMER

Contents

List of plates

Notes on contributors

June Balshaw is currently working on a PhD thesis, funded by the British Academy, at the University of Greenwich where she also completed her BA in Humanities and a Masters degree in Historical Studies. She teaches a range of subjects including history and media studies.

Claire Eustance has a BA from Portsmouth Polytechnic and a DPhil from the University of York. She is currently a Research Fellow in the School of Humanities at the University of Greenwich and co-ordinator of the Research Project on Men's Support for Women's Suffrage. She also teaches history and gender studies at Greenwich. Her publications include a chapter in J. Purvis and M. Joannou (eds), *The Women's Suffrage Movement. New Feminist Perspectives*, Manchester, Manchester University Press, forthcoming, and 'Protests from behind the Grille: Gender and the Transformation of Parliament, 1867–1918', for *Parliamentary History*. She is currently working on a book based on her thesis on 'The Evolution of Women's Political Identities in the Women's Freedom League, 1907–1930'.

Sandra Stanley Holton is an Australian Research Council Fellow in the History Department at the University of Adelaide. Her publications include *Feminism and Democracy. Women's Suffrage and Reform Politics in Britain, 1900–1918*, Cambridge, Cambridge University Press, 1986 and a series of articles in *Australian Historical Studies*, *Women's History Review*, *American Historical Review* and *Victorian Studies*. Her most recent book is *Suffrage Days. Stories from the Women's Suffrage Movement*, London, Routledge 1996 and she is currently working on a life of Alice Clark, industrialist, suffragist and pioneering historian of women's work.

Angela V. John is Professor of History at the University of Greenwich and directs the project on Men's Support for Women's Suffrage. She is a founder member of the editorial collective of the journal *Gender & History* and chairs *Llafur*, the Welsh Labour History Society. Her publications include *By the Sweat of Their Brow. Women Workers at Victorian Coal Mines*, London, Croom Helm, 1980, and London, Routledge, 1984; with Revel Guest, *Lady Charlotte. A Biography of the Nineteenth Century*, London, Weidenfeld, 1989; and *Elizabeth Robins. Staging a Life*, London, Routledge, 1995. She edited *Unequal Opportunities. Women's Employment in England 1800–1918*, Oxford, Basil Blackwell, 1986 and *Our Mothers' Land. Chapters in Welsh Women's History 1830–1930*, Cardiff, University of Wales Press, 1991. She is currently investigating women's and men's lives in the context of familial biography.

Carolyn Spring gained her BA from Sheffield Hallam University then undertook a Masters degree at Lancaster University in Women's Studies and Sociology. She jointly organized the international conference 'Seeing Through Suffrage' held by the University of Greenwich at Dartford in April 1996. Her current interests include exploring the language men employed in support of women's suffrage.

Paul Stigant is the Head of the School of Humanities at the University of Greenwich. He was a founding editor of the journal *Literature and History* and has a particular interest in the history of gender and forms of consciousness. He coedited *Popular Fictions. Essays in Literature and History*, London, Methuen, 1986.

John Tosh is Professor of History at the University of North London. His publications include *The Pursuit of History*, London, Longman, 1984 and, with Michael Roper, he coedited *Manful Assertions: Masculinities in Britain since 1880*, London, Routledge, 1991. He is currently writing a book on men and domesticity in Victorian England.

Laura Ugolini was born in Italy and moved to Britain to attend the University of Wales, Cardiff where she obtained a BA and an MA, later specializing in women's history. She is currently completing a PhD at the University of Greenwich on 'Independent Labour Party Men, 1891–1914'.

Foreword: Whose history?

From the start it was always the intention that this book would be the product not just of individual research but also of shared debate and discussion. A team of young researchers, under the direction of Angela John, was formed at the University of Greenwich to take the project forward. That research team included Sean Mortimer. His brutal murder meant that the group lost a much valued colleague and friend, and historical research lost a young scholar of immense potential. The power of ideas and their role in the construction of 'reality' fascinated Sean, but if his tragic death meant that he could take his research no further, the research team were determined that his voice should not be silenced. This book is affectionately dedicated to him, and this Foreword contains many of the ideas he discussed and shared with me as the supervisor for his PhD on 'Demasculinizing the Public?: The Challenge to the Political by the Women's Suffrage Movement in Britain'. I have tried here to capture the essence of much of Sean's thinking, and to offer that thinking as an interesting context in which the rest of this book can be read.

The necessity for a struggle over women's suffrage in Britain has, on the whole, received a favourable historical press. This is not surprising. It is difficult to argue in a liberal democratic pluralist society that one half of the population should be (or even should have been when it asked) denied the vote. Moreover, when that vote was won, partially in 1918 and more fully in 1928, it did not bring in its wake any revolutionary change in the political character of British society. Indeed the political dominance of the Conservative Party since 1918 might suggest that in simple party political terms, those who were among some of the strongest opponents of women's suffrage had least to fear from its being gained, whilst the continuing problems women face nearly eighty years on in gaining access to the male bastion of Parliament itself suggests the relative ease men have had in resisting a fairly basic political equality between the sexes.

In one sense this stands in marked contrast to the hostility and violence heaped upon many suffragettes and even suffragists before 1914. This argues for a deeper threat; one that passed beyond a mere alteration to the franchise, one that touched rawer nerves of gender, power and sexual politics. But this contrast between the anger and bitterness of the events themselves and the history that followed may be more apparent than real. It may depend upon within which broad historical 'narrative' we choose to locate the suffrage struggle. Four such 'narratives' immediately suggest themselves.

The most conventional narrative, and the one that explains why the struggle has been so readily accepted as part of our *national* history, is that which places the women's suffrage campaigns in the context of the growth of Britain as a politically democratic society. In this story, full female suffrage by 1928, in addition to universal male suffrage in 1918, are the final major stepping-stones on the road to a true British democracy. As part of this history even militancy can (just) be made acceptable and respectable since, as hindsight has shown, the forces of 'reaction' were resisting and denying a *safe* as well as a legitimate demand. Thus, the struggle for women's suffrage is incorporated into the 'evolutionary' narrative that conventionally explains the historical development of modern British democracy. This may not in itself detract from the more radical aspects of many of the demands that women made, but it does tend to emphasize formal political equality ahead of no less important, but not so easily achieved, claims for social and economic equality.

Interestingly, but not surprisingly, the story of women's suffrage has been located less comfortably in the historical narrative shaped by concepts of class and class struggle. Here for the most part the campaigns for women's suffrage have been pictured as a diversion (and an overwhelmingly middle-class diversion at that) from the forward march of labour. A march that, with some honourable exceptions, was very much undertaken by a male working class. This story-line was challenged in a fundamental way in the late 1970s by Jill Liddington and Jill Norris.[1] And yet the result has been the production of what might be categorized as two types of history: one that seeks to understand the gendered nature of labour and working-class history, the other that, at best, equates gender with women and thus adds an extra 'and women' chapter to its narrative. Moreover, the presentation of the struggle for women's suffrage as a distraction from the mainstream objectives and interests of the working class, raises interesting issues of what constitutes 'radical' activity, and touches the sensitive relationship of class and gender. Thus, just as the first narrative can include the women's suffrage struggle by essentially ignoring the centrality of gender, so this narrative has effectively to exclude women's suffrage in order to avoid the painful problems of class, gender and radical politics.

The keyword in the third narrative is 'crisis'. This locates the struggle for women's suffrage, and, rightly, feminism more generally, within what is seen as a major crisis of the British state and society in the late nineteenth and early twentieth centuries. There is more to this historical explanation than simply George Dangerfield's pioneering, yet misogynist, book *The Strange Death of Liberal England*.[2] But essentially women's suffrage and feminism (or broadly the politics of gender) become ingredients in a heady mix of forces and events that converge to produce a major structural and ideological transformation of the British state and civil society. It is a very different story from the first two for, whereas they stress the struggle for women's suffrage as part of an evolutionary history, the crucial feature of 'crisis' is *discontinuity*. In this respect feminism and women's suffrage play a vital role in the fragmentation and disintegration of the mid-Victorian state and civil society. Moreover, the vitality of that role goes some way towards explaining the contemporary hostility and anger directed at the women's movement.

A narrative of crisis is useful in other respects. First, it stresses that the breakup of the mid-Victorian consensus is about more than structures and organizations. It is also about *ideas*. Hence, not only do the campaigns for women's suffrage help to change the very idea of what constitutes the 'political nation', but being part of a wider women's movement they are also central to the disintegration and reformation of ideas around the 'public and private'. Second, an emphasis on the importance of ideological forces points to a loss of intellectual confidence and certainty. The significance of this, it can be argued, is that the loss of intellectual control, which can be seen as a key characteristic of masculinity, becomes as potent a force in the politics of gender as the challenge to male political and social authority. Third, a narrative of crisis allows for a strong element of autonomy for the constituent parts that make up the totality of forces feeding the crisis. Thus, the politics of gender can be given as important an explanatory role as the politics of class or the politics of party in an analysis of historical change.

In the fourth narrative the struggle for women's suffrage holds a special place. Feminist History has enabled the development of a historical narrative that can stress, among much else, difference and conflict, oppression and subordination, not determined solely by the grand explanatory device of class. In a narrative that directs attention to other, often ignored, forms of stratification and tension, any moment when those divisions are challenged in fundamental and public ways can expect to be privileged. The focus, of course, as with the overwhelmingly masculine narrative of class, is one of conflict and struggle. And this in itself raises interesting questions about the foregrounding of a moment in women's history when many women can be seen to be acting most 'like men'. Does it mean, for example, that some men begin to enact a more thorough role reversal and to behave more 'like women'? To what extent, in other words, is there embedded within stories of conflicts initiated by women another set of narratives about men that involve negotiation and compromise, hesitant comprehension and uncertain understanding, partnership and support?

The question 'whose history?' can also be approached from another direction. This book took as its problematic that the analysis of gender is crucial to an understanding of historical change. It also began with the premise that the writing of history has much to gain from collective research and discussion. It was, conspicuously, a book about men and masculinity written for the most part by women. From the start this was an issue to which the research group was sensitive and Sean's murder, which in itself confronted us with one violent and vicious aspect of masculinity, left a group of women debating and questioning more than ever before, their 'qualifications' to write about masculinity in all its complex and varying forms. It was no answer to that questioning to reflect that few male historians appear to have the same problem in reverse. It was a questioning that certainly brought to mind E. H. Carr's directive, laid down over thirty years ago in *What Is History?*: 'Before you study the history study the historian.'[3]

History is a social construct produced in a particular time and place. Does it, should it, affect the quality of the history written here that, for the most part, it is by women about men? Perhaps Edward

Thompson, as part of another debate which occurred in the late 1970s, provides one answer:

> A feminist will say, or ought to say, that this history book is wrong, not because it was written by a man, but because the historian neglected contiguous evidence or proposed conceptually inadequate questions: hence a masculine 'meaning' or bias was imposed upon the answers.[4]

Two immediate thoughts flow from this that are pertinent to this book. If we believe that an analysis of gender is crucial to an understanding of historical change, and we believe, along with Carr, that no historian stands outside time and place, is it really legitimate to regard the category 'historian' as gender-free? The question will be, for historians of gender, familiar and rhetorical. What needs to be asked is how far a wider historical establishment has yet accepted any such connection – or problem?

The second is Thompson's use of the concept 'masculine "meaning"'. Feminine 'meaning' might be thought to derive from theories peculiar to feminism, or from particular 'readings' of women's history. But what theories might there be peculiar to masculinism, or to 'readings' of men's history? The very way the word 'masculinism' jars, not to mention the thought of a separate branch of history for men, suggests some of the very real theoretical and conceptual problems encountered in writing a history book about men and masculinity. Moreover, once the concrete object of study becomes the struggle for women's suffrage, and a central concept is the notion of 'male *support*', we potentially enter very unfamiliar territory. It is not common in most history-writing to encounter men in what might be thought of as relatively passive, and certainly secondary, roles. Perhaps in this respect, if no other, it is appropriate that a group of female historians should be mainly responsible for this book.

It could be argued, however, that this book is exploring a fairly unique moment in the historical relationship between women and men, and that such moments have few long-term consequences. But how do we know? Unlike the story of our political democracy, there is no accepted narrative or chronology of gender relations for twentieth-century Britain, and certainly men as a consciously conceived entity have remained (for the most part) 'hidden from history'. It is difficult to know, therefore, what story or whose story this book is telling; or, perhaps more grandly, of what meta-narrative it is a part.

This is important. Or, at least, it is important if the purpose of writing history is to better understand our own present and act upon it. Stuart Hall and Bill Schwarz argued in 1985 that 'the significance of the 1880s–1920s . . . is that although its epochal character is not so well established or studied, it is, nevertheless, the period most immediately formative *for us*'.[5] Their interest was the genesis of the crisis in late twentieth-century social democracy. That 'crisis', it has to be admitted, includes public concern, fear and debate about male roles and identity, and, by implication, gender relations more generally. This is not to argue for some simple causal link or comparison between the 1880s–1920s and now, but it is to suggest that many of the questions asked then of men, as men, have not been fully raised let alone comfortably resolved. Moreover, how they were addressed and 'contained' has informed our present. What stands out in the period of the 1880s–1920s is that the challenge to male roles and identity came from women, and it was a challenge mounted in the context of a series of 'crises' that included British imperialism, political authority and state power.

This book is a contribution to research on the transformation of men, concepts of masculinity and male identities between 1890 and 1920. Further research is clearly needed on how thoroughgoing that transformation may, or may not, have been. It is clear, however, that women taking the lead, setting agendas and determining tactics was a significant aspect of *a* transformation in gender identities. Men may have learnt during this period how to contain that transformation so that fundamental changes in gender relations were avoided. But it was a matter of *containing* change, not stopping it altogether. There is much evidence in this book of even the male supporters of women's suffrage desperately seeking to bring events and ideas within their terms of reference, within their ideological universe. But containment of necessity requires negotiation, compromises and concession. It is something wrought with ambiguities and paradoxes and it can create some strange political and social alliances.

A history of gender relations is not easy to write for all too often it crosses the conventional wires of history, and can upset some comforting 'truths'. It is not a history essentially conceived through great set pieces: no wars, no general strikes, no mass popular rebellions. It is a history with few conventional heroines or heroes, few 'great' public figures. A history played out more often than not at the meeting of public and private lives; at the point at which major structural change in society interacts most sensitively with the 'meanings' women and men seek to ascribe to their personal lives. In the late nineteenth and early twentieth centuries, for example, major demographic change, in part the result of a declining birth rate, was in some measure driven by very personal, intimate decisions taken in tens of thousands of middle-class and working-class homes. This book explores another aspect of this interaction between public and private lives, giving a very immediate meaning to the old dictum that 'the personal is political'.

Moreover, though it is a history that hardly excludes struggle, conflict and tension, it is not one that can use such concepts as a central narrative device. 'Containment' is probably no better a term, except that it suggests the historical resilience and survival of male power at one extreme and the constant public and private negotiations around that power at the other. Men's support for women's suffrage may be one specific (though in the context of the fundamental issues the suffrage questions raised, very important) illustration of this point. The wide variations in the nature of the support, from those socialists who would countenance it only as part of their own class-determined agenda to those men prepared to face prison and forcible feeding, suggests the extent to which even 'support' becomes a matter of contested and differing masculinities.

How far those contested and differing masculinities were recognized by men at the time is what this book questions. We also need to ask to what extent the winning of the vote was more symbolic than real in the changing relations between women and men. Formal political equality, once partially established in 1918, took little time to become one of the core principles of liberal democracy. The speed with which a once hotly contested political idea was assimilated into the political and intellectual mainstream, indeed into everyday political 'common sense', might suggest the extent to which in itself it presented few problems to male authority. But at the end of the day, the suffrage campaigns were essentially campaigns of women about the creation of a better society for everyone, and men could choose only to give or not give their support. And yet, of course, the actual granting of the vote was a male prerogative however female the protest. Thus, men had the power as well as the luxury of support or opposition. Perhaps this was one of the points at which the containment of a genuine and radical change in the relationship between the sexes began?

Paul Stigant

NOTES

1   J. Liddington and J. Norris, *'One Hand Tied Behind Us.'* *The Rise of the Women's Suffrage Movement*, London, Virago Press, 1978.
2   G. Dangerfield, *The Strange Death of Liberal England*, London, MacGibbon & Kee, 1935.
3   E. H. Carr, *What Is History?*, Harmondsworth, Penguin Books, 1978 edition, p. 44.
4   E. P. Thompson, *The Poverty of Theory and other essays*, London, Merlin Press, 1978, p. 233.
5   S. Hall and B. Schwarz, 'State and Society, 1880–1930', in M. Langan and B. Schwarz (eds), *Crises in the British State 1880–1930*, London, Hutchinson, 1985, p. 8 (pp. 7–32).

Acknowledgements

We are grateful to many people for assistance in the preparation of this book and would like to mention in particular Diane Atkinson, Joanne Cayford, Anna Clark, Katharine Cockin, David Doughan, June Hannam, H. Stephen Housman, June Purvis, Peter Searby, Mabel Smith and Mary Worley.

We thank the University of Greenwich for its support for our three-year group research project on men's support for women's suffrage and thank all those who contributed to our regular project seminar held in the School of Humanities where so many of the ideas in this book were first discussed.

We are also grateful to the following for assistance/permission to use material: BBC Written Archives, Caversham; the Backsettown Trust and Fales Library at New York University Library (Elizabeth Robins Papers); the Bodleian Library, Oxford (H. W. Nevinson, Evelyn Sharp and Gilbert Murray Papers); the British Library; Greater London Record Office (Dickinson Papers); the Fawcett Library (Franklin Papers); Harry Ransom Humanities Research Center at the University of Texas at Austin; the Museum of London (Suffragette Fellowship Collection); the National Library of Wales (S. T. Evans Papers); the Public Record Office; the Master and Fellows of Trinity College, Cambridge (Pethick Lawrence Papers); Street Public Library (Housman Papers); and the University of Illinois, Urbana-Champagne and A. P. Watt Ltd on behalf of the Literary Executors of the Estate of H. G. Wells; the British Library for Plates 1, 2, 3, 4, 5 and 7 and the Museum of London for the jacket illustration.

We thank Claire L'Enfant and Heather McCallum and the Routledge team for their support and work.

Abbreviations

CD Acts	Contagious Diseases Acts
DORA	Defence of the Realm Act
ILP	Independent Labour Party
LCC	London County Council
MIAWS	Men's International Alliance for Woman Suffrage
MLWS	Men's League for Women's Suffrage
MPU	Men's Political Union
NMF	Northern Men's Federation
NUWSS	National Union of Women's Suffrage Societies
PEN	Poets, Essayists, Novelists
PSF	People's Suffrage Federation
TUC	Trades Union Congress
US	United Suffragists
WFL	Women's Freedom League
WSPU	Women's Social and Political Union
WWSL	Women Writers' Suffrage League

Shared histories – differing identities

Introducing masculinities, male support and women's suffrage

Angela V. John and Claire Eustance

I

In May 1912 the wealthy barrister Frederick Pethick Lawrence provided a spirited defence of women's suffrage militancy at the Old Bailey, London. He was in the dock. This was published and called 'The Man's Share'. In 1960 the elderly Lord Pethick Lawrence, Labour peer, reworked his pamphlet of nearly half a century earlier, now calling it 'The Men's Share'.[1] Here he presented the struggle for women's suffrage in Britain as a battle for human rights. He paid tribute to the 'ancillary' yet important part played by men who had stood with the women during 'the strenuous years'. He alluded to the moral support of sympathetic fathers, husbands, brothers and sons, the physical violence some men encountered in the streets, their inquisition of Cabinet Ministers, their imprisonment, their sacrifice of positions. As in 1912, he denied that there was a sex war though argued that there might easily have been one had women been left to struggle on their own.

Pethick Lawrence is probably the best-known male supporter of women's suffrage, the exemplar, though, as we shall see, unlike many male activists, he chose to work for (he could not actually be a member of) the Women's Social and Political Union (WSPU) rather than joining an all-male suffrage society. How he sought to rethink his own gentlemanly gestures is the subject of one of the chapters in this book. Here he is viewed as part of the political partnership he shared with Emmeline Pethick Lawrence. His claims and assumptions form a vital part of our project but we are particularly concerned with considering how his and other men's support for women's suffrage aids our understanding of how masculinities are expressed. And recognizing that masculinity/ies must be a relational construct, we see here a valuable opportunity for analysing gender relations in the context of a well-known historical movement led by women.

Recently some concern has been voiced about studies of men and masculinity running the risk of subsuming women within a dominant male frame of reference.[2] Such wariness is warranted. After all, History has been about men for so long. Yet it has not tended to be about men qua men. As John Tosh has put it, 'In the historical record it is as though masculinity is everywhere but nowhere'.[3] Moreover, much depends on the starting-point, aim and degree of sensitivity deployed as well as the nature of the subject. If a study develops from and is informed by feminist historical analysis, and is conscious of the need to question how power is developed and maintained, then surely there is little danger of its ultimately subsuming women? There is anyway a problem in reading 'gender' as 'women' since it exculpates men and masculinity from critical examination and somehow suggests that men are gender-free.

By looking at men's relationship to a movement essentially defined and operated by women, but in a society saturated with structural inequality, we can ponder anew the connections between the exercise of power and the construction of masculinities. We can consider how pro-suffrage men navigated their way through situations where they were, unusually, not the ones primarily responsible for taking the initiative, instigating action and getting publicity, though at the same time women and men alike were only too aware that their fate ultimately depended on an élite group of men within Parliament. What effect did being prepared to declare themselves pro-suffrage have on these men and on their sense of worth? How did they cope with the jibes of the 'antis' and could a movement organized by and for women threaten male space and destabilize notions of male protection and authority? And how far did the men not just aim to improve society and alter the position and even meanings of the category 'woman' but also seek to change themselves and rethink their own sense of manhood? These are the sort of questions the contributors to this book seek to provoke, whether through the close reading of a newspaper written by and for those on the left, via analysis of the ideas and actions of individuals and organized groups, or by more synoptic explorations of their formative experiences, their language and ideals.

Men's campaigns for women's rights were the subject of '*Traitors to the Masculine Cause*' (1982) by the American historian Sylvia

Strauss.[4] Here she traced 'male feminists' from the late eighteenth century, linking their views to enlightenment notions concerning progress and civilization, including some consideration of the men who demanded votes for women in Britain and the United States. This provided a valuable recognition of the need to move beyond women's history *per se*. Yet, leaving aside debates about whether men *can* rightly be labelled feminists, her resuscitation of male champions of women's rights results in the occlusion of the women. Male thinkers, albeit largely progressive, replace them though we see less of their political ideas translated into action. This tends to ignore the fact that 'gender always operates in the relationship of one category to the other'.[5] And it is perhaps only with the very recent work on the construction of masculinities by sociologists and historians that truly gendered analyses are becoming possible, the sort of binocular focus that Peter Filene has called 'a dialectical drama of the sexes'.[6]

In her book *White, Male and Middle Class*, Catherine Hall considers notions of competing masculinities in relation to gender and ethnicity via the mid-century case of Governor Eyre in Jamaica.[7] In the process she reveals the similarities and differences between Thomas Carlyle and John Stuart Mill, both public men sharing the 'manly conviction that they could be knowers and doers, teachers and improvers'. She examines their differing notions of what constituted a proper English manhood (though Carlyle was, of course, Scots-born). Carlyle couched his exculpation of Eyre in terms which cast him as a hero: man of action, power and authority. Mill, in contrast, built on a myth of independence which, as we shall see, was dear to the civic humanist tradition. Yet, as Hall observes, despite Mill's egalitarian impulse in *The Subjection of Women*, he 'still falls back on a notion of the natural division of labour between the sexes'.[8]

These two middle-class intellectuals prefigure in some ways the debates over women's suffrage, which in turn reveal competing, yet not always divergent, notions of masculinity. Male opponents of suffrage saw themselves as worthy defenders of a faith, celebrating and demonstrating a tough masculinity that would concede neither authority nor power. They spoke of preserving civilization, the empire, chivalry and the 'natural' order. Yet, as Carolyn Spring's chapter demonstrates, the language of the pro-suffrage man also drew on similar themes though with differing inferences. The latter presented the 'antis' as antediluvian, the 'Hithertos' (to use Israel Zangwill's words) as opposed to the 'Henceforwards'.[9] Pro-suffrage men were concerned about women's needs; not only were there many controversial ways in which suffrage might be endorsed but the extent to which they were actually prepared to confront their own conceptions of masculinity is also open to question. Indeed, the claims of effeminacy by 'antis' – American supporters were taunted as 'Aunt Nancy boys'[10] – provoked some pro-suffrage men into exhibiting what they saw as suitably manful assertions.

Manliness was seen as the civic virtue *par excellence*. It was constantly adapted according to factors such as time, place and class but it is probably best remembered today in its 'muscular Christianity' version associated with the Rev. Charles Kingsley. Stefan Collini has shown how ideals of manliness played a vital role in defining the political attributes and later memorialization of the pro-suffrage political economist and Liberal MP, Henry Fawcett.[11] By the late nineteenth century the neo-Spartan, stoical qualities fostered in the public schools were celebrated, and increasingly significant, too, was the code of imperial manliness.[12] In the eyes of the influential Baden-Powell, the ability to endure physical hardships constituted an essential prerequisite for manliness.[13]

John Tosh's opening chapter discusses the culture of the public schools, which formed an important and somewhat painful part in the shaping of the sensibilities of pro-suffragists such as the writers considered in Angela John's chapter. The manly ideal was frequently tied to a reworked Christian code of knightly conduct and Chapter 3 shows how this influenced the literary suffrage men's sense of responsibility towards women. In Chapter 7, Claire Eustance explores how manly pride could influence pro-suffrage sentiments.

An emphasis on manliness was enhanced in the cosy world of clubland which appealed to both pro- and anti-suffrage men. However, for the latter, it seemed imperative to stress the maintenance of order and discipline. For antis, a manly role meant remaining in charge, permitting no breach of public or sexual authority through challenges such as women seeking the vote.[14]

Jeff Hearn's refreshing reading of the period 1870–1920 has alerted us to the reshaping of masculinities over these years through a spate of laws such as the Married Women's Property Acts 1870 and 1882 and the Punishment of Incest Act 1908 which helped shift the authority of the man as father, private patriarchies being 'rolled back' by public state legislation.[15] This, however, did not fundamentally question the patriarchal structure of domestic relations or conceptions of masculine and feminine but merely readjusted them with possible consequences for how men would view their stake – and that of women – in public life. Against this sort of background, and influenced by the institutions explored by John Tosh, we can consider the men who were active in promoting women's suffrage and so see how they began to confront the realities of public patriarchies.

And what of working-class men? How were their masculine identities shaped during these years? Here again state legislation was important, further protective legislation, for example, influencing men's conception of women's right to waged work and their own sense of familial protection. Working-class men had opportunities to consolidate their public gender identity and influence through trade unions, now reinforced through the TUC and legislation of the 1870s. The continued emphasis on organization at the workplace marginalized many women who worked in other people's homes as servants or in sweated labour in their own homes. The threat of emasculation thought to be posed by the 'invasion' of women clerical workers is but one example of how, through language, ritual and practice, men sought to assert their masculinity in the face of perceived threats. Sonya Rose has demonstrated how, in work and during strikes, male practices helped ensure that women's exclusion from the franchise was reflected in a perception of their role as secondary whilst the ideology of the family wage provided a neat, if unrealistic, corollary to the notion of the middle-class householder elector protecting his wife.[16]

Laura Ugolini's chapter on *The Workman's Times* in the early 1890s examines how, in the context of drumming up support for the principle of independent labour representation immediately prior to the establishment of the Independent Labour Party (ILP), a particular masculine identity was constructed, one which would empower workers yet essentially collapsed the categories of 'working man' and 'workers'. Although readers of the paper supported both the need for some women to work and women's right to the vote, because women were categorized as separate from the central notion of male workers requiring proper representation, their interests were invariably relegated and subordinated to this imperative. More generally the rhetoric of masculine political discourse still treated the working class as male (Keith McClelland's work on the 1867 Reform Act is illuminating in this context)[17] and in style, language and assumptions it was a language of exclusion, women's issues being linked in the public eye with social policy and gender-specific needs as opposed to 'real' political issues.

David H. Morgan has briefly considered men and women's suffrage.[18] Although based on secondary sources, his discussion helpfully situates the movement in the context of a sociological examination of men. He proceeds, as does Christine Bolt in her historical survey of British and American 'feminist ferment',[19] from anti-suffrage men to a brief survey of those in favour. Indeed, it is the 'antis' who are the better known in British history, thanks in large part to Brian Harrison's study of 1978.[20] Yet the biggest and most powerful of the men's pro-suffrage societies, the Men's League for Women's Suffrage (MLWS), was founded in the spring of 1907 and the inaugural meeting of the Women's National Anti-Suffrage League, in part reacting against this, was not held until July 1908. The Men's League for Opposing Women's Suffrage (which would ultimately amalgamate with women antis to create a National League) was not formed until the end of that year, well after the rival whose name it sought to subvert.

Recent studies of women suffragists' attitudes and actions (from the later nineteenth century through to the 1920s) have shown how the suffrage campaign was neither static nor focused solely on the single issue of votes for women.[21] In order to understand something of the pro-suffrage men's attitudes we need to encompass a broader perspective than concentrating only on the years of the most intense activity. This book therefore covers the thirty years from 1890 to 1920 (for the key dates in suffrage developments see Appendix 1). John Tosh who, along with Michael Roper, has done much to make men visible as gendered subjects in History,[22] provides here a discussion of the making of masculinities, examining influences which many pro-suffrage men would have experienced in their youth. His consideration of their socialization encompasses the family, school and bachelor life in the latter part of the nineteenth century. The literary pro-suffrage men considered by Angela John exemplified a number of the more general traits and trends also discussed by Tosh; for example, in their marriage patterns.[23]

The 1890s have recently been associated with a decadent *fin de siècle* culture and a crisis in masculinity (first identified by Michael Kimmel in relation to America).[24] Oscar Wilde's trials of 1895 turned the spotlight on male homosexuality which had been criminalized a decade earlier and publicized in the Cleveland Street homosexual brothel scandal of 1889. The trials helped mark a pointed shift in gender identity as inscribed in language – for example, until then the word 'effeminate' signified a man who spent too much time in the company of women. Post 1895 it assumed its modern meaning and censure.[25] The writings of the sexologists in this same decade categorized relationships as normal or deviant.

Definitions of heterosexuality had already been redrawn by the Contagious Diseases Acts of the 1860s which in turn provided a valuable platform for women protesters. The Acts also aroused hostility from men such as the former moral-force Chartist William Shaen and the MP James Stansfeld,[26] although the figure most associated with Victorian women's rights, John Stuart Mill, objected to any link being made between the cause of repeal (though he did oppose the Acts) and the demand for women's suffrage.[27] Interestingly, in a number of places in South Wales, clergy, outraged by the Acts, chaired early suffrage societies and their views of woman's mission and superior moral function helped shape an essentially incrementalist and cautious approach to women's suffrage.[28]

The formation of men's chastity leagues moved concern from the violation of women's bodies to the problem of male lust. This aggressive form of social purity deployed military metaphors, and by the 1890s the work of Ellice Hopkins in particular resulted in an amalgamated White Cross League and Church of England Purity Society boasting many thousands of members. One of their texts, 'True Manliness', sold over a million copies.[29] In place of maleness connoting a physical expression of male sexuality was a sense that masculinity could be expressed by restraint. Men, however, were, in the main, unresponsive to such arguments. When later Christabel Pankhurst drew attention to 'Chastity for Men', her appeal was not favourably received by the majority of men.

It is important to consider the relationship of masculinity to the winning of the vote by the 1890s, a time when only 59 per cent of the male population over 21 were registered to vote, fuelling considerable debate about priorities and tactics in relation to gender. Whilst the Lockean tradition had asserted the natural right of the individual man, this man was emphatically a head of household. Civic humanists' classical model stressed the primacy of independence, linking this to the economic independence and worth of the middle-class man. In contrast Painite radicalism had drawn on a theoretically egalitarian notion which did not emphasize the citizen as a head of household. Yet not only had Paine himself actually conceived of the citizen as male but, as Anna Clark has shown, working-class radicals, influenced both by the fraternal solidarity of artisan culture and by civic humanism, also equated citizenship with men and, despite some glimpses of wider visions, settled for a 'People's Charter' demanding *manhood* suffrage.[30]

Clark has examined the evolution of gendered notions of the vote in constitutional debate, showing how the claim to vote was part of the construction of the male identity of citizens.[31] The Reform Acts of the nineteenth century show how masculine definitions of the vote impoverished women at the same time as many men were being denied rights. Yet with legislation attaching rights to property rather than persons, women property-holders appeared to have a claim to be represented. Moreover single female householders gained the municipal vote in 1869. Now exposed, however, was the vulnerability of married women who lacked property rights. And the emphasis on the male householder, the 'fathers of families' taking care of their dependants, which lay behind the Second Reform Act of 1867, underscored the link between property and masculinity. That Act also enfranchised a million urban men. Suffragists began demanding that in place of manhood or, rather, a class-based conception of fit manhood, the basis for the vote should be taxation and property – many male suffragists would pick up on the 'no taxation without representation' adage, thus effectively seeking the vote for women on the same terms as men. By 1911 with MPs being remunerated for the first time (one of the points of the 1838 Charter), the professionalism of members was stressed, marking a further division between voters and the unenfranchised.

As Clark recognizes, the independence of the male vote meant the obverse for women, their dependence.[32] So suffragists now challenged the basis of the men's vote, the belief that citizens were synonymous with male heads of households who represented women's interests. The energetic pro-suffragist MP W. H. Dickinson questioned the notion that the vote enriched domestic life.[33] His view was that it was given to men because it admitted the right of the people to a say in the affairs of state, because man was a citizen. By the same token women wanted the vote because it was the badge of citizenship. Recognizing how much was at stake here helps explain just how much some men feared they would lose by women gaining the vote. It raised fundamental issues about how masculinity was and might be exercised. In 1910 the Liverpool barrister W. Lyon Blease of the MLWS published *The Emancipation of English Women*. Here he praised Mary Wollstonecraft's *Vindication of the Rights of*

Women (1792) and wrote of the 'slow and reluctant recognition by man of the fact that woman is not merely an appendage to him but a separate individual'.[34]

Clark points out that a refusal to accept that representation should continue to be equated with manhood revealed the sham of protection, exposing a male citizenship predicated upon women's subordination.[35] In fact it was a subordination which would not even simply disappear with the instigation of formal political equality. Taking a slightly different focus, Claire Eustance's chapter on the Northern Men's Federation explores how the connections between masculine identity and citizenship were negotiated by male supporters of women's suffrage in Scotland directly prior to and during the First World War. Instead of seeing female citizenship as a threat to their manly status, members of the federation identified government treachery over women's suffrage as a factor in debasing the value of male citizenship and male votes.

At the beginning of our period there were already a number of women's suffrage organizations with some experience behind them – 1890 marked the death of one of their most devoted adherents, the Manchester campaigner Lydia Becker. The Isle of Man, influenced by the Manchester National Society for Women's Suffrage, had already made international history in 1881 by extending the parliamentary franchise to female propertied householders.[36] A key role in this had been played by Richard Sherwood, a member of their House of Keys. He argued for the deletion of the word 'male' from the election bill as a matter of justice, stressing the 'no taxation without representation' principle. When the 700 pioneer women were enfranchised, all those in his district voted for him.

Notable amongst those advocating women's rights in the British Parliament was Jacob Bright who, with Sir Charles Dilke, had introduced in 1870 the first women's suffrage bill, drafted by the barrister Richard Marsden Pankhurst. Bright was part of that remarkable circle of Quakers whose politics were informed by anti-slavery and anti-corn law traditions. Research is now drawing more attention to the networks of women and men suffragists in mid-nineteenth-century Britain, their transatlantic links, connections between the Kensington Society, the 1866 Women's Suffrage Petition and Mill, and the importance of family, kinship and radical sects such as the Unitarians.[37]

Dr Pankhurst spoke at the first meeting of the Women's Franchise League in 1889, founded to advocate women's right to vote in parliamentary and other elections and the first suffrage organization specifically including married women in its demands.[38] It worked to secure the 1894 legislation which gained the local government vote for all qualified married women and committed itself to fight for civil and political equality, Pankhurst's inaugural speech urging not only the vote for women but also divorce reform. Its council included such figures as Professor Gilbert Murray (discussed in Chapter 3), Jacob Bright and Ben Elmy. Elmy also became treasurer to the Male Electors' League for Women's Suffrage, formed in 1897. Here was a men's society formed expressly to work for the 'abolition of sex distinction in the allotment and exercise of the Parliamentary franchise'.[39] And in 1903, the year that Mrs Pankhurst founded the WSPU, the men from this society presented a suffrage petition to the House of Commons.

II

So, who were the men who supported women's suffrage in the early years of this century and how and why did they commit themselves? Support came in various forms but it would seem as though much of it was orchestrated through a range of societies. Men could be members of Mrs Fawcett's umbrella organization, the National Union of Women's Suffrage Societies (NUWSS). In Oxford, for example, men played a key role in the local Women's Suffrage Society (WSS).[40] A number of prominent Tories were honorary vice-presidents of the Conservative and Unionist Women's Franchise Society.[41] Those who believed in universal suffrage rather than votes for women on the same terms as men might be members of the People's Suffrage Federation (PSF). As Appendix 2 shows, there also existed a range of men-only or predominantly male societies between 1890 and 1920. Most were formed between 1907 and 1913 and tailored to specific interest groups and political affiliations. We have identified just over 1,000 men who were members of one or other of these societies and some were active in more than one. Chapter 7 provides an interesting insight into the roles women took in one of the men's societies.

The major men's society was undoubtedly the MLWS, which prided itself on being independent, non-party and non-political.[42] It was formed on 2 March 1907 by Herbert Jacobs, a London barrister specializing in banking law who also became its chairman. Its purpose was to 'promote the enfranchisement of women' and its executive committee included T. Mortimer Budgett, Mrs Pankhurst's brother-in-law. Using diaries, autobiographies, personal papers, newspapers, the *Suffrage Annual* (1913) and the MLWS's own records, we have identified 930 members during its seven-year existence. The league's own analysis of the occupations of its first 300 members revealed that 20 per cent were in commerce and finance, 16 per cent were clergy and writers, 10 per cent lawyers and an equal number scholars. Our research threw up little on the first category who may anyway have been more coy about revealing their affiliations outside the society but it did confirm the support of the other groups who, in the main, are anyway more easily discerned by titles or fame. For many members occupations could not be traced but from those who were identifiable, we discovered over fifty MLWS clergy members, ranging from nonconformist ministers and Anglican vicars and curates to a sprinkling of bishops. The Rev. Canon Hicks who was president in Manchester became the Bishop of Lincoln in 1910 and a MLWS vice-president the following year. He also presided over the Church League for Women's Suffrage which contained many MLWS members including its founder, the Rev. Claude Hinscliff.

We can get a clue as to possible clergy motivation from a short story by Margaret Wynne Nevinson of the Women's Freedom League (WFL), the daughter of a Leicester clergyman. She wrote about a High Anglican parson in the Midlands, a confirmed bachelor, who had a reputation as a mean boxer. In an episode which drew heavily on the famous Manchester Free Trade Hall suffrage intervention of 1905, Norman was converted to the cause when he witnessed the reaction to a 'frail little girl' asking for Votes for Women at a meeting at the Corn Exchange. The 'girls' were 'brutally and shamefully handled' and 'all the chivalry in his nature revolted at the violence of the stronger towards the weaker'.[43] He protested in the name of 'our common manhood'. The women had one other champion and protector, Solomon, a burly radical who opposed taxation without representation.

The Scottish Churches' League for Women's Suffrage included a large number of clergy on its council whilst the president and many of the vice-presidents of the Free Church League for Women's Suffrage were also in the MLWS. Herbert Jacobs was Jewish and so were many MLWS members. One well-known member was Israel Zangwill who founded the Jewish Territorial Organization. He was a vice-president of the Sussex Men's League. Like many of his league colleagues, he was a professional writer.

Some writers used their literary skills to advocate the cause. Laurence Housman, for example, drew on the Mad Hatter's tea party as a means of advocating the vote in his play *Alice in Ganderland* (1911).[44] Recent feminist evaluation of the work of dramatists such as St John Hankin and Shaw suggests not only the limitations of their self-confessed feminism but also, Sheila Stowell argues, vital differences between themselves and their female equivalents in the representation of themes and presentation of character types with implications for dramatic form, social intent and effect.[45] Yet the impetus for much of the suffrage theatre which was popularized by the Actresses' Franchise League (AFL) came initially from the Barker–Vedrenne production at the Royal Court Theatre, London, of Elizabeth Robins's 1907 play *Votes For Women!*. Indeed, Granville Barker suggested the play's title. He also wrote plays such as *The Madras House* which raised important social issues concerning women, though Stowell has pointed out that during his years in management he presented only three plays by women. Pro-suffrage men such as the actor-manager Johnston Forbes-Robertson (a vice-president of the MLWS) whose wife Gertrude was president of the AFL, and playwrights, novelists and poets such as John Masefield and John Galsworthy, spoke at meetings of societies like the Women Writers' Suffrage League (WWSL) as Angela John's chapter shows. Fittingly for writers, words were their weapons. They expressed their support publicly in speeches though in private they articulated their reservations.

With a barrister as chairman it is not surprising that lawyers were prominent in the MLWS. Their numbers included Judge H. Yorke Stanger MP who introduced a private member's bill for women's suffrage in 1908. The war correspondent Henry Nevinson commented that, as a lawyer, Pethick Lawrence was especially sensitive to the implications and necessity of preserving and therefore challenging law and order.[46] For principled lawyers, the need to explain and defend the cause could be seen as part of their duty as professionals. Lawyers had played a valuable role in the Law Amendment Society, encouraging Victorian married women's property reform.[47]

A high proportion of MLWS members were graduates and a number of distinguished academics were members of the London Graduates' Union for Women's Suffrage. When, in 1909, women suffragists organized a list of pro-suffrage men to combat a list of supporters of the 'antis', they too found many academics and teachers[48] prepared to support the cause. Both Oxford and Cambridge Universities formed their own MLWS branches, the Cambridge men, along with the women suffragists, performing Shaw's futurist playlet *Press Cuttings* (1909), satirizing the Prime Minister's anti-suffrage sentiments and the madness of militarism. Other eminent MLWS scholars included the historian Professor Tout (Manchester), the classicist Professor T. Hudson-Williams (Bangor) and the Arabic scholar Professor Margoliouth (Oxford) who was also vice-president of the Oxford WSS.

We have identified over thirty medical men who were MLWS members. Some were presumably stung into support by the blatant sexism of colleagues and the spurious pseudo-scientific ideas in circulation about women's apparent inferiority, ideas which made woman, rather than the vote, a problem. A deputation of medical men to the Commons stated fifteen objections to the treatment of suffrage prisoners, including the insult to their profession inherent in medical officers' brutal punishments. The Home Secretary McKenna urged the Royal College of Surgeons to discipline the eminent surgeons Sir Victor Horsley and Charles Mansell Moullin (a MLWS vice-president) for criticism of fellow doctors but no action was taken. These two men also voiced their opposition to forcible feeding in the medical press. Mansell Moullin, who was married to the leader of the London Welsh suffragettes, performed the unsuccessful emergency operation on Emily Wilding Davison after she was trampled by the king's horse at the 1913 Derby.[49] He told Nevinson that most doctors were hostile to the cause and that he and Horsley were 'cut by nearly everyone'.[50]

Twenty-five men boasted military titles, including several commanders, naval captains, colonels and a major-general. At the end of 1911, Captain Gonne of the MLWS, a former artilleryman and relative of Maud Gonne, and the London Irishman Albert Jamrach, a stockbroker, founded the Men's Society for Women's Rights. The following year they organized a deputation of 300 men to the Prime Minister to demand the immediate enfranchisement of women.

Along with a few titled figures, the MLWS boasted some famous names such as Ebenezer Howard who joined the new Letchworth branch in 1913, Sir Arthur Quiller-Couch, Sir Ernest Rutherford, Fenner Brockway, William de Morgan and Bertrand Russell who had sat on the NUWSS executive between 1907 and 1909, fighting the

Wimbledon by-election on a women's suffrage/Liberal ticket. In his early twenties Russell had given a paper entitled 'Lövborg or Hedda' to the exclusive Conversazione Society of Cambridge University, better known as the Apostles. This paper discussed and advocated admitting women as members.[51]

By their own admission, league members were a 'sober, grey-coated, and somewhat grey-haired' group. Nevinson who, with H. N. Brailsford, resigned from the *Daily News* over women's suffrage and edited the MLWS newspaper for a time, was not infrequently impatient with the society's procedural and legalistic tone, seeing their AGMs as 'endless discussions and resolutions on policy'.[52] The league largely represented those who were voters, who had a stake in society and believed their voices should be heard, since, unlike the women, they could argue that they were unselfishly working for others. They also felt that responsible men should set an example. In November 1911 they stressed that 'It lies with men who are voters already to insist that their members play straight'.[53] Such language permeated the men's societies. Victor Duval of the MLWS, then of the Men's Political Union (MPU), declared that 'it would be difficult to conceive of Englishmen, renowned throughout the world's history for their love of fair play, deliberately setting their minds against the freedom of their sisters'.[54]

League members spoke at joint suffrage events, tried men-only meetings, held open air rallies and could be found in processions 'toiling manfully with banners'.[55] They saw themselves as ready for combat. Just after Black Friday in 1910, Nevinson, who spent his working life observing enemies at war, accompanied a deputation to Downing Street, headed by Mrs Pankhurst:

> We drove the two lines of police more than halfway up the street, and for about twenty minutes there was a terrible conflict. Other police came and slowly drove us back out of the street. One policeman struck me violently on the back of the neck from behind and knocked me silly for a few minutes.[56]

These men did, however, mainly participate in less dramatic engage-ments, helping, for example, to organize petitions. They even used gimmicks such as having MLWS members walk the streets of London sporting top hats and carrying sandwich-boards to advertise a meeting.[57] In their columns they urged members to do their bit, praising men like Theodor Guggenheim who gave up ten days of his holiday to organize twenty-two meetings.[58]

They kept an eye on MPs whose statements were 'somewhat scrappy'. Members of the Manchester committee each had responsibility for scrutinizing different sections of the press.[59] Journalists such as Nevinson bombarded newspapers with indignant letters. Leaguers wrote pamphlets and from 1912 had their own literature department. They also offered candidates at by-elections – the NUWSS women were anxious for a MLWS man to stand against Hilaire Belloc at South Salford though in the event the latter withdrew and was replaced by a candidate prepared to support suffrage. They provided over 200 speakers (giving an average of five speeches each) for George Lansbury. This Labour MP had been outspoken in his defence of militancy and in 1912, after a clash in the Commons with Asquith over suffrage prisoners, he resigned and ran at Bow, East London as a women's suffrage candidate. Despite the efforts of the Men's League and the East London Federation of Suffragettes, he lost by 700 votes though the former declared that 'A handsome minority of the men of Bow rose to his challenge to their manhood'.[60]

For over two years, the views of the MLWS were advocated weekly in two pages in the suffrage newspaper *Women's Franchise*, printed and owned by J. E. Francis who became the first man to have his goods sold for tax resistance. From October 1909 they had their monthly paper which lasted until July 1914. From the start the league encouraged branches, soon evident in places such as Bournemouth, Edinburgh, Dublin, Bristol, East Grinstead and Pontypridd. Their degree of independence varied, with some being essentially local groupings of the parent society whilst others were considerably more independent or even autonomous leagues. For example, by 1911 the Manchester men had had enough of being answerable to London and contributing to it a substantial proportion of members' annual subscriptions. They therefore set up on their own.[61]

The MLWS liked to see itself as a broad-based, tolerant society representing views 'from the bluest Tory to the reddest socialist'. Its president was the Tory Earl of Lytton. An Irishman, he also had a radical pedigree in that he was descended from Anna Wheeler who, with William Thompson, had formulated in 1825 the powerful *Appeal* for women's equality. Moreover he was brother to Lady Constance Lytton. He chaired the all-party Conciliation Committee which worked hard to produce a compromise measure of women's suffrage, proposing to enfranchise single women householders (and married women if the house were in the wife's name).

The league's parliamentary members included the socialist Philip Snowden whose father was a Lancashire weaver enfranchised in 1884. He became a vice-president in 1912 and was on the Conciliation Committee. Probably the majority of the MLWS members were disappointed Liberals. Some pro-suffrage (and less disaffected) Liberals could belong to the Men's Liberal Society or later the Men's Liberal Associations. Yet within the Men's League, with the editorship of the monthly paper passing to the political journalist Brailsford early in 1912 and the Labour Party's endorsement of women's suffrage in that year, the drift towards Labour became more marked.

The league's own policies made the situation quite difficult for prospective Liberal MPs. In 1907 John Raphael, an Oxford double blue who was reading for the Bar, stood as the government candidate for Croydon. The Labour Party fielded an adult suffrage candidate. Through the columns of *Women's Franchise*, the MLWS urged support for Raphael, presenting him as an active and brilliant advocate for the cause. Yet others, equally understandably, protested that the league must stick to its agreed policy of neutrality. In the event Croydon remained a Tory stronghold. Raphael was elected to the MLWS's executive the following year.

Organized pro-suffrage men varied their tactics according to the political climate. In September 1910 with the government refusing to provide facilities for the Conciliation bill, the MLWS changed its policy. From then until July 1911 (when Grey made some encouraging assurances), it took on a definite anti-government stance. It would now support Liberals only if they in turn pledged to support women's suffrage and were in favour of the Conciliation bill. This meant that H. G. Chancellor, a Liberal MP on the executive, felt obliged to resign though he did become a vice-president as did that stalwart supporter of women's issues, Walter S. B. Maclaren, who had moved the 1884 women's suffrage amendment. The new policy did, however, help those who felt frustrated by the league's tendency to sit on the proverbial fence.

The crisis over Asquith's announcement (in November 1911) of a Manhood Suffrage bill with dire implications for the future of the Conciliation bill (its 36-strong committee included many MLWS stalwarts) provoked major new debates and disagreements about tactics.[62] The Earl of Lytton was conspicuous by his absence from the AGM in April 1912 when discussion of a new policy of concentrating on contests where there was a chance of gaining a Labour MP rather than simply putting pressure on elections and by-elections generally, resulted in a compromise agreement whereby Labour candidates were to be supported where they were standing against 'antis'.

By this time some of the more militant members had already joined the MPU. As early as 1908 Nevinson had attended meetings to consider forming a 'fighting men's league'.[63] In January 1910 this happened with about fifty men, 'all hard and straight and promising', meeting at Eustace Miles's restaurant in London where Brailsford proposed, and Nevinson seconded, a resolution to oppose government candidates at the forthcoming election. From the start, then, the MPU had a definite anti-government policy and a pledge. Its membership card unequivocally stated that 'To acquiesce in a non-committal attitude on the question from any government is to be in league with the worst enemy of the cause'.[64] Its members were to put women's enfranchisement before any other political question. It prided itself on its militant stance, its second annual report boasting, as though they had proved their manliness, that members had to 'undergo more ridicule, more contempt, and far more blows than those who are the advocates of Party questions'.

Its more confrontational expression of masculinity contrasted with the more cautious MLWS as well as worrying many women suffragists as Holton demonstrates in Chapter 4.[65] In a sense the MPU saw itself as a (big) brother society to the WSPU, sporting its colours of purple, white and green. Branches were formed in Birmingham, Dundee, Newcastle, Bradford, Leicester, Reading, Barnsley, Southampton and elsewhere, in towns with and without MLWS support. Nevinson who, slightly reluctantly, became chairman, saw its members as 'young bloods thirsting for rows'. They tended to be somewhat younger than men in the Men's League though, in the main, they too were aspiring or actual professionals. The more mature and dignified Nevinson was not infrequently embarrassed by their exhibitionism and sense of spoiling for a fight.[66] He intervened to stop them throwing bags of flour over Cabinet Ministers and enjoyed deflecting their anger. After addressing the Oxford MPU he commented, 'they expected serious rage and I gave them humorous remarks and memories'.[67] Early in 1913 when Duval proposed a raid from the gallery of the House of Commons, Nevinson put his foot down. They reluctantly agreed to an outer lobby protest. By this point Nevinson believed that Duval was trying to oust him from the society. Victor Duval was the MPU's founder and secretary, author of 'An Appeal to Men' in *Votes For Women* in 1910. He had resigned from the Young Liberals and from the MLWS (having been secretary of the Clapham branch and in their Stewards League). He was twice imprisoned.

Sandra Holton, who has written widely on women's suffrage, examines in Chapter 4 the motives of and reactions to those men prepared to place themselves on the line, both through passive resistance and physical activism.[68] One such man was Hugh Franklin who was gated at Cambridge after being caught chalking pavements with women's suffrage slogans. He graduated from student 'pranks' such as smashing up punts to actions which landed him in prison and even embarrassed the MPU. Franklin saw himself as a soldier fighting for a cause.[69] The MPU's treasurer Henry Harben was another privileged, flamboyant figure, 'Fabian, Etonian, wealthy, a little overbearing'.[70] He was a barrister, an ex-member of the Liberal League who, as Brian Harrison remarked, belatedly and suddenly became converted to militant suffrage with motives 'as much sporting and chivalrous as feminist'. He described forcible feeding as 'unmanly, ungentlemanly, unsportsmanlike and uncivilised'.[71]

In contrast there were some working-class men in the male societies, perhaps the best-known being William Ball of the Transport Workers' Federation whose sad case is discussed by Holton. Nevinson's diaries are also full of praise for John Scurr of the Independent Labour Party (ILP), secretary of the Dockers' Union. He possessed real powers of oratory as well as physical strength, both of which Nevinson felt he personally lacked. Displaying both skills, Scurr rescued Nevinson when he was surrounded by hostile crowds as he tried to advocate the cause in Hyde Park.

Better represented in both the MLWS and MPU was the well-educated man whose sympathies lay with the working class. Joseph Clayton was such a person though his personal experience of manual labour post-Oxford gave him better credentials than most.[72] He had been secretary of the Gasworkers' and General Labourers' Union as well as secretary to the Leeds ILP before editing the Southampton *Labour Chronicle* and *The New Age*. He was now a novelist living in Hampstead whose independent tactics were not always appreciated by the Men's League. His announcement of a deputation to test police treatment was roundly condemned. In 1913, in despair at the treatment of suffrage prisoners, he suggested to Nevinson the possibility of getting together a party of men 'to threaten to thrash McKenna'.[73]

The Manchester MLWS felt snubbed when their offer of an

academic to address the TUC on the relationship between the women's movement and the labour movement was turned down.[74] Yet because the working class was not well represented within the formal men's societies, which, after all, did not espouse universal suffrage and must have exuded a sense of class assurance, we should not thereby presume that working men were hostile or even apathetic towards votes for women. Quite apart from Sylvia Pankhurst's ability to appeal to women and men in London's East End, at the local level the WSPU and ILP seem to have worked quite well together in organizing local meetings.[75] Jill Liddington's study of the mill worker Selina Cooper reveals her husband Robert's support for suffrage. He not only worked with her in the NUWSS but was also an active member of the MLWS.[76]

And in 1906, years before the miners formally backed women's suffrage, Vernon Hartshorn, miners' agent for the Maesteg district of the South Wales Miners' Federation, was asked by a group of miners' delegates to write to their MP, S. T. Evans, who had 'talked out' a women's suffrage resolution in Parliament.[77] Hartshorn's letter expressed the miners' realization that it was pointless asking him to vote for the Women's Franchise bill but added that they hoped he would at least 'see the way to abstain from placing any obstacle to the Second Reading'. Hartshorn added, 'as far as I have been able to gauge the opinions of the Miners of Maesteg on the subject there is a preponderance in favour of the measure'. When the suffragette Mary Gawthorpe attended two of Evans's meetings in his mid-Glamorgan constituency to give him a taste of his own medicine and talk *him* out, a strong force of men gathered round to protect her when stewards evicted her.[78]

In 1912 brutality was demonstrated by young men (such as Ben Evans a solicitor's clerk) against the suffragettes who interrupted Lloyd George in his native Llanystumdwy in North Wales.[79] Yet the following year, commentating on a demonstration of Bangor suffragists with stone quarrymen, the *North Wales Chronicle* commented:

> We find it everywhere the same – the genuine working man is sympathetic with the women's cause. Their difficulties are in many ways the same, and they do not let prejudiced and preconceived ideas stand in the way of a fair and sympathetic consideration of the question.[80]

Such a comment, however, cloaked as much as it revealed. The adherence of the key female and male suffrage societies to a position demanding votes for women on the same terms as men seriously complicated the situation and created tensions between them and the labour movement, only too aware that over 40 per cent of men still lacked the vote. By contrast, in, for example, South Australia, at the time the vote was won by women, manhood suffrage had already been secured. For many in Britain the primacy of class and socialist issues spelt a commitment to adult suffrage. As with the writers in *The Workman's Times* during the early 1890s (discussed in Chapter 2), such priorities meant that serious consideration of gender inequality was inevitably relegated. This was not to be confused with being anti-women, but it did mean a disparagement of what could be dismissed as 'fine lady suffrage'. And although Arthur Henderson MP, who chaired the PSF and the Joint Committee for Securing the Enfranchisement of Women on Broad and Democratic Lines, contributed to the 1912 MLWS *Handbook* (designed to show the MLWS's broad approach and containing articles with very different emphases by figures such as Lytton and Brailsford), Henderson's contribution was an advertisement for the adultist position.

Arthur Craven, founder and secretary of Bradford's MLWS, tried to tackle the issue head-on in 1907, holding a debate with the local branch of the Social Democratic Federation on whether the workers should support the present women's suffrage movement.[81] He stressed the importance of justice and the advantages for the whole nation promised by women becoming voters. Adult suffrage, he warned, was too great a leap for many to be prepared to endorse.

This debate emphasizes the value of not only considering the big names associated with men's support, but also examining how men and women used the structures of local government to press for change. A number of MLWS members were local councillors, accustomed to respect and a voice in local communities. In South Wales the *Caerphilly Journal* reported a suffrage meeting in 1910 where Alderman Evans argued that 'the women would also help the men to be men'.[82] Opponents in turn attacked local representatives when they spoke out, portraying them, like women, as lesser beings who should not meddle in national affairs. One Brighton elector denounced his council:

> I shall find out which Councillors voted for Women's Suffrage and I shall not vote for them and do all in my power to get allies to do likewise . . . The men of this country are not going to have

feminine control of the Empire thrust upon them at the bidding of Gentlemen whose proper concern is with the parish pump.[83]

Claire Eustance's chapter reveals the levels of Scottish men's support, in particular among local government dignitaries in Glasgow and Edinburgh.[84] There are important narratives of Scottish, Welsh and Irish suffrage work, often complicated in varying degrees by commitments to Liberalism, nationalism and religious belief. Moreover the opposition of Asquith, who represented East Fife, and the 'betrayal' of Welsh-bred Lloyd George, were particularly keenly felt by suffrage supporters in Scotland and Wales. The significance of Irish Home Rule, in shifting the balance in Parliament and the Liberals' dependence on the Irish vote, cannot be overstressed.

Quite apart from grass-root or societal support, there were of course sympathizers within Parliament. After the resounding Liberal victory of 1906, a majority of MPs from all parties pledged support and 1908 saw a majority of 179 for the second reading of the suffrage bill. Yet the replacement of Campbell-Bannerman with H. H. Asquith in that year lost the cause 'a weak friend and gained [it] a determined enemy' in the words of the suffragette Elizabeth Robins (see Chapter 3).[85] Women's suffrage debates had been more or less annual events since the 1870s but when it came to turning assurances into action, it was another matter. This had been demonstrated back in 1884 when 104 pledged Liberal supporters actually voted against the bill. Only a very small number of MPs could really be relied upon and Carolyn Spring's examination of the language of parliamentary support is revealing.

One of the most faithful supporters in Parliament was the barrister W. H. Dickinson. As a Liberal MP from 1906, he introduced a suffrage bill into the Commons in 1907, and in subsequent years took part in almost every debate on the subject.[86] A former chairman of the London County Council, his work there demonstrated his belief in women's equality, trying, for example, to equalize women and men teachers' salaries. He perceived women's suffrage as part of the general progress of civilization and, as we have seen, stressed the natural rights of men and women as citizens of the state. For Sir Alfred Mond MP (a vice-president of the MLWS), women's suffrage was essentially a state question and this industrialist described the suffrage struggle as 'an effort of co-partnership' rather than a sex war.[87]

Dickinson urged the need to move with the times. Pro-suffragists liked to see themselves as modern men. As Ephraim Lipson stressed in the MLWS paper, 'the world has moved since Victorian days' and those who did not share their views were dismissed as atavistic early Victorians or worse: 'Biologically considered the Anti-Suffrage man belongs to a period of human evolution that is nearly at an end.'[88] Dickinson also urged recognition of women as a force in international politics. In 1893 New Zealand had become the first self-governing country to pass legislation granting universal women's suffrage. Yet this victory was then used to counteract the scaremongering of the 'antis' and demonstrate that what might be seen as a colonial experiment had neither destabilized society nor disturbed gender roles.[89]

Sir John Cockburn KCMG, the former premier of South Australia, now settled in London, spoke to the MLWS at the Queen's Hall in 1908.[90] South Australia got full state suffrage in 1894 and women could also stand for Parliament. On the MLWS executive and an honorary vice-president of the National Political League for Men and Women, Sir John epitomized the more conservative element of pro-suffrage support, believing, as had Macaulay in 1832, that you should reform in order to preserve. In his speech he emphasized that the franchise in Australia (federal franchise had been granted in 1902 but denied to Aborigines) had not interfered with home life. There was no decline in chivalry, men still surrendered seats on omnibuses and tramcars and he reassured listeners by stressing that 'women's action is always gradual, persistent, prevailing'.

For Cockburn, matrimony and motherhood represented 'the crown of a woman's life' and for many male supporters of women's rights, the vote was a key to strengthening family life. Back in 1891 John Gibson, editor and owner of the *Cambrian News*, had also drawn attention to women's rights and motherhood. In *The Emancipation of Women* he demonstrated his belief that equality in law would result in 'a higher tone of family life'. He was critical of current marriage laws but hopeful for a greater emphasis on motherhood. Full emancipation, in his view, meant that 'the family will have its King and its Queen and the rule will be a joint rule'.[91] Yet his stress on current inequality in order to urge the necessity of legislation exaggerated gender difference – his claim that women 'do not seem to have the power of men to organize' was soon being proved wrong – and he placed too much emphasis on the efficacy of the legal process.

Much suffrage propaganda from both men and women linked legal change to imperialist concerns. Leaguers were told that 'If England still wishes to retain any primacy among nations, let her grasp at this last chance of asserting her lost leadership by being the First Great Power to call women to her councils'.[92] The pro-suffrage position seemed to invite a sense of superiority with the men claiming the moral high ground. Zangwill declared to the MLWS (at their first major meeting at the Queen's Hall), 'If ever a person had a right not only to a quiet hearing, but to an almost pharisaic self-satisfaction – if anybody could exclaim "I am not as other men", it would be a member of this League.'[93]

The British MLWS was the first such society in the world. The Dutch followed in 1908 and in Stockholm in 1911 a Men's International Alliance for Woman Suffrage (MIAWS) was formed during a meeting of the sixth International Woman Suffrage Alliance.[94] Sir John Cockburn became its president and its first congress was held in London the following year organized by the MLWS, the MPU and the newly formed Men's Federation for Women's Suffrage. Affiliated were men's leagues in France, Hungary, Sweden, Germany, Denmark, the Netherlands and the United States (where there existed both a New York and a national society which developed thirty branches).

The women's suffrage societies hosted a number of social occasions during the week-long congress, including a visit to Shaw's *Fanny's First Play* in which suffragettes are compared very favourably with boisterous students. As Holton observes in Chapter 4, the organized men could be valuable mediators between the various interests involved in suffrage. Although the women could not vote on resolutions, a large number of societies sent 'fraternal' delegates including Mrs Fawcett, Laurence Housman (Women's Tax Resistance League and WWSL), the Rev. Llewelyn Smith (London Society for Women's Suffrage) and Gustav Spiller (Union of Ethical Societies). European delegates included Rosika Schwimmer (co-president of the Hungarian Society for Women's Suffrage) and Italy, Norway, Switzerland, Finland, Japan and Russia were all represented. A unanimous resolution called the attention of men of all nations to the problems of women's employment and wages. By 1913 when the MIAWS met in Budapest, Bohemia, Galicia and Canada were also affiliated. British delegates included Dr Drysdale and Keir Hardie. In the same year Hardie offered to put up the exhausted Franklin after his temporary release from prison.

Dr Charles Vickery Drysdale DSc, MIEE had previously

UWE LIBRARY SERVICES

represented the Men's League at a women's international conference in Amsterdam. Along with his father Dr Charles Robert
Drysdale MD, FRCS, MRCP he had been a founder member of the
MLWS and was an honorary secretary for a couple of years. He also
sat on the Men's Committee for Justice to Women. Drysdale senior
had stood bail for Annie Besant and Charles Bradlaugh at their 1877
trial, was the first president of the Malthusian League, founder and
editor of *The Malthusian*, and gave pioneer medical lectures to
women.[95] His common-law wife Dr Alice Vickery qualified in
pharmacy, becoming the first British woman chemist, then a doctor.
Their son published pamphlets on women's suffrage and his wife
Bessie Ingham Edwards was in the WSPU, then the WFL. Picking
up on concern about women undercutting men in the labour market,
Drysdale junior presented the solution not in terms of banning
women's work but in a recognition that they deserved the same
human rights as men. Women's enfranchisement should lead to
their greater remuneration and to the prosperity of the working
class. Thus women's suffrage was in the interests of all. In the final
issue of the MLWS paper (July 1914) he stressed that automatic
and excessive child-bearing lay at the root of many problems and,
like others in his family, urged family limitation as an essential
prerequisite to women's true emancipation.

The Drysdales provide a vivid example of a radical network of
support for women's rights including suffrage. There are many other
examples of partnerships between advocates of women's rights,
perhaps the most famous being those of Harriet Taylor and John
Stuart Mill, the Fawcetts, the Pankhursts and the Pethick Lawrences.
Many others could be mentioned specifically in relation to suffrage;
for example, Sir John Rhys, Celtic luminary who chaired the first
public women's suffrage meeting in Oxford, Lady Elspeth Rhys and
their two daughters, the family being moving spirits in the Oxford
WSS for a number of years. It has, however, been noted that in
Oxford at least, active familial support tended to involve the
daughters rather than the sons of pro-suffrage parents.[96] The very
different gender politics of siblings such as John and Jacob Bright,
or Laurence and Clemence Housman and their brother Alfred,
remind us, however, that we do need to exercise caution in forging
links between family upbringing and pro-suffrage sentiments.[97]

June Balshaw's chapter on the Pethick Lawrences raises questions
about how far politics embraced a couple's personal relationships.
Some suffragists saw their own marriages as opportunities to imple-

ment – at least publicly – their conception of equality. In 1912 Una Dugdale whose father, a commander, was in the MLWS and whose mother was a suffragette, married Victor Duval whose own family was active in suffrage. They had a big wedding at the Royal Chapel of the Savoy, London. The Archbishop of Canterbury sent along two priests to insist on her saying 'obey'. Although they persuaded the Rev. Hugh Chapman (a MLWS member), who officiated, to utter the word, the bride demurred and later wrote a pamphlet called 'Love and Honour but NOT Obey'.[98] Duval's sister Elsie later married Hugh Franklin.

Differences over suffrage tactics threatened the marriage prospects of a Dublin couple, Samuel Kingston a civil servant and constitutionalist and Lucy Lawrenson a post office worker.[99] When Kingston spoke out against militancy, stressing the moral superiority of women, Lawrenson, who joined the militant Irish Women's Franchise League, temporarily had second thoughts about marrying him. For some men and women, marriage appears to have been a catalyst for, rather than response to, change and suffrage commitment. Apparently the decisive factor in making Louise Mary Peters a suffragette was her marriage to Dr A. R. Eates in 1901.[100] A general practitioner, he interested her in public questions and in suffrage in particular. She became secretary of the Kensington branch of the WSPU between 1906 and 1910 and was imprisoned for one month.

As June Balshaw discusses, the Pethick Lawrences were a couple whose generosity towards the WSPU was cut short only by Mrs Pankhurst's peremptory decision to break with them in 1912. Brian Harrison portrays their partnership as 'one of the most significant marriages twentieth-century Britain has so far seen'.[101] Fred Pethick Lawrence's complicated relationship to the WSPU without the safety net of the MLWS, put him in an ambivalent position. Yet there were times when he demonstrated remarkable sensitivity (as well as expediency) such as stressing when on trial that 'I am a man and I cannot take part in this women's agitation'.[102] Yet, as Balshaw recognizes, it is of course impossible to know how far the Pethick Lawrences put their principles into practice in private. It is, nevertheless, interesting to note that commentators, at the time and since, rarely mention one without the other.

Fred Pethick Lawrence's suffrage support grew, as did that of a number of fellow sympathizers, out of a wider radical commitment. The public platform was familiar to them. Henry Nevinson, who witnessed the curtailing of freedom in many corners of the world, spoke for one cause or another most nights of the week when in England. Women's suffrage could therefore be seen as a natural extension to a liberal agenda though, as autobiographies show, it was one cause amongst many. Men such as Brailsford who, for example, later became vice-president of the Abortion Law Reform movement, were and remained seasoned campaigners and a number of them became pacifists.

Women's suffrage could offer a degree of commensality and a way of being seen as progressive which actually worked through homo-social networks. In the case of men's society members it was not dissimilar to belonging to a club. It is, however, worth stressing here that suffrage also gave women a sense of belonging. One former suffragette called it 'our Eton and Oxford, our regiment, our ship, our cricket match'.[103]

Several chapters discuss the concept of chivalry and how it could be adapted. Franklin's imprisonment might have been presented in the daily press as emasculating but it could also be interpreted as a chivalrous, manly gesture. Charles V. Drysdale explained that true chivalry was not dead but involved standing up for rights.[104] Here were the *real* men in contradistinction to the 'hooligans' and 'loafers' who heckled at suffrage meetings (an element of class pride could also be detected here). During the 1908 Pembrokeshire by-election when a heckler interrupted a woman speaker with 'Don't you wish you were a man?', her retort was 'Don't you?'[105]

Yet, how conditional was all this support? The escalation of women's militancy and the threat to gender roles which this appeared to imply (exacerbated by 'antis' denouncing masculine women), proved to be a real test for manly men who either retreated into condemning the wrong turn and reappropriated control through their mastery of words, or, as in the case of the MPU, sought to take action into their own hands, in their own way.

Like the Female Chartist Associations of the 1840s, much of the male societies' work was supportive, complementary and gender-specific. There were, however, times when tensions surfaced between them and the WSPU in particular. In 1910 Christabel told the Conciliation Committee, 'This is a women's movement and can only be conducted by women.'[106] Yet in his diary Nevinson added the crucial rider to this: 'unhappily the vote can only be won through men.'[107] During the Conciliation crisis the MLWS asked Asquith to receive a joint deputation from the women's societies. This provoked 'WSPU rage' for seizing the initiative.[108] Pethick Lawrence's comment on the lack of a sex war depends on whom he was referring to and when. Whereas women like Maud Arncliffe Sennett (see Chapter 7) could declare in 1909, 'If anything could console us for the suffering inflicted on us, it would be the real chivalry and manly attitude of the MLWS'[109] and even Christabel Pankhurst could tell Franklin in 1911 that 'We are very proud of our men friends who are fighting so bravely for us',[110] by the time Nevinson saw her in Paris in November 1912, she was stating that she 'rather disapproved of men's intimate concern in the movement'.[111] Holton discusses Christabel Pankhurst's growing determination to exclude men from involvement and the increased militancy, as both Holton and John show, posed new pressures which were crucial to the gendered nature of suffrage and definitions of 'the movement'.

Towards the end of 1913, from different perspectives, Christabel and the MPU were attacking the MLWS whilst Nevinson was suspected of being in league with Lloyd George. Although the latter had, a few years earlier, appeared to confide in an ever-wary Nevinson, the situation had changed considerably and Nevinson dismissed such claims as 'a kind of spy-mania, a terror and blindness due to Christabel's absence'.[112] Dismayed by what he now saw as Christabel's 'suspicion and hatred of all men',[113] Nevinson encouraged discussions amongst MPU members in particular for creating a mixed-sex society espousing a 'new and milder militancy'.[114] The writer Gerald Gould would have liked it to be broader than concerned with women's suffrage alone, wanting 'an industrial revolution', but he was overruled and after a dinner with the Pethick Lawrences, the basis for what would become the United Suffragists (US) was laid. By January a manifesto was being discussed and the twelve-member executive included Nevinson, the Pethick Lawrences and Lansbury.

The United Suffragists' desire for men and women to work together for women's suffrage was mirrored in the growing strength of other mixed membership organizations, notably the Church Leagues. Nevertheless, it was within the women's societies that the most extensive discussions took place on the future path of the women's suffrage movement after the vote had been won. WFL president Charlotte Despard had stated as early as 1911:

> I see the Vote won and I see beyond it . . . I see those who have been the most earnest students of social conditions – those who have felt most deeply the power of feminism and its part in the

growing humanism of to-day refusing to loosen the bands of comradeship that hold them together.[115]

The men's societies, in the main, failed to consider the future of their organizations with such vigour, and the period from the end of 1913, when the MPU folded, until shortly after the end of the First World War witnessed the demise of much organized male support for women's suffrage. This was in stark contrast to the numbers of female organizations that had origins in the suffrage campaign and continued to organize in the 1920s and beyond. Yet it was not necessarily the women activists who rejected male support: in what was a gesture of gratitude, together with a desire to harness the potential of men and women's co-operation, the WFL opened its membership to men in 1918. It was revealing that no men took up the WFL's offer.

The national MLWS ceased to exist soon after the outbreak of war. Former stalwarts such as Major Gillespie (MPU then US), 'always a stand-by in a fight',[116] were soon distinguishing themselves on another kind of battleground, at Ypres and elsewhere. Yet despite the depletion of numbers of younger men now fighting, war did not mark the end of men's work for women's suffrage, and the final chapter on the Northern Men's Federation considers factors – besides the war – that contributed to the end of organized male support for women's equality. The United Suffragists and the Manchester MLWS also continued to be active in wartime.[117] Fiona Montgomery has shown how the latter espoused a wide range of social issues including protesting against the cutting of separation allowances and the banning of women from public houses.[118] They also furnished a Girls' Club with educative books including Elizabeth Robins's chilling novel of middle-class white slavery and works by John Stuart Mill and Olive Schreiner.[119]

In February 1918 a limited vote was finally given to women householders or wives of male householders over the age of 30.[120] Some eight million women were enfranchised along with adult males previously denied the vote. The following year the Sex Disqualification (Removal) Act enabled women to take up a number of public posts such as becoming magistrates and jurors.

The horrors and hopelessness of war along with its results, not least the image of 'shell-shocked' men, fractured some ideas about masculinity, whilst women's war work questioned gendered notions of skill and women's association with staying at home rather than going out to work.[121] Militarism also put militancy and the concept of fitness for a vote in a new light. Although women did not enjoy complete enfranchisement until 1928, the world that they and men inhabited in the 1920s was markedly different from that prewar. It therefore seems a fitting point to end our study in 1920 after the legislation of 1918 and 1919.

III

What might men's articulation of support reveal about their own understandings of masculinity and femininity and how deep was their critique of this? How far was their desire to liberate women – or to enable women to liberate themselves – tempered by their own instincts, inculcated since childhood, to protect the female sex? Physical protection remained important in the men's societies. For example, the main means of support for organized men was through meetings to which they offered their minds and bodies, as speakers and as stewards in their own rallies at the Queen's Hall, London and at countless meetings throughout the country. They subverted yet also reinforced tradition, escorting women to functions where votes would be demanded, once again assuming the role of protector. The 'Men's Share' could, however, assume many forms and pro-suffrage men's politics was therefore expressive of different masculinities. Despite all the efforts of women campaigners, it was men's socialization, their experience in public life and the confidence this generated that combined to place them in a powerful position to advocate the vote for others.

As the chapters in this book show, British male suffragists might exert themselves for women's suffrage but, on the whole, they did not examine the basis of their own masculinity. In contrast the sex radicals of Greenwich Village, New York appear more progressive. Here couples such as Max Eastman and Ida Rauh sought personal equality and a critique of gender and class relations. Eastman was secretary of the New York MLWS founded in 1910. Looking back on this period in the 1930s (and therefore possibly with greater awareness from hindsight), Eastman recalled that it was extremely difficult for him to stand up and be counted as a 'male suffragette'. It meant 'not only that I had asserted my manhood, but that I had passed beyond the need of asserting it'.[122]

Yet there were a few British men who began to provide similar critiques. John Tosh draws attention to Edward Carpenter who was in the MLWS whilst several chapters consider Laurence Housman, whose homosexuality helped him to confront dominant notions of sexuality. The Men's Society for Women's Rights had a much wider agenda than suffrage alone (see Sandra Holton's chapter) and, for example, in June 1913 held a public meeting in Ealing on the 'White Slave Traffic and Kindred Evils'.[123] The Rev. Hugh Chapman declared that women's suffrage meant 'the whole reconstruction of the attitude of the sexes towards one another'.[124]

Another remarkable supporter, not least because he was that unlikely creature a suffragist metropolitan police magistrate, was Cecil Chapman. He explained at the Queen's Hall in 1911 that

> The spirit of dominance in man and the spirit of subservience in women must both be removed; civilisation demanded from men something of the gentleness associated with women, but also from women something of the fearlessness and independence which this manliness implied.[125]

Chapman briefly chaired the MLWS in 1911 and was a leading light in the New Constitutional Society for Women's Suffrage. Known as 'just and tender on the bench to the poor and them that are helpless',[126] during the publicity surrounding the publication of the Royal Commission on Divorce he wrote a challenging article for the MLWS on obedience in marriage, arguing that freedom and equality should replace obedience and domination.[127]

Ever ready with the stirring line, Israel Zangwill declared that women's suffrage involved 'a complete re-reading of life, a re-evaluation of all values, a transformation of the whole political area'. He announced, 'We have done with this man-ridden world.'[128] Yet such rhetoric tended to lack real substance.

Perhaps, however, we should not in retrospect judge such pro-suffrage men too harshly. As all the chapters in this book demonstrate in differing ways, by their very concern about women's rights and representation these men were nevertheless drawing attention to fundamental questions about male behaviour. Although the sacrifices they made did not, on the whole, involve in such numbers the courage displayed by women claiming 'male space', and although men's support tended not to encompass a fundamental critique of masculinity which really confronted the basis of gender relations, these men were at least seeking to change society for the better. Compared with the 'antis' or even those not prepared to speak out, they at least recognized the need for equal voting rights and many men were not just ideologues but also prepared to take action. And it is possible that the very process of meeting with like-minded men as well as committed women, may have helped to further men's views on a range of issues concerning gender past, present and future.

All this is particularly worth bearing in mind today when, in the United States and now in Britain, it is possible to discern a male backlash against the achievements of modern feminism. Anti-feminist men conceive of themselves as part of a Men's Movement.[129] The twentieth century began and looks like ending with men organizing themselves, prompted by women's actions. These men who now declaim against women's jobs, laws on marital rape, the feminist lobby and much else seem to have more in common with the Edwardian antis than with the subjects of this book.

Yet, now as then, vocal male groups with radically different agendas have also laid claim to the same language but invested it with other meanings. Since the early 1980s, some self-avowed 'New Men' have seen themselves as part of a Men's Movement.[130] They have radically different conceptions and expectations of masculinity, femininity and the 'Men's Share' from the anti-feminist men. In some ways these 'New Men' may be seen as the inheritors of the ideas of Pethick Lawrence and other enlightened pro-suffrage men of a century ago.

NOTES

1 Frederick Pethick Lawrence Papers, Trinity College, Cambridge, P-L 5/133(1). The original pamphlet, based on the defence of 20 May 1912, sold for 1*d*. His later version was for a BBC talk which does not appear (from the BBC Sound Archive records at Caversham) to have been broadcast. Although the Pethick Lawrences themselves tended (particularly in later years) to hyphenate their names, for consistency we have not done so in this book.

2 J. Purvis, 'Women's History in Britain. An Overview', *European Journal of Women's Studies* 2 (1995), pp. 15–16 (pp. 7–19).

3 J. Tosh, 'What should Historians do with Masculinity? Reflections on Nineteenth-Century Britain', *History Workshop Journal* 38 (Autumn 1994), p. 180 (pp. 179–202).

4 S. Strauss, *'Traitors to the Masculine Cause'. The Men's Campaigns for Women's Rights*, Westport, CT, Greenwood Press, 1982.

5 L. Davidoff, *Worlds Between. Historical Perspectives on Gender and Class*, Oxford, Polity Press, 1995, p. 12.

6 P. Filene, 'The Secrets of Men's History', in H. Brod (ed.), *The Making of Masculinities. The New Men's Studies*, Boston, MA, Allen & Unwin, 1987 (pp. 103–19).

7 C. Hall, *White, Male and Middle Class. Explorations in Feminism and History*, Oxford, Polity Press, 1992, p. 268.

8 ibid., p. 288.

9 Suffragette Fellowship Collection, Museum of London, 50/82/105.

10 M. S. Kimmel and T. E. Mosmiller, *Against the Tide. Pro-Feminist Men in the United States 1776–1990*, Boston, MA, Beacon Press, 1992, p. 6.

11 S. Collini, *Public Moralists. Political Thought and Intellectual Life in Britain, 1850–1930*, Oxford, Clarendon Press, 1991, pp. 170–96.

12 J. A. Mangan and J. Walvin (eds), *Manliness and Morality. Middle-class Masculinity in Britain and America 1800–1940*, Manchester, Manchester University Press, 1987, Introduction and p. 200.

13 T. Jeal, *Baden-Powell* (1989), London, Pimlico edition, 1995, p. 29.

14 B. Harrison, *Separate Spheres. The Opposition to Women's Suffrage in Britain*, London, Croom Helm, 1978, especially Chs 4 and 5.

15 J. Hearn, *Men in the Public Eye. The Construction and Deconstruction of Public Men and Public Patriarchies*, London, Routledge, 1992, Ch. 6.

16 S. O. Rose, 'Gender Antagonism and Class Conflict: Exclusionary Strategies of Male Trade Unionists in Nineteenth-Century Britain', *Social History* 13, (1988), pp. 131–208; S. O. Rose, *Limited Livelihoods: Gender and Class in Nineteenth-Century England*, London, Routledge, 1992.

17 K. McClelland, 'Rational and Respectable Men. Gender, the Working Class and Citizenship in Britain 1850–1867', in L. Frader and S. O. Rose (eds), *Gender and the Reconstruction of Working-Class History in Modern Europe*, Ithaca, NY, Cornell University Press, forthcoming.

18 D. H. Morgan, *Discovering Men*, London, Routledge, 1992, Ch. 7.

19 C. Bolt, *Feminist Ferment. 'The Woman Question' in the USA and England, 1870–1940*, London, UCL Press, 1995, Ch. 4. O. Banks, *Becoming a Feminist. The Social Origins of First Wave Feminism*, Brighton, Wheatsheaf, 1986 includes only one man (Brailsford) in her sample of feminists born between 1872 and 1891.

20 In 1908, an anti-suffrage petition was signed by 337,018 people; Harrison, *Separate Spheres*, p. 120.

21 See N. Cott, *The Grounding of Modern Feminism*, New Haven, CT, and London, Yale University Press, 1987; J. Purvis and M. Joannou (eds), *The Women's Suffrage Movement. New Feminist Perspectives*, Manchester, Manchester University Press, forthcoming; and C. Daley and M. Nolan (eds), *Suffrage & Beyond. International Feminist Perspectives*, New York, New York University Press, 1994.

22 See J. Tosh and M. Roper (eds), *Manful Assertions. Masculinities in Britain since 1800*, London, Routledge, 1991.

23 Of the seven men considered, one never married, one was divorced, one married late his divorced cousin and at least two had 'semi-detached' marriages. Only two had more than two children.

24 E. Showalter, *Sexual Anarchy. Gender and Culture at the Fin de Siècle*, Harmondsworth, Penguin, 1991; M. Kimmel, 'The Contemporary "Crisis" of Masculinity', in Brod (ed.), *The Making*, p. 150 (pp. 121–53).

25 We are grateful to John Tosh for this information.
26 Strauss, *Traitors*, pp. 60–6.
27 S. S. Holton, 'From Anti-Slavery to Suffrage Militancy: The Bright Circle, Elizabeth Cady Stanton and the British Women's Movement', in Daley and Nolan (eds), *Suffrage & Beyond*, p. 222 (pp. 213–33).
28 R. Wallace, *Organize! Organize! Organize! A Study of Reform Agitations in Wales, 1840–86*, Cardiff, University of Wales Press, 1991, Ch. XI.
29 E. Cohen, *Talk on the Wilde Side. Towards a Genealogy of a Discourse on Male Sexualities*, London, Routledge, 1993.
30 A. Clark, *The Struggle for the Breeches. Gender and the Making of the British Working Class*, London, Rivers Oram Press, 1995.
31 A. Clarke, 'Gender, Class and Nation: Franchise Reform in the Long Nineteenth Century', in J. Vernon (ed.), *Rereading the Constitution*, Cambridge, Cambridge University Press, forthcoming. We are grateful to Anna Clark for letting us read a draft version of her chapter. See too C. Hall, K. McClelland and J. Rendall, *Defining the Nation: Race, Gender and the British Reform Act of 1867*, Cambridge, Cambridge University Press, forthcoming.
32 Clark, 'Gender, Class and Nation'.
33 W. H. Dickinson Papers, Greater London Record Office, F/DCK/29/5/1–2.
34 Strauss, *Traitors*, p. 243.
35 Clark, 'Gender, Class and Nation'.
36 M. A. Butler and J. Templeton, 'The Isle of Man and the First Votes for Women', *Women and Politics* 4, 2 (Summer 1984), pp. 33–47. For a useful survey of the main developments in women's struggle for the vote see S. S. Holton, 'Women and the Vote', in J. Purvis (ed.), *Women's History, Britain, 1850–1945. An Introduction*, London, UCL Press, 1995, pp. 277–305.
37 Holton in Daley and Nolan, *Suffrage & Beyond*; J. Rendall, 'Citizenship, Culture and Civilisation: The Languages of British Suffragists 1866–1874', in *ibid.*, pp. 127–50; A. Dingsdale, '"Generous and Lofty Sympathies": the Kensington Society, the 1866 Women's Suffrage Petition and the Development of Mid-Victorian Feminism', PhD, University of Greenwich, 1996 and K. Gleadle, *The Early Feminists. Radical Unitarians and the Emergence of the Women's Rights Movement 1832–51*, London, Macmillan, 1995.
38 Fawcett Library, UDC 396. 11 (06) A.
39 ibid., UDC and Suffragette Fellowship Collection, Museum of London, 56.8 2/416. 11.
40 Katherine Bradley. Paper given to University of Greenwich Research Project Seminar (U of G.RPS).
41 For example, Sir Edward Busk (who was also on the MLWS executive) and chief honorary secretary to the Repeal the Act Committee – the Act being the infamous Prisoners' (Temporary Release for Ill-health) Act or 'Cat and Mouse' Act (see Chapter 4).
42 Material on the social composition etc. of the MLWS is based on their annual records in the Fawcett Library, UDC 396.11.B, their pamphlets

and 1912 *Handbook* in the Suffragette Fellowship Collection, Museum of London, *Women's Franchise (WF)*, the MLWS *Monthly* and AJR (ed.), *The Suffrage Annual and Women's Who's Who*, London, Stanley Paul, 1913 (this lists sixty-nine men, mostly in suffrage societies).

43 M. W. Nevinson, 'In a Midland Parish', in her *Fragments of Life*, London, Allen & Unwin, 1922, p. 74. One Leicester clergyman called Donaldson led a deputation of parsons to Asquith in July 1913. In this year Bishop Maud told Evelyn Sharp that 'militancy is the only thing after all'. H. W. Nevinson Diaries, Bodleian Library, Oxford, MS Eng. Misc., e618/1,16 October 1913.

44 C. Hirshfield, 'The Suffragist as Playwright in Edwardian England', *Frontiers* ix, 2 (1987), p. 4 (pp. 1–6).

45 S. Stowell, *A Stage of Their Own. Feminist Playwrights of the Suffrage Era*, Manchester, Manchester University Press, 1992, pp. 6–7.

46 H.W. Nevinson, *More Changes, More Chances*, London, Nisbet, 1925, p. 319. Other prominent pro-suffrage lawyers included Arthur Marshall and the Irish MP Tim Healy who defended Mrs Pankhurst.

47 Dingsdale, 'Generous and Lofty Sympathies', p. 218.

48 Hilda Kean, U of G.RPS.

49 A. V. John, '"A Draft of Fresh Air". Women's Suffrage, the Welsh and London', *Transactions of the Honourable Society of Cymmrodorion for 1994*, new series, 1 (1995), pp. 80–93 for the Mansell Moullins.

50 B. Harrison, 'Women's Health and the Women's Movement in Britain 1840–1940', in C. Webster (ed.), *Biology, Medicine and Society 1840–1940*, Cambridge, Cambridge University Press, 1981, p. 49.

51 K. Blackwell *et al.* (eds), *The Collected Papers of Bertrand Russell*, Vol. 1, London, Allen & Unwin, 1983, p. 83. We are grateful to Liora Lukitz for this reference.

52 Nevinson Diaries, e617/4, 25 April 1913.

53 MLWS *Monthly* 25 (November 1911).

54 Victor D. Duval, *An Appeal to Men*, 1910, Suffragette Fellowship Collection, Museum of London.

55 MLWS *Monthly* 5 (July 1910), M. Durham, 'Suffrage and After', in M. Langan and B. Schwartz (eds), *Crises in the British State, London, Hutchinson, 1995, pp. 182–4; M.A. Richardson, Laugh a Defiance*, London, Widenfeld, 1953, pp. 31, 44.

56 Nevinson Diaries, e616/2, 22 November 1910.

57 L. Housman, *The Unexpected Years*, London, Jonathan Cape, 1937, p. 278.

58 MLWS *Monthly* 5 (February 1910).

59 F. Montgomery, 'Gender and Suffrage: The Manchester Men's League for Women's Suffrage 1908–1918', *Bulletin of John Rylands University Library of Manchester* 77, 1 (1995), p. 225.

60 MLWS *Monthly* 39 (December 1912).

61 Montgomery, 'Gender and Suffrage', pp. 223–41.

62 For an excellent discussion of the workings of the Conciliation Committee see F. W. Leventhal, *The Last Dissenter*, Oxford, Clarendon Press, 1985, pp. 82–91.

63 Nevinson Diaries, e615/1, 22 June 1908 and e615/4, 13 January 1910 for the following quote.

64 The MPU material is in the Fawcett Library, UDC 396.11 (06) B.
65 See too Nevinson Diaries, e617/1, 19 January 1912. Referring to Lloyd
    George, Duval stated: 'We in the Men's Political Union give a man one
    chance, but we do not give him two or three'; Victor D. Duval, 'Why I
    went to Prison' in Franklin Papers, Fawcett Library, HFD, Box 227.
66 Nevinson Diaries, e616/3, 29 June 1910.
67 ibid. e618/1, 3 October 1913.
68 See especially, S. S. Holton, *Suffrage Days. Stories from the Women's
    Suffrage Movement*, London, Routledge, 1996.
69 Franklin Papers, HFD, Box 226, Folder 1, 1910.
70 Nevinson Diaries, e617/3, 3 January 1913.
71 B. Harrison, *Prudent Revolutionaries. Portraits of British Feminists
    between the Wars*, Oxford, Clarendon Press, 1987, p. 226.
72 Deian Hopkin, 'The Newspapers of the Independent Labour Party', PhD,
    University of Wales College, Aberystwyth, 1981, pp. 83, 442–3.
73 Nevinson Diaries, e617/1, 8 March 1912.
74 Montgomery, 'Gender and Suffrage', p. 229.
75 Linda Walker, U of G.RPS.
76 J. Liddington, *The Life and Times of a Respectable Rebel, Selina Cooper
    (1864–1946)*, London, Virago Press, 1984, pp. 150–5.
77 Samuel T. Evans Papers, National Library of Wales, V. Hartshorn to
    Samuel T. Evans, Letter 24.
78 S. Pankhurst, *The Suffragette*, London, Gay & Hancock, 1911, p. 98.
79 A. V. John, '"Run like Blazes". The Suffragettes and Welshness',
    Llafur, Journal of Welsh Labour Society 6, 3 (1994), pp. 28–43.
80 *North Wales Chronicle*, July 1913.
81 *WF*, 8 August 1907. For the SDF see K. Hunt, *Equivocal Feminists.
    The Social Democratic Federation and the Woman Question 1884–1911*,
    Cambridge, Cambridge University Press, 1996.
82 Quoted in M. Lieven, *Senghennydd. The Universal Pit Village*, Llan-
    dysul, Gwasg Gomer, 1994, p. 81.
83 *Brighton Herald*, 17 June 1911.
84 See also, L. Leneman, *A Guid Cause. The Women's Suffrage Movement
    in Scotland*, Aberdeen, Aberdeen University Press, 1991; and L.
    Leneman, 'Northern Men and Votes For Women', *History Today* 41
    (1991), pp. 33–41.
85 E. Robins, *Way Stations*, London, Hodder & Stoughton, 1913, p. 70.
86 W. H. Dickinson Papers, F/DCK/52/6/1–2, F/DCK/28/9.
87 MLWS *Monthly*, 38 (November 1912).
88 ibid., 4 (May 1913); *Women's Franchise*, 25 February 1909.
89 R. Dalziel, 'Presenting the Enfranchisement of New Zealand Women
    Abroad', in Daley and Nolan, *Suffrage & Beyond*, pp. 42–64.
90 Suffragette Fellowship Collection, Museum of London, 5–7.116/2.
91 J. Gibson, *The Emancipation of Women* (1891), Llandysul, Gwasg
    Gomer, 1992 edn, pp. 78, 101.
92 Suffragette Fellowship Collection, Museum of London, Unaccessioned.
93 ibid.
94 For international reports see especially the MLWS *Monthly* 38

(November 1912), 47 (August–September 1913). Keir Hardie's letter is in the Franklin Papers, HFD, Box 226, Folder 4, 29 April 1913.

95 For the Drysdales see L. Bland, *Banishing the Beast. English Feminism and Sexual Morality 1885–1914*, Harmondsworth, Penguin, 1995, pp. 202–9; C. V. Drysdale, 'The Wages and Employment Question', 1912, Suffragette Fellowship Collection, Museum of London; MLWS *Monthly* 56 (July 1914).

96 K. Bradley, '"Odd Men". The Role of Men in the Oxford Suffrage and Anti Suffrage Societies 1870–1914', paper given to 'Seeing Through Suffrage' Conference at the University of Greenwich, April 1996.

97 See Holton, 'From Anti-Slavery to Suffrage Militancy', p. 217 and Housman, *The Unexpected Years*. For an interesting, progressive partnership see S. S. Holton, 'Victorian Feminism: The Divers Matrimonials of Elizabeth Wollstoneholme Elmy and Ben Elmy', *Victorian Studies* 37, 2 (1994), pp. 199–222.

98 Nevinson Diaries, e617/1, 12 January 1912.

99 D. Lawrenson Swanton, *Emerging from the Shadow. The Lives of Sarah Anne Lawrenson and Lucy Olive Kingston*, Dublin, Attic Press, 1994, pp. 58–65.

100 Book of Suffragette Prisoners – Questionnaire replies, 1931, Suffragette Fellowship Collection, Museum of London, 58, 87/65.

101 Harrison, *Prudent Revolutionaries*, p. 272. Interestingly, contemporaries tended to refer to him as Pethick and to her as Mrs Lawrence.

102 See Chapter 5, p. 145.

103 Rachel Ferguson, quoted in J. Beckett and D. Cherry (eds), *The Edwardian Era*, London, Phaidon Press and Barbican Art Gallery, 1987, p. 19.

104 Drysdale, 'The Wages and Employment Question'.

105 A. Philpin, 'Crime and Protest 1815–1974', in D. Howell (ed.), *Pembrokeshire County History*, vol. iv *Modern Pembrokeshire 1815–1974*, Haverfordwest, Pembrokeshire Historical Society, 1994, p. 331.

106 Nevinson Diaries, e616/2, 1 December 1910.

107 ibid.

108 ibid.

109 *WF*, 25 February 1909.

110 Franklin Papers, HFD, Folder 4, 7 April 1911.

111 Nevinson Diaries, e617/3, 23 November 1912.

112 ibid., e618/1, 11 October 1913. For earlier dealings with Lloyd George see, for example, e615/3, 27 July 1909.

113 ibid., e618/1, 28 November 1913.

114 ibid., e618/1, 24, 28 November 1913, e618/2 December 1913–January 1914 for the USA.

115 *The Vote*, 18 February 1911, p. 201.

116 Nevinson, *More Changes*, p. 336.

117 *The Vote*, 26 May 1916, p. 1046.

118 Montgomery, 'Gender and Suffrage', pp. 229–32.

119 F. Montgomery, '"Women Who Dids, and all that kind of thing . . ." Male Perceptions of "Wholesome Literature"', in C. Parker (ed.),

Gender, Politics and Sexuality in Victorian Literature, Aldershot, Scolar Press, 1995, pp. 172–87.

120 A woman over 30 who occupied a home or had landed property of an annual value of at least £5, of which she or her husband was a tenant, could now vote. Female graduates of universities (or the equivalent where degrees were not yet conferred on women) could vote for a university member as well as in their own constituency.

121 See, for example, J. Bourke, *Dismembering the Male: Men's Bodies, Britain and the Great War*, London, Reakton Books, 1996.

122 Kimmel and Mosmiller, *Against the Tide*, p. 77. Not all American suffragists were progressive. In the south, for example, some supported women's suffrage to counteract recently emancipated blacks; ibid., p. xxi.

123 *The "Awakener"*, 14 June 1913. In the personal papers of June Purvis to whom we are grateful.

124 H. Carter (ed.), *Women's Suffrage and Militancy*, London, Frank Palmer, 1911, p. 9.

125 MLWS *Monthly* 18 (March 1911).

126 ibid., 9 (June 1910). Chapman's second wife, his divorced cousin, Adeline, was president of the New Constitutional Society for Women's Suffrage.

127 ibid., 43 (April 1913); reply, 44 (May 1913).

128 Suffragette Fellowship Collection, Museum of London, Unaccessioned and 50/82/105.

129 P. Baker, 'Who's Afraid of the Big, Bad Women?', *Guardian*, 24 January 1994. The UK Men's Movement was launched in April 1994.

130 See, for example, *Achilles Heel* and the *Anti-Sexist Men's Newsletter*.

Chapter 1

The making of masculinities
The middle class in late nineteenth-century Britain

John Tosh

In late twentieth-century Britain male support for the cause of women's liberation has included some quite searching critiques of masculinity itself. Writers and activists have drawn the conclusion that, however overdue attention to women's demands may be, sexual inequality will remain intact unless the spotlight is turned on to the dominant sex as well. Men have been fully involved in this endeavour, producing critiques of surprising harshness, as well as more celebratory forms of self-appraisal.[1] Before 1914, however, this aspect of male solidarity with the women's cause was conspicuously absent. Much has been made in recent years of Edward Carpenter, socialist, homosexual and supporter of women's rights. In *Love's Coming of Age* (1896) Carpenter argued that 'woman the serf' and 'man the ungrown' were two sides of the same coin of bodily and spiritual denial, and that human progress depended on a radical reform of both.[2] But Carpenter was one of the very few male polemicists seriously to address these issues. Other supporters of women's rights tended to justify their crossing of gender lines in ways which left their own gender unscrutinized. For example, in the Men and Women's Club, a small group of progressive intellectuals of both sexes who met in London in the 1880s, female members complained that the subject of male sexuality was ignored while the men repeatedly directed attention to woman's nature.[3] Women were still 'the sex', and men the unstated standard by which the world was judged. Compared with present-day debates on sexual politics, masculinity seems to have been almost invisible in the classic era of women's suffrage.

In the light of this reticence it is perhaps understandable that the actions of male suffragists still tend to be interpreted in terms of their personal relationships or their adherence to general (and gender-free) political principle. Yet if there is one conclusion on which all recent work on masculinity concurs, it is its relational quality. Neither masculinity nor femininity is a meaningful construct without the other; each defines, and is in turn defined by, the other. Men do not decide to work for a major change in the position of women without experiencing a modification in their own gender identity. Some male suffragists, as Angela John explains in her chapter, interpreted their role as one of protection due to the other sex, which might be weaker in physical terms but was superior to men on moral grounds. This required a reworking of the traditional ideal of chivalry. Others like Laurence Housman saw women's disfranchisement as symptomatic of a wider malaise which distorted men's natures too. They looked for a dissolution of sexual difference, for comradeship in place of patriarchy. Whatever their conception of the women's cause, male supporters from John Stuart Mill to Frederick Pethick Lawrence had to court the charge of sexual treason; in Housman's words, they dared 'to be thought unmanly and cowardly'.[4] No man could maintain his public support for women's suffrage without reflecting on what really constituted his manhood.

Historical analysis requires a comparable focus. What manhood really consisted of, both in social practice and in cultural representation, is an essential starting-point for setting in context the male suffragist, as well as his opponent. And manhood cannot be considered apart from the gender order as a whole. Just as women's position was disclosing dramatically new possibilities during this period, so too some of the most fundamental constituents of masculinity were called into question, in many cases as a direct result of changes in the position of women. The crisis over women's suffrage between 1905 and 1914 was the latest and most dramatic stage in a destabilizing of gender boundaries which had been gathering pace since the 1870s. The issue of votes for women had been a focus of debate throughout that time, but seldom the dominant one; in practical terms far more had been achieved with regard to women's education, employment, life-style and marital status. Many men were disturbed and threatened by these changes. Others experienced them as liberating. But all participants in the struggle for women's suffrage were marked by that experience. Masculinity, no less than femininity, had shifted ground as a result.

Changing codes of manliness offer one clearly marked point of entry into this neglected field. Masculinity may have been scarcely visible in critical discourse, but its approved forms were endlessly proclaimed. The voluminous late nineteenth-century literature on 'manliness' is testimony to that: it documents some significant shifts in thinking over the period, and has provided the most accessible material for historians of masculinity.[5] But there is a limit to how much we can learn from a fundamentally didactic body of texts. For this period they tell us more about the rise of secular imperialism at the expense of religion than about masculinity itself. A deeper and more comprehensive enquiry is needed which engages with men's gender identity at three levels. First, and most fundamentally, masculinity is formed within the family, in intimate relations of desire and dependence. How those relations are structured affects both the gender conditioning of boys and their subsequent attitude to family life as adults. Secondly, from puberty (and often earlier) masculine identity is developed, and partly validated, through participation in male peer-groups, school usually being the first arena in which boys are exposed to a competitive masculine ethos. Winning recognition from one's fellows is critical to socially valid masculinity, which partly explains why male bonding continues to be such an important feature of men's adult lives, notably at the workplace or in leisure activities. Thirdly, masculinity is constructed by a perception of women, not so much as individual family members, but as a social category bound by patriarchal relations to the dominant sex. In most societies the exercise of patriarchal power, both individually and collectively, is so inseparable from masculine identity that changes in the structure of sexual relations usually have a very direct – and sometimes undermining – impact on masculinity. The later nineteenth century saw significant changes in each of these areas: in family life, in schooling and associational life, and in relations between the sexes. In this chapter I consider these changes as they affected men in the middle class, from which the majority of men prominent in the suffrage movement were drawn.[6]

I

The most fundamental, but also the least understood, trend affecting domestic relations in this period was the reduction in family size. Beginning in the 1860s among doctors and clergy, family limitation soon spread to professional people in general, followed by the commercial and industrial classes. Upper- and middle-class couples who married during the 1880s were having 3.5 children on average, compared with 6.4 for those married in the 1850s.[7] There has been much debate among historians as to where the initiative for this process came from, and what were the respective inputs of husband and wife.[8] Wives were influenced by the continuing perils of childbirth and by the anticipated gain in the quality of mothering if concentrated on fewer recipients. Sometimes husbands co-operated out of deference to their wives' wishes. But they were also keenly aware of the rising cost of providing each child with the socially appropriate level of domestic comfort and schooling. The man holding the purse-strings was likely to be highly susceptible to the argument that fewer children would avert the dangers of spreading family resources too thinly.[9] Yet what made good economic sense exacted an emotional cost too. Virility was a traditional test of masculinity, and men who had no children suffered definite loss of reputation.[10] As Peter Gay has pointed out, to limit the number of one's offspring raised insistent, if largely unconscious, doubts about the capacity to make children.[11] Becoming a father was no less central to traditional notions of household headship. Both attributes were most effectively demonstrated by fathering a quiverful of children. The alternative construction, which saw reduced fertility as a mark of manly self-reliance, probably had more meaning for working-class husbands with a tenuous hold on respectability than for their middle-class counterparts.[12] Having fewer children might also modify the power dynamic within marriage. A wife with fewer burdens of childbirth and childcare was in a stronger position to extend the scope of her parenting and to contest her husband's authority in other ways.[13] But given the extreme reticence of the Victorians on sex within marriage, little more than speculation is possible here.

We are on firmer ground in assessing the changing appeal of domesticity. In late Victorian Britain the sanctification of home was alive and well across a wide swathe of society. To live in domesticity continued to be a compelling aspiration for men on the margins of 'respectable' society who were anxious to better their social status. The non-working wife, the terraced house and the front room were becoming the hallmarks of the skilled working man, with rhetoric to match from his trade union.[14] Much the same was true of the rapidly expanding ranks of clerks and office workers among the lower middle class – like the fictional Mr Pooter who struggled so hard to make reality conform with his vision of domestic decorum.[15] But higher up the social ladder the situation was different. Men of the middle and upper classes expressed mounting reservations about the proper place of domesticity in their lives. Reluctance to marry was a demographic fact. The age of first marriage rose gradually but steadily in the second half of the nineteenth century; for professional men it had reached 31.2 years by 1885.[16] Many well-established families, like the Gladstones or the Rhodeses, faced possible termination of the family name because of their sons' preference for bachelorhood.[17] Thousands of young men avoided their marital fate by embarking on careers in the colonies as single men. Much was made by contemporaries of the deterrent effect of the rising cost of marriage, defined as the level of expenditure needed to set up a household in accordance with the bride's expectations.[18] But rejection of domesticity was also strongly written into the culture of the period, suggesting a deeper alienation from the married state. The arrival of Robert Louis Stevenson and H. Rider Haggard on the London literary scene in the mid-1880s signalled the rapid rise of a new genre of men-only adventure fiction, in which the prevalent concern of the English novel with marriage and family was quite deliberately cast aside in favour of a bracing masculine fantasy of quest and danger, a world without petticoats.[19] What Arthur Conan Doyle called 'the modern masculine novel' accounted for many best-sellers.[20] The bachelor had become, in Eve Kosofsky Sedgwick's phrase, 'the representative man' in English literature.[21] The same tendencies were at work on the persona of the popular hero. The new paragons of imperial manliness, like Gordon and Kitchener, were represented as men without female ties, in contrast to Nelson's passionate private life or Henry Havelock's acute sense of family duty.[22] Domesticity, in short, had a much more equivocal place in the lives of English middle-class men by the 1890s than had been the case in the High Victorian era.

This ambivalence makes sense only if we register the full extent of what the late Victorians were reacting against. Their grandfathers had made a bigger investment in family life than their counterparts in any other country. In all settled communities family and household furnish the beginnings of masculine identity; but in Victorian England, foreign observers were agreed, home life had a place in the construction of men's lives without parallel in, say, France or America. The Englishman was perceived as a home-loving soul who preferred the tender ministrations of wife and children to life on the town. It was because public men drew so much of their identity from the familial sphere that R.W. Emerson regarded domesticity as the 'taproot' of the English nation.[23]

Domesticity had conferred many benefits on the early Victorian bourgeois or professional man. The home was a protected zone for the exercise of masculine authority over those defined as inferior on account of sex, age, or class, at a time when authority relations in society as a whole were being redrawn in unpredictable ways. There was the possibility of greater intimacy within marriage, in conformity with the companionate and romantic ideals which had grown up since the late eighteenth century. Above all, for the many men who were alienated or exhausted by their labours in the counting-house or the factory, home was touted as the one place where they could fully express their humanity. 'We cease the struggle in the race of the world, and give our hearts leave and leisure to love', was how J. A. Froude put it.[24] The centrality of home in Victorian culture reflects its heightened meanings for men, as much as its exclusive claim on the priorities of women.

At the same time, however, home was always an ambivalent marker of masculinity. Traditionally the man who withdrew from male conviviality and spent his time at home in the company of women was exposed to the charge of effeminacy. Worse still, his capacity for independent action might be undermined and his governance of the home surrendered to his wife or daughter. Evangelicalism, which had such a profound influence on early Victorian family life, gave a new twist to this fear of female control by emphasizing woman's superior moral nature and her role as Angel Mother. But this higher profile for women was offset by the more traditional Protestant idea that the household head stood in place of God to his family and was charged with responsibility for their moral and spiritual progress – an ideal symbolized by the father presiding over daily family prayers. As Leonore Davidoff and Catherine Hall have shown, it was primarily the teachings of evangelicalism which enabled middle-class men to be both domesticated and manly. Time spent at home was compatible with manhood, provided the man was in command.[25]

In the 1880s the prevailing social conditions which had accounted for so much of the appeal of domesticity in the 1830s had not significantly shifted. It may be that urban spaces now appeared a little less threatening as commercial and leisure amenities improved.[26] But the working life of most middle-class men continued to be as stressful and alienating as before – indeed probably more so in view of the economic anxieties current during the Great Depression of the 1880s and early 1890s. The domestic conventions inherited from the early Victorians were still sustained by the doctrine of separate spheres, now freshly decked out in the fashionable garb of evolutionary science.[27] But among men the consensus in favour of those values was no longer so overwhelming. There was mounting evidence of frustration and *ennui*. What W. R. Greg in 1869 called 'the decent monotony of the hearth' had long been an occupational hazard of domesticity for men.[28] But this complaint became more pronounced in the 1880s, with observers tending to notice the boredom rather than the bliss of the married state: like the anonymous man-about-town who remarked 'I would sooner dine in public, with a play of life and character around me . . . I consider the domestic dinner gruesome', or the youthful Robert Louis Stevenson who complained that in marriage 'the air of the fireside withers out all the fine wildings of the husband's heart'.[29]

Much of the boredom was no more than the acceptable face of sexual antagonism. Men resented what they perceived as a negative shift in the balance between female service and female authority, and their evaluation of domesticity changed accordingly. It has often been pointed out that Victorianism became more rigid and formulaic with every decade, and this was certainly true of the middle-class home, where ceremonial diversified and rigidified. Since the wife had the management of these routines, her role came to seem more obtrusive. She controlled the increasingly elaborate domestic rituals, from the dinner-table to the Christmas tree. Her ascendancy within the home was most evident in the drawing-room, perhaps most of all in the institution of five o'clock tea, which the journalist T. H. S. Escott called 'the symbol of the ascendancy of the softer over the sterner sex'.[30] Of course, as Edward Carpenter correctly deduced, there was a mockery about this drawing-room homage, in that the lady's sovereignty was more apparent than real, but even the appearance of masculine inferiority was galling, not to mention the time expended on sustaining the fiction.[31] Men therefore sought avenues of escape. The late nineteenth century was, according to Mark Girouard, the great age of the smoking-room and the billiard-room in country houses – men-only sanctums where husbands and bachelors alike could indulge in masculine pleasures.[32] Wealthy London bourgeois husbands often maintained bachelor pads in places like the Inns of Court or the Albany.[33] Lower down the social scale, husbands were urged to set aside a 'den' to be reserved for their old mementoes and photographs – and for a quiet pipe. 'The tired master should have one place secure from the seamy side of domesticity', as one advice-book writer put it.[34] Thus at the very time that young middle-class women were revolting against the stifling conventions of the drawing-room, their fathers and brothers were in many cases making their own, less obtrusive protest. Some were staking out autonomous territory in or near the home, while others were postponing marriage indefinitely.

Reactions of this kind were themselves partly conditioned by family upbringing. One of the deepest though most intangible influences on masculine identity in the late nineteenth century was the sharp divide experienced in childhood between the roles of mother and father. The culture of separate spheres not only meant a strong demarcation of gendered spaces; it also tended to polarize the character traits of men and women, and in the home this was a crucial aspect of gender conditioning. While making due allowance for the variety of both character and parenting styles, the structure of bourgeois family life tended to push parental roles in opposite directions of love and discipline. Sons often experienced from their mothers warmth, affection and a degree of emotional openness – qualities which were fully validated by the mystique of the Angel Mother. But fathers, whether or not they spent much time in the home, were constrained by different priorities. Their most pressing concern was to prepare their sons for an adult world which many saw as more challenging and dangerous than they themselves had ever faced as young men. The moral qualities required for survival in this world were summed up by the word 'manliness', which meant courage, resolution, tenacity, and self-government or 'independence'. How far these qualities could be instilled in a domestic environment was a question which much troubled Victorian fathers, but whether or not they opted for boarding education for their sons, their own role was clear: guidance and discipline must be clearly laid down, and emotional closeness avoided in the interests of instilling manly independence.[35] Of course by no means all fathers acted according to these austere principles, and family memoirs of the period recall many instances of openly affectionate fathers or ineffectual ones who had virtually abdicated their parental authority.[36] But the reproduction of masculinity was a serious business, and fathers tended to be over-serious in consequence. Edmond Demolins who visited England regularly in the 1890s noted that, whereas French parents continued to treat their sons as children long after it was appropriate, English parents sought to hasten their emancipation; 'a father's conversation with his children bears on serious, real, manly topics . . . they vaunt the Struggle for Existence and Self-Help.'[37]

In a domestic regime where the mother stood for love (and often indulgence) while the father represented the discipline needed for survival in the outside world, growing sons often experienced a gulf between the characters of father and mother. They identified readily with the stern and undemonstrative father and learned to associate tenderness and emotional support exclusively with women. The display of affection – even the awareness of inner feeling – became incompatible with a masculine self-image, and while a son might sentimentalize these qualities in his mother he could not express them in his own demeanour. This was the background which produced some of the characteristic masculine traits of the period. The stereotype of the 'stiff upper lip' approximates pretty well to the emotional repression which marked so many men of the upper and middle classes at this time – 'man the ungrown' in Carpenter's telling phrase. Lord Kitchener, son of a martinet and of an adored mother who died when he was 14, fits the mould; as a colleague later recalled:

> He loathed any form of moral or mental undressing. He was even morbidly afraid of showing any feeling or enthusiasm, and he preferred to be misunderstood rather than be suspected of any human feeling.[38]

Then there were those who craved more emotional warmth than their fathers had ever given them, and who found it in intensely homo-social settings, and sometimes homosexuality. The three surviving sons of Edward Benson (born between 1862 and 1871) had experienced a particularly acute temperamental divide between mother and father; all of them conducted their adult lives outside the normal confines of domesticity in bachelor quarters or collegiate communities, and all of them were drawn to 'Uranian' notions of love between males.[39] Other men – an increasing number in this generation – were drawn to a career in the colonies not only for economic reasons but also because of the freedom it offered from home ties. Their response, and that of countless others, to the distorting emotional field of the conventional bourgeois family was to renounce domesticity, including the patriarchal privileges that went with it.

This trend must not of course be exaggerated. The reproduction of patriarchy did not grind to a halt. Large numbers of men continued to contemplate matrimony happily, and many were satisfied with the results. But even their conventional contentment was played out against a new backdrop. From the 1880s, as never before, the merits of the married state were open to question. The fact that they were vociferously denied in some quarters, while legal judgments and media comment pointed to more exacting standards for husbands, caused a great deal of heart-searching among the young. Marriage could certainly not be taken for granted. For an unprecedented proportion of upper- and middle-class men, avoidance of marriage was a real option, and bachelorhood a recognized pattern of life.

II

The socialization of boys and young men by their peers can take many forms. In the past it had been associated with apprenticeship, often a byword for rowdy group behaviour of a precocious and exaggerated kind. In the late nineteenth-century urban working class, peer-group discipline was imposed in the street. But for middle- and upper-class boys school was the critical arena of peer-group recognition, and more and more the boarding public school. The overwhelming dominance of these schools over the education of boys from 'good families' was a recent phenomenon. At the beginning of the century, seven public schools had catered mainly for the landed aristocracy and squirearchy. By 1890 their number had leaped to some seventy, and they attracted boys from the professional classes, and a rising number from the business classes.[40] The private tutor was now a rarity, and attendance at day school among the affluent middle class was the exception. For the public service and professional elites, public school had become the defining initiation into manhood. This function was directly addressed by the official ethos of the schools. Thomas Arnold of Rugby, who had a huge posthumous influence on the new foundations around mid-century, aimed to push boys into moral and intellectual maturity as quickly as possible, so that they would leave school with a fully formed sense of Christian public duty and the inner discipline to fulfil it. By the 1880s the initiation was seen differently. The school's job was to mould and direct a phase of life now seen as fundamentally healthy. Under the influence of evolutionary biology, educationalists developed a new respect for the instinctual aspects of boyhood. Boys were admired for their animal spirits, their testing of physical limits, their primitive loyalties and their presumed sexual innocence. Whereas Arnold had aimed to compress the transition from child to man by forcing the pace of maturation, public school headmasters at the end of the century thought nothing of indulging 'boyishness' until the age of 19 or 20. In practice this meant encouraging team games and physical toughness at the expense of intellectual and moral growth.[41]

But the importance of the public schools to the construction of late Victorian masculinity lay not so much in the programme of the educators as in the values instilled in each other by the boys themselves. The schools were ruled by peer-group pressure with a vengeance. A boy's standing – often his access to food and whatever physical comforts the school provided – was at the mercy of his fellows. This was what explained the enduring appeal of the public schools through all the changes of fashion from the eighteenth century onwards. A middle-class father's decision to adopt the expensive expedient of sending his son to public school might be influenced by academic or professional ambitions, or by the hope that the boy would acquire the patina of a gentleman, but the bedrock of the schools' appeal was the training which they provided in self-government and self-reliance. Learning to stand on one's own feet, to rub shoulders with all sorts, to have the guts to stand out against the crowd – these qualities were integral to manliness, and they were not likely to be acquired at home. Provided the worst excesses were avoided, hard knocks and salutary neglect at school were acceptable to parents as the best means of teaching their son to 'shift for himself'.[42] Analogies with ancient Sparta drew attention to this aspect of the public schools.[43]

The boy culture of the public schools despised intellectual ability and aesthetic sensibility; it elevated athletic prowess to become a fetish; and it cultivated a strong but somewhat mechanical group loyalty, easily adapted to an unthinking patriotism and a secular sense of public duty.[44] Two attitudes proved particularly relevant to men's responses to women's suffrage. In the first place, public school enforced a crude pecking order of privilege by seniority and by muscular might. Anti-suffrage men placed great weight on the contention that, since government rested on the use or threat of force, it could not concern the weaker sex.[45] Pro-suffrage activists like Laurence Housman who struggled to counter this 'physical force' argument were well aware that undue respect for force was one of the most pernicious legacies of a school culture which taught boys to endure cruelty and then inflict it on those weaker than themselves.[46] Secondly, the public schools intensified a preference for the company of males. Women were confined to the humble servicing role of matron or maid. Mother and sisters were not to be spoken of, or displayed in photographs. Those who breached this convention were branded as weak and effeminate. For every boy who pined for home there were others for whom the home and its female inmates seemed increasingly unreal and who would never adapt to a conventional domestic environment. Behaviour associated with the opposite sex succumbed to the same fate. This was particularly true of emotional disclosure. Already, as we have seen, the gender polarization of many middle-class homes discouraged the display of feeling in boys; school tended to make the ban absolute. Sir Francis Younghusband recalled of his days at Clifton in the late 1870s, 'to betray any sort of sentiment was a crime'.[47] In the words of a colonial educationalist in 1903: 'the manly man is to stand like a bluff headland unshaken by the waves of emotion.'[48]

The dominant code of manliness in late Victorian Britain accurately expressed the public school values of the time. Chivalry towards women was *de rigueur*, but it was secondary. Manliness was essentially a code which regulated the behaviour of men towards each other. It extolled action rather than reflection, duty to one's country rather than one's conscience, and physical pluck rather than moral courage. The manly ideals propagated in the 1880s and 1890s made less allowance for the inner man or for transparency in personal relations; they emphasized instead conformity of opinion and correctness of behaviour – or 'good form'. Of course the public school did not just produce an elite of rigid conformists. More critical spirits who survived its rigours were ready for anything, as the career of Frederick Pethick Lawrence testifies: at Eton in the 1880s 'the very fact that I stood then against the stream strengthened my spirit of independent judgement and gave me self-reliance'.[49] But Carpenter's estimate of public school manliness was surely right: a narrow and conventional sense of honour, which might comprehend the call to duty, and even self-sacrifice, but was deaf to the dictates of the heart.[50]

Beyond public school lay a range of openings which beckoned the young man inured to men-only living. The universities and the armed services maintained their traditional appeal; colonial administration and teaching in public schools both offered many more openings during this period; while settlement houses and Anglican celibate orders were entirely new. All of these occupations provided a total homosocial environment reminiscent of public school. But this was also the golden age of the gentleman's club, especially in London's West End. Here bachelors could conduct social life on their own terms, and married men could find a reassuringly masculine refuge from the over-feminine ambience of home. Closer to the margins of respectable society, London also spawned its own version of Bohemia, composed of artists and writers who were either too poor to marry or too fearful that domesticity would sap their talent. As Brian Harrison has put it, the period before the First World War was 'an age of bachelors, or of married men who spent a large part of their lives as though they were bachelors'.[51]

This preference for bachelor living begs important questions about the ties between men. Social purists attacked the public schools as dens of homosexual vice where boys were corrupted by their seniors into a life of perversion. London and other big cities had their rent-boy sub-culture which was well patronized by men of the governing classes, and the colonies offered further exotic (and inexpensive) possibilities. But relations between men of the same class were much more inhibited. As Eve Kosofsky Sedgwick has pointed out, a fine but critical line separates being 'a man's man' from being 'interested in men': male friendship in an institutional setting strengthens patriarchy, but exclusive sexual relationships between men introduce division and jealousy, as well as undermining the vital reproductive mechanism of marriage. According to Sedgwick, it was during the second half of the nineteenth century that this schism between friendship and sex in homosocial relations became absolute. Darwinism rehabilitated the healthiness and normality of sex in the scheme of evolution, while branding non-reproductive forms of sex as pathological. Concern about the evidence of a declining rate of population growth from 1881 tended to the same effect. Imperial concerns also lent their weight: an educated class reared on the classics was sensitive to the argument that empires are brought low as much by moral canker within as by barbarian incursions from without. By the 1880s a crescendo of protests against vice of all kinds, especially in the young, was reaching its climax, and in 1885 homosexual acts in private were outlawed by the Criminal Law Amendment Act.[52]

These were the conditions for homosexual panic, causing men not only to proscribe homosexual behaviour in others, but anxiously to scrutinize their own emotional life for signs of illicit desire. When Oscar Wilde was convicted in 1895 under the 1885 Act, the journalist

W. T. Stead (not a homosexual himself) presciently remarked to Edward Carpenter:

> A few more cases like Oscar Wilde's and we should find the freedom of comradeship now possible to men seriously impaired to the permanent detriment of the race.[53]

Close relations between men were much more circumscribed than in the early Victorian period. Too much effusiveness or physicality was open to misinterpretation. Idealistic young men from Oxford and Cambridge were attracted in a steady stream to settlement houses and churches in slum areas, where they could enjoy an extension of common-room comradeship with their fellow graduates, and at the same time savour the rough manliness of working-class lads.[54] But decorum was usually observed. For some, residence in an all-male institution was only a phase, to be followed by marriage and domesticity. For others it became a permanent commitment and the focus of their emotional life. But even these men usually behaved as 'asexuals'. Arthur Benson, whose entire working life was spent as an Eton master and a Cambridge don, could declare only a small part of his feelings for the succession of attractive young men who came his way; he seemed always to be 'on the edge of Paradise'.[55] Middle- and upper-class men of this generation often yearned for 'man-talk and tobacco'. They did not, by and large, conduct erotically explicit friendships. They were probably happier with Kipling's image in *The Light That Failed* (1891) of 'the austere love that springs up between men who have tugged at the same oar together'.[56]

III

Growing up male is not only about establishing one's standing in the company of men and learning the appropriate codes of masculine behaviour; it is also about taking one's place in a social order designed to deliver power and privilege to men at the expense of women. For most, but not all, men patriarchy is an immediate personal agenda, a standard by which relations of dominance with wife, daughters, or female employees are to be measured. But since all men benefit collectively from the structure of sexual inequality, patriarchal values matter to the overwhelming majority of men, whether or not they share their everyday lives with women. The stake which men have in patriarchy is materially so valuable and culturally so pervasive that one may indeed question whether masculinity can exist apart from patriarchy: not that it is entirely subsumed in patriarchy, but that it would be a radically different kind of identity in a situation of sexual equality.

The suffrage movement was shocking because it openly challenged public patriarchy. When after 1905 militant suffragettes literally invaded the public sphere, the threat was even more disturbing. But this was not the first time that women had stepped out of their allotted role and challenged the conventional separation of spheres. In fact the suffrage campaigns would be hard to imagine without the earlier assault on the Contagious Diseases Acts (CD Acts) in the 1870s and early 1880s, when the Ladies National Association attacked medical and state power as men's power, in public meetings where both the platform and audience were female. The movement also drew attention to the double standard of sexual conduct, relentlessly exposing the damage which young men of loose morals did to prostitutes and to their brides. After the temporary repeal of the CD Acts in 1883, this second aspect of the movement's agenda was developed by Social Purity feminists (in alliance with leading evangelicals) into a call for the state repression of brothels. The Criminal Law Amendment Act 1885 raised the age of consent to 16 and outlawed brothel-keeping, leading to a massive increase in prosecutions against brothels. As a restraint on the traditional sexual freedoms of young men, the Act was a good deal more significant than the repeal of the CD Acts themselves.[57]

Sexual behaviour on the street was not the only aspect of masculinity to be regulated by the state. The structure of family life itself came under critical scrutiny in ways which could be interpreted as fulfilling a feminist agenda at the expense of men. Despite the protests of laissez-faire purists, the wall of domestic privacy was breached in important ways during this period, and limits were set on the sway of private patriarchy. First came the change in the law of divorce. The reform enacted in 1857 was certainly not intended to make for a more equal balance between husbands and wives. It upheld the traditional double standard which required wives to prove other offences (such as cruelty, incest, or desertion) besides infidelity, while husbands could secure a divorce on grounds of adultery alone. But the greater accessibility and lower costs of the new Divorce Court, as compared with the old ecclesiastical courts, encouraged more wives to initiate proceedings: between the 1860s and 1911 the percentage of women petitioners gradually rose from 38 per cent to 46 per cent.[58] As A. James Hammerton has movingly shown, the plight of wives who sought redress in the courts against years of abuse or neglect made a deep impression on judges – and on newspaper readers. Judges responded by extending the existing grounds of physical cruelty to include mental cruelty as well. The newspaper-reading public, who were given every detail of the more lurid cases, reacted in effect by subscribing to higher minimum standards for husbands – a tendency also reflected in the copious advice literature on marriage which now placed the greater responsibility for marital harmony on the husband rather than the wife.[59]

The reform in the law on married women's property was in some ways even more profound. Accomplished in two main stages, it was the second Act in 1882 granting 'separate property' to wives in the form of capital which meant most to the middle and upper classes. It was conceived by the Liberal government as a reform of anomalies in the relationship between equity and common law, but contemporaries were agreed that the social consequences were likely to be profound. The Act's opponents were wide of the mark in predicting an open season for domestic tyranny by wives. But feminists were right to hail the principal outcome – wives' control of their own property – as the end of one of the key props of patriarchy. Moreover, as many commentators pointed out at the time, separating out wives' property was not merely a financial matter; it was bound to enlarge the individuality and autonomy of wives in general.[60] Marriage would never be quite the same again, a judgement borne out by Hammerton's account of the marriage of Henry and Elizabeth Ashbee. Elizabeth left her husband in 1893 because of a growing divergence of tastes and interests, but her son makes it clear that she was a beneficiary of the changes in the 1880s. The Married Women's Property Act 1882 did not add to her legal or financial power to leave her husband, but it had contributed significantly to the more egalitarian climate in which such a drastic step could be contemplated.[61] Equally, greater legal constraints on husbands' authority influenced the way men weighed up the advantages of marriage. The suggestion made by one last-ditch opponent of the 1882 Act that the application of the measure be postponed for two years 'in order to give people who were contemplating matrimony time to change their minds when they find the law altered' may have been facetious, but it voiced real doubts about the attractions for men of marriage under the new dispensation.[62] It was in psychological dimensions of this kind that marriage changed most, adding to the dignity of wives while bringing time-honoured patriarchal assumptions into question. That process was extended by the widening scope of feminist critiques of marriage. Initially targeted in the 1870s at the economic subordination of the wife compared to her spinster sister, by the 1890s the attack was breaching the taboo on discussing sex in marriage.[63]

A different kind of challenge to patriarchy was thrown down by the New Woman. This label did not primarily denote an active feminist politics, though many who fitted the description certainly joined the ranks of the suffragists or the social purists and became 'platform women'. The term 'New Woman' originated as a media invention of the 1890s,[64] but it referred to trends which had been discernible since the 1880s. The New Woman was usually a young middle-class woman who enjoyed a measure of personal independence in ways which affronted patriarchal propriety. Behind the smoking and cycling which identified her in public was someone who lived on her own, or with other young women. She usually worked for her living, often in teaching or journalism. Somewhat lower down the social scale, the large numbers of women who were recruited into office work at this time – over 20 per cent of all clerks in some cities by 1901 – scarcely rated as 'middle class', but they posed a direct threat to the men who had hitherto monopolized clerical jobs.[65] The New Woman also asserted her freedom to be unchaperoned both in private and in public. She was increasingly likely to attend secondary school, and even university, and to play in the competitive team sports which these institutions encouraged. In these and other aspects of her life-style, the New Woman was highly visible, perhaps more so than her actual numbers warranted. Her claim to both intellectual and economic equality was highly provocative. Above all, in rejecting men's protection, the New Woman was refusing to lead her life by the patriarchal rules.[66]

Late nineteenth-century culture was permeated by images which expressed a fear of female power. Beneath the ridicule heaped on the New Woman by the press lay the anxiety instilled by women who flouted paternal authority and refused or postponed marriage. This was expressed in the almost morbid fear of women's sexuality which characterized the visual arts of the period, with their recurrent images of predatory seduction.[67] In avant-garde literature, the stories published in *The Yellow Book* between 1894 and 1897 reflected keen anxiety about women's assertion within marriage.[68] As Elaine Showalter has pointed out, the novels of masculine quest in the 1880s and 1890s, like those of Rudyard Kipling, Rider Haggard and Joseph Conrad, expressed acute fears of 'manly decline in the face of female power'.[69] Their analogue was the New Women novelists whose merciless portrayal of venereally diseased husbands and sexually assaulted wives only intensified male anxieties. The changing character of manliness conformed to the same pattern: as Peter Gay has argued, the more strident tone of manly discourse towards the end of the century was, in part at least, a defence mechanism designed to bolster men against increasing female intrusion into 'their' sphere.[70]

IV

The question that remains is just how pervasive and undermining this sense of masculine insecurity was. Surveying the political scene in 1888, the editor of the *Spectator*, Meredith Townsend, expressed his unease as follows:

> Whether for good or evil, a great change is passing over Englishmen. They have become uncertain of themselves, afraid of their old opinions, doubtful of the true teachings of their consciences. They doubt if they have any longer any moral right to rule anyone, themselves almost included. An old mental disease, the love of approbation, has suddenly risen among them to the height of a passion. . . . That is the real root of the great change which has passed over the management of children, of the whole difficulty in Ireland, of the reluctance to conquer, and of the whole of the new philanthropic social legislation.[71]

This ascription of specific national problems to a general failure of will and a weakening of backbone speaks the language of gender crisis. When men grow soft, the body politic disintegrates. Similar responses were sparked by the physical unpreparedness of British manhood for the Boer War.[72] And, like the lax management of children, craven concessions to women and the canker of homosexuality were both seized on as part metaphor, part cause, of the unsettled face of public life. The *fin de siècle* is now in fact commonly seen as a period of crisis in masculinity, when evidence from many different directions seemed to confirm that men were under threat and losing control of themselves and others. The consequence was a growth of irrational and paranoid responses in both society and culture.[73]

Against this must be set the plentiful evidence of unruffled masculine composure. The British upper and middle classes continued to boast a large number of men who were secure in their wealth and positions of power, untroubled by wifely independence, and unreflecting in their enjoyment of club life. So far as their personal circumstances were concerned, patriarchy operated as smoothly as before. But the notion of 'crisis' does not mean that all men were personally confronted by a collapsing gender order – in the way that, for example, some sections of the lower middle class were by the rise of female clerical workers. What counted was the perception of social instability mediated in cultural terms. Here it was increasingly difficult to retain a confident sense that men's position was strong or unchanged. New social actors were at large, voicing new challenges. The hierarchy of family life was more openly questioned than at any time within living memory and had been partly modified by legislation. The spotlight had been thrown on the covert conventions of patriarchal sexual practice, and significant restraints imposed by law. Public spaces, including the workplace and educational institutions, were more open to women, and public life itself was subject to periodic female incursions. The journals of the day were open to radical feminist polemic, aided by feminist novels of sexual discontent and sometimes frank sexual antagonism.

Men's responses to the campaign for women's suffrage were firmly located in this context. At one extreme stood the rigid upholder of the patriarchal order, convinced that the suggested extension of the franchise was the most serious infringement of separate spheres yet proposed, with appalling consequences likely in each. In the domestic sphere, Frederic Harrison warned, the truth and spirituality of woman would be swept aside 'by gruesome cant about equal rights and adult suffrage'.[74] The whole structure of woman's moral mission was in jeopardy. As for the public sphere, votes for women would introduce feminine susceptibilities into the heart of government where a masculine mind was most needed – they would, in other words, compound the very problem of collapsing backbone that Townsend had identified. Imperialists like Curzon and Cromer were particularly drawn to this argument.[75] They found plentiful support in the ranks of those educated at the public schools, and among the denizens of Clubland, a terrain which of course included both Houses of Parliament.

At the other extreme were those men whose personal experience and social principles had led them to regard conventional forms of masculinity as a cruel constraint rather than a support. Gender identities as polarized as late nineteenth-century manliness and femininity were bound to produce a counter-discourse of androgyny. Many pro-suffrage writers of both sexes rejected the straitjacket of 'tough' manhood and 'soft' womanhood, either by reclassifying all the gendered virtues as 'human', or by recommending that each sex incorporate some of the qualities associated with the other.[76] Many men felt they had been personally damaged by the separation of spheres in family and education. Some, like Thomas Hardy and George Gissing, welcomed the possibilities of greater openness in relations between men and women since the 1870s, and they saw women's suffrage not only as an overdue entitlement for women, but as a step towards the reform of sexual mores. For Laurence Housman and Edward Carpenter, support for militant suffragism amounted to a rejection of the stifling conventions of bourgeois family life. Others believed that votes for women would achieve a transformation in British political culture. The majority of leading pro-suffragists were anti-imperialists, and many (like Richard Pankhurst and Henry Nevinson) fervently hoped that women's suffrage would sound the death-knell of imperialism and militarism – even of capitalism itself.[77]

Both the inflexibility of the reactionary and the visionary optimism of the enthusiast were in their different ways the consequence of a generation of change in gender relations. Each was grounded not just in a narrow reading of the suffrage issue, but in a consciousness of shifting gender relations over a broad front. Historically men's power *vis-à-vis* women has partly depended on maintaining a veil over masculinity itself. The fact that so many of the constituents of masculinity, by becoming the subject of public discourse, were made visible during this period affected the gender identity of all men who had access to that discourse. Their reactions to the campaign for women's suffrage were framed accordingly.

NOTES

1 This strand is best represented by the magazine *Achilles Heel* (1978–), and by the writings of Victor Seidler. See especially his *Rediscovering Masculinity*, London, Routledge, 1989.

2 E. Carpenter, *Love's Coming of Age*, London, Methuen, 1914 (first published in 1896). Recent examinations of Carpenter include

S. Rowbotham and J. Weeks, *Socialism and the New Life*, London, Pluto, 1977, and T. Brown (ed.), *Edward Carpenter and Late Victorian Radicalism*, London, Frank Cass, 1990.

3 L. Bland, *Banishing the Beast: English Feminism and Sexual Morality 1885–1914*, Harmondsworth, Penguin, 1995, pp. 40–1; J. Walkowitz, *City of Dreadful Delight: Narratives of Sexual Danger in Late-Victorian London*, London, Virago, 1992, p. 146.

4 L. Housman, 'Militancy: and No Mistake', *Votes for Women*, 15 March 1912; see Ch. 3 by Angela John, below.

5 This approach to the study of masculinity is best represented by J. A. Mangan and J. Walvin (eds), *Manliness and Morality: Middle-Class Masculinity in Britain and America, 1800–1940*, Manchester, Manchester University Press, 1987. For a critique, see editors' introduction in M. Roper and J. Tosh (eds), *Manful Assertions: Masculinities in Britain since 1800*, London, Routledge, 1991, pp.1–4.

6 The points made in this paragraph are considered more fully in J. Tosh, 'What Should Historians Do with Masculinity? Reflections on Nineteenth-Century Britain', *History Workshop Journal* 38 (1994), pp. 179–202.

7 These figures are adapted from those of the Registrar-General in 1911 by J. A. Banks, *Victorian Values: Secularism and the Size of Families*, London, Routledge & Kegan Paul, 1981, pp. 40, 98. See also M. Anderson, 'The Social Implications of Demographic Change', in F. M. L.Thompson (ed.), *Cambridge Social History of Modern Britain*, Vol. 2, Cambridge, Cambridge University Press, 1990, p. 44.

8 The debate is conveniently reviewed in F. M. L. Thompson, *The Rise of Respectable Society*, London, Fontana, 1988, pp. 51–68.

9 This is the argument of J. A. Banks, *Prosperity and Parenthood*, London, Routledge & Kegan Paul, 1954.

10 Ruskin and Mill are well-known examples.

11 P. Gay, *The Bourgeois Experience*, Vol. 1, New York, Oxford University Press, 1984, p. 274.

12 W. Seccombe, 'Starting to Stop: Working-Class Fertility Decline in Britain', *Past & Present* 126 (1990) (pp. 151–88).

13 A. J. Hammerton, *Cruelty and Companionship: Conflict in Nineteenth-Century Married Life*, London, Routledge, 1992, p. 165.

14 K. McClelland, 'Masculinity and the "Representative Artisan" in Britain, 1850–80', in Roper and Tosh, *Manful Assertions*, pp. 74–91.

15 G. and W. Grossmith, *Diary of a Nobody*, London, 1894.

16 Anderson, 'The Social Implications of Demographic Change', p. 34.

17 P. Jalland, *Women, Marriage and Politics 1860–1914*, Oxford, Oxford University Press, 1986, p. 97; R. I. Rotberg and M. Shore, *The Founder: Cecil Rhodes and the Pursuit of Power*, New York, Oxford University Press, 1988, pp. 21, 92.

18 Banks, *Prosperity and Parenthood*.

19 E. Showalter, *Sexual Anarchy: Gender and Culture at the Fin de Siècle*, London, Bloomsbury, 1991, Ch. 5. In *King Solomon's Mines* (1885) Haggard's narrator, Allan Quatermain, reassures his readers: 'there is not a petticoat in the whole history.'

20 Arthur Conan Doyle, quoted in J. A. Hammerton (ed.), *Stevensoniana*, London, Grant Richards, 1903, p. 243.
21 E. Kosofsky Sedgwick, *Epistemology of the Closet*, Berkeley, CA, University of California Press, 1990, p. 247.
22 G. Dawson, *Soldier Heroes: British Adventure, Empire and the Imagining of Masculinities*, London, Routledge, 1994, pp. 134–51.
23 R.W. Emerson, *English Traits*, London, Routledge, 1856, pp. 62, 71–2, 164. See also Hyppolite Taine, *Notes on England* (trans. Edward Hyams), London, Thames & Hudson, 1957, esp. pp. 5, 61, 78.
24 J. A. Froude, *The Nemesis of Faith*, London, J. Chapman, 1849, p. 113.
25 L. Davidoff and C. Hall, *Family Fortunes: Men and Women of the English Middle Class, 1780–1850*, London, Hutchinson, 1987, Ch. 2.
26 Walkowitz, *City of Dreadful Delight*, pp. 46–50.
27 C. E. Russett, *Sexual Science: the Victorian Construction of Womanhood*, Cambridge, MA, Harvard University Press, 1989.
28 W. R. Greg, *Why are Women Redundant?*, London, Trubner, 1869, p. 21.
29 'One of Us', 'Why We Men Do Not Marry', *Temple Bar* 84 (1888), p. 219 (pp. 218–23); R. L. Stevenson, *Virginibus Puerisque*, pocket edition, London, Chatto & Windus, 1918, p. 5.
30 T. H. S. Escott, *England: Its People, Polity and Pursuits*, 2nd edition, London, 1885, p. 309.
31 Carpenter, *Love's Coming of Age*, pp. 44–5. See also E. Carpenter, 'The Drawing-Room Table in Literature', *The New Age*, 17 March 1910, p. 464.
32 M. Girouard, *Life in the English Country House*, Harmondsworth, Penguin, 1980, pp. 292–8.
33 See, for example, A. Crawford, *C. R. Ashbee: Architect, Designer and Romantic Socialist*, New Haven, CT, Yale University Press, 1985, p. 6; B. Caine, *Destined to be Wives: the Sisters of Beatrice Webb*, Oxford, Oxford University Press, 1986, p. 137.
34 M. Haweis, *The Art of Housekeeping: a Bridal Garland*, London, Sampson Low, 1889, pp. 33–4.
35 L. Krenis, 'Authority and Rebellion in Victorian Autobiography', *Journal of British Studies* 18 (1978), p. 117 (pp. 107–30).
36 J. Tosh, 'Authority and Nurture in Middle-Class Fatherhood: the Case of Early and Mid-Victorian England', *Gender and History* 8 (1996, forthcoming); Caine, *Destined to be Wives*, Ch. 8.
37 E. Demolins, *Anglo-Saxon Superiority: To What It Is Due*, London, Leadenhall, 1898, p. 100.
38 E. Cecil, *The Leisure of an Egyptian Official*, London, Hodder & Stoughton, 1921, p. 184.
39 J. Tosh, 'Domesticity and Manliness in the Victorian Middle Class: the Family of Edward White Benson', in Roper and Tosh, *Manful Assertions*, pp. 59–68.
40 Banks, *Prosperity and Parenthood*, pp. 189, 228–9.
41 J. R. de S. Honey, *Tom Brown's Universe: the Development of the Victorian Public Schools*, London, Millington, 1977; J. A. Mangan,

Athleticism in the Victorian and Edwardian Public School, Cambridge, Cambridge University Press, 1981.

42 Honey, *Tom Brown's Universe*, pp. 209–17.

43 W. Pater, *Plato and Platonism*, London, Macmillan, 1893, pp. 200–2; R. Baden-Powell, *Rovering to Success*, London, Herbert Jenkins, 1922, p. 24.

44 See, for example, Harold Nicolson's reminiscences of Wellington in Graham Greene (ed.), *The Old School*, Oxford, Oxford University Press, 1934, especially pp. 91–2.

45 B. Harrison, *Separate Spheres: the Opposition to Women's Suffrage in Britain*, London, Croom Helm, 1978, pp. 73–8.

46 L. Housman, *Articles of Faith in the Freedom of Women*, London, A. C. Fifield, 1910, p. 15.

47 Quoted in G. Seaver, *Francis Younghusband*, London, John Murray, 1952, p. 10.

48 J. E. Adamson, *The Theory of Education in Plato's Republic*, London, Swan Sonnenschein, 1903, p. 51.

49 F. W. Pethick Lawrence, *Fate Has Been Kind*, London, Hutchinson, 1943, p. 29.

50 Carpenter, *Love's Coming of Age*, p. 29.

51 Harrison, *Separate Spheres*, p. 97.

52 E. Kosofsky Sedgwick, *Between Men: English Literature and Male Homosexual Desire*, New York, Columbia University Press, 1985, p. 89. See also her *Epistemology of the Closet*.

53 Quoted in J. Weeks, *Coming Out: Homosexual Politics in Britain from the Nineteenth Century to the Present*, London, Quartet, 1977, p. 21.

54 S. Koven, 'From Rough Lads to Hooligans: Boy Life, National Culture and Social Reform', in A. Parker *et al.* (eds), *Nationalisms and Sexualities*, New York, Routledge, 1992, pp. 365–91.

55 D. Newsome, *On the Edge of Paradise: A. C. Benson the Diarist*, London, John Murray, 1980.

56 R. Kipling, *The Light That Failed*, Harmondsworth, Penguin edition, 1988, pp. 58, 89.

57 E. J. Bristow, *Vice and Vigilance: Purity Movements in Britain since 1700*, Dublin, Gill & Macmillan, 1977, pp. 154–74; Bland, *Banishing the Beast*, pp. 95–110.

58 G. Rowntree and N. H. Carrier, 'The Resort to Divorce in England and Wales, 1858–1957', *Population Studies* 11 (1958), table 2, p. 201 (pp. 188–233).

59 Hammerton, *Cruelty and Companionship*, Ch. 4.

60 L. Holcombe, *Wives and Property*, Oxford, Martin Robertson, 1983, pp. 201, 218. See also M. Lyndon Shanley, *Feminism, Marriage and the Law in Victorian England, 1850–1895*, London, I. B.Tauris, 1989.

61 Hammerton, *Cruelty and Companionship*, pp. 143–9; C. R. Ashbee, 'Grannie', Oxford, privately printed, 1939, p. 62.

62 Holcombe, *Wives and Property*, p. 201; Shanley, *Feminism, Marriage and the Law*, p. 124.

63 Bland, *Banishing the Beast*, Ch. 4.

64 D. Rubinstein, *Before the Suffragettes: Women's Emancipation in the 1890s*, Brighton, Harvester, 1986, pp. 12–34.
65 G. Anderson, *Victorian Clerks*, Manchester, Manchester University Press, 1976, pp. 56–60.
66 Rubinstein, *Before the Suffragettes*, Chs 2–4; Walkowitz, *City of Dreadful Delight*, esp. Ch. 2.
67 B. Dijkstra, *Idols of Perversity*, Oxford, Oxford University Press, 1986.
68 F. Harrison (ed.), *The Yellow Book: an Anthology*, Woodbridge, Boydell, 1982.
69 Showalter, *Sexual Anarchy*, p. 83.
70 P. Gay, *The Cultivation of Hatred*, London, Harper Collins, 1994, Ch. 1.
71 M. Townsend, 'Will England Retain India?', *Contemporary Review* 53 (1888), p. 811 (pp. 795–813).
72 A. Davin, 'Imperialism and Motherhood', *History Workshop Journal* 5 (1978), pp. 9–65.
73 Showalter, *Sexual Anarchy*, pp. 9–15; R. Gagnier, *Idylls of the Market-place: Oscar Wilde and the Victorian Public*, Stanford, CA, Stanford University Press, 1987, p. 98. See also M. S. Kimmel, 'The Contemporary "Crisis" of Masculinity in Historical Perspective', in H. Brod (ed.), *The Making of Masculinities*, London, Allen & Unwin, 1987, pp. 121–53.
74 F. Harrison, 'Family Life' (1893), in his *On Society*, London, Macmillan, 1918, pp. 45–6.
75 Harrison, *Separate Spheres*, pp. 60, 75–6.
76 See, for example, L. Housman, *What Is Womanly?*, London, Women's Freedom League, 1914, and J. E. Harrison, *'Homo Sum' : Being a Letter to an Anti-Suffragist from an Anthropologist*, London, National Union of Women's Suffrage Societies, 1913.
77 S. Strauss, *'Traitors to the Masculine Cause' : the Men's Campaigns for Women's Rights*, Westport, CT, Greenwood Press, 1982, pp. 195–202, 224–5.

Chapter 2

'By all means let the ladies have a chance'

The Workman's Times, independent labour representation and women's suffrage, 1891–4

Laura Ugolini

During its life-span *The Workman's Times* struck a responsive chord among its audience. Inaugurated only a few years before the better-known *Clarion*, it was, admittedly, neither as successful nor as long-lived. Lasting only five years, between 1889 and 1894, it was hardly ever out of financial difficulties. It can best be described as the poor relation of successful northern papers such as the *Cotton Factory Times* and *Yorkshire Factory Times*, whose owner it shared until 1892.[1]

Yet, most notably, it could boast that it was the appeal to its readers to send in names pledging support to the principle of independent labour representation which set into motion the events which led to the Bradford Conference and the establishment of the Independent Labour Party in 1893.[2]

Edited by Joseph Burgess, a Lancashire piecer and poet turned journalist (and between 1885 and 1889 sub-editor and then manager of the *Yorkshire Factory Times*), *The Workman's Times* represented one of a number of attempts in the early 1890s to establish a national labour paper.[3] Although the columns of the paper were open to socialists and Burgess considered himself to be one, the paper's editorial policy was not distinctively socialist: a wider audience was clearly hoped for.[4]

It is impossible to calculate with any precision the extent of the paper's readership. It seems that on 9 January 1891 *The Workman's Times* was receiving 10,077 orders, increasing to 13,464 by 5 June, and then suddenly jumping to 51,284 on 3 July. The last given figure was that of 62,517 on 2 October. Apparently, though, circulation continued to grow until the time of the 1892 general election, after which it started to fall (although the rate was not revealed).[5]

On more than one occasion *The Workman's Times* was defined as a 'family paper'. Moreover, the presence of a column on 'Household hints' and serialized romantic fiction was presumably designed to attract a female readership. Nevertheless, the paper's main audience was clearly meant to be not only one of waged workers, but also of those among them who were already members of a trade union. Burgess himself did not believe that many unorganized workers read his paper.[6]

It was the shift from a concentration on purely trade union to political matters, and the advocacy of labour's political action independently of either Liberal or Tory parties (particularly from 1892), that marked the beginning of the paper's difficulties. Ironically, the fundamental contribution of *The Workman's Times* to the establishment of the Independent Labour Party ultimately served to spell its own destruction, as support from the party was not sufficient to allow it to survive.[7]

Although many causes were advocated, or merely discussed, in the columns of this paper – for example, trade unionism, the eight-hours day and co-operation – it is in its guise of independent labour representation advocate that I shall consider the attitude of its male contributors towards women's suffrage.

The involvement of labour activists within the women's suffrage movement has already attracted considerable attention from historians. Early suffrage historians chose to place varying degrees of emphasis on Labour's role within the campaign, according to their own sympathies: in Sylvia Pankhurst's *The Suffragette Movement* the labour and suffrage movements appeared almost inseparable, while in Ray Strachey's *The Cause* the former was far less in evidence.[8] More recent works have taken the shape of detailed studies, recognizing the geographical, organizational and ideological variations within the labour movement. Quite understandably, considering their neglect within standard labour histories, these works have tended to concentrate on women activists.[9] None the less, they point the way for a study of male activists. Just as such studies demonstrated the need to explore the female activists' backgrounds rather than regarding their involvement in the suffrage movement in isolation, so the men's attitudes towards women's suffrage cannot be divorced from their identities as male labour activists. Although these identities were clearly made up of other factors apart from their masculinity, it is with issues of gender that this chapter is centrally concerned.[10] The construction of a particular masculine identity by labour activists through media such as *The Workman's Times* was central to the development of an ideology which aimed at the empowerment of 'workers' through independent labour representation. Attitudes towards women's suffrage cannot be considered in isolation from such efforts.[11]

This chapter does not concentrate exclusively on the male contributors' arguments in favour of women's suffrage, but adopts a broader approach. An investigation of the paper's aims in advocating independent labour representation reveals the primary importance of the association of the 'worker' (whose representation was being sought) with a masculine identity. Not all men may have belonged to the category of 'workers', but all women were excluded. It is necessary to reassess the extent to which the achievement of women's own enfranchisement and political emancipation could be accommodated within this ideology. The picture which emerges does not simply highlight the support (or lack of it) for women's suffrage within *The Workman's Times*, but rather throws new light on the nature of the terms upon which support was given.

The paper's male contributors were remarkably supportive of women's right to vote. Although the paper was not always above caricaturing suffrage activists, it welcomed the introduction in Parliament of Haldane's suffrage bill in April 1891, and warned that politicians could not be trusted. Furthermore, although in some cases women's suffrage was advocated within the context of adult suffrage, this was by no means always the case: Haldane's bill, for example, would have granted women the vote on the same limited terms as men.[12]

And yet, when one turns to the question of independent labour representation, it seems that the claims of women to political representation were forgotten. By 1891, the paper was strongly advocating the representation of workers independently of the main political parties in both Parliament and local government. This was symptomatic of a growing feeling of discontent towards working-class MPs such as Henry Broadhurst, who were characterized as 'men who masquerade in Labour garb and dance obedience to party whips'. It was felt that MPs should have been able to act in the interests of workers, irrespective of either Liberal or Conservative party lines.[13]

It is clear that class issues were central to such aspirations. The opposition of interests between 'workers' and those who controlled the main political parties was emphasized. In some cases the latter were explicitly identified with capitalists, while it was thought that genuine working-class MPs would naturally legislate in the interests of their own class.[14] Very occasionally, a commitment to socialism was explicitly proposed as the distinguishing feature of a new party.[15]

Much more often, though, the emphasis was on the difference between those who had experience of work and those governing the country who lived in an 'intellectual heaven'.[16] The main parties were dominated by 'men of wealth' and 'parasites', while the workers were those who produced all the wealth of the country and who had, at least at some point in their lives, experienced the harshness of the labour market. The true representatives of labour would thus 'deal with public questions from the point of view of those who have to work with their hands for scanty pay, and who know where the shoe pinches'.[17]

And yet, if one considers the extent of the franchise as late as 1911, when only roughly 59 per cent of the adult male population was registered to vote in parliamentary elections, it can hardly be said that the proposed party of workers would have represented the working class as a whole, unless one wished to define the latter as exclusively male, and selective at that.[18] Contributors to *The Workman's Times* thus called for a type of empowerment for workers which depended on the possession of the vote, and from which women (and some men) were in fact debarred. And while women's right to the vote was recognized, franchise reform was never advocated as a preliminary step towards independent labour representation.

Quite the opposite: *The Workman's Times* was more likely to emphasize the power of the working class at the ballot-box and the adequacy of the contemporary franchise; an editorial of May 1891, for example, pointed out that a change in the personnel of government should come before a change in the system.[19] Even when the limitations of the present franchise were lamented, no mention was made of women's suffrage. Joseph Burgess himself, writing under the pseudonym of 'Autolycus', emphasized that the great number of non-voters were welcome to join the Independent Labour Party, but then simply advocated a reform of the registration laws. On the whole, independent labour representation as envisaged by *The Workman's Times* seems to have left little space for women's own political representation.[20]

An understanding of such apparently contradictory attitudes towards women's claims to political representation lies in the meaning attached to the terms 'workers', 'toilers', 'labour' and so on, as used when advocating independent labour representation. Although these had an obvious class connotation, they also carried gendered understandings developed in relation not only to the paper's contributors' own views, but also to those of its readership. As this was assumed to be comprised mostly of trade unionists, it is clear that despite the recent advances in so-called 'New Unionism', it would have represented not only a minority of the working population, but also a minority from which, outside the cotton industry, women were virtually absent. It is thus necessary to assess how the 'workers' to whom *The Workman's Times* appealed, were in fact defined.

I shall start by examining the ideas expressed by the male contributors to *The Workman's Times* in relation to what was perceived to be the 'proper' role to be played by women within society, the fundamental question being whether women were in fact included in the category of 'workers'.

There was no blanket condemnation of women's work anywhere on *The Workman's Times*. Their participation in the labour market was often taken for granted and in February 1892 a section of the paper on 'Women's work, wages and organisation' was started, proposing to cater for their special needs. In the case of young or single women such participation was even commended. For example, in a short story entitled 'Two Girls' Plans', the girls were described as they discussed their plans on leaving school. Both were mechanics' daughters, but the mother of one of them had told her that it was not genteel for women to work, while the other wanted to become a dressmaker to help her family's finances. In the end the first one died miserably, having become unfit for any activity, while the second started a prosperous dressmaking business, later in a telling twist giving that up to marry an even more prosperous manufacturer.[21] By the 1890s it was considered the norm for such girls to go out to work before marriage. Shop-work in particular provided working-class girls with a relatively high-status occupation without requiring more than an elementary education, although, as the story indicates, marriage continued to be considered girls' ultimate goal in life.[22]

Occasionally the necessity (if not the advisability) of married women's work was admitted. Contemporary social commentators had increasingly come to the conclusion that married women's work was not an evil *per se* but the result of evil circumstances. Similarly *The Workman's Times* recognized that women such as the London matchbox makers worked because, for various reasons, the bread-winning husband could not provide for the family.[23] Much emphasis was placed on the importance of forming strong trade union organizations among working women, in sympathy with the trend towards mixed, general unions, rather than the exclusive practices of many craft societies: united, women would 'be the better able to command proper respect due to labour of all sorts, and gradually but surely elevate themselves socially, morally and politically'.[24] The work of women such as Lady Dilke of the Women's Trade Union League was warmly praised.[25]

And yet, underlying most discussions of women's waged work was the belief that while the latter may at times have been a necessity, and in the case of young girls even a praiseworthy activity, work was essentially a masculine right and duty. A division of labour was seen as desirable whereby the men could support their families with married women not being forced to seek work outside the home. In this *The Workman's Times* reflected the increasingly wide acceptance, at least among certain sections of the working class, of the desirability for the male worker to be able to support a family on his sole earnings, while at the same time securing the wife's domestic services.[26] Despite the fact that investigations such as those carried out by the Women's Industrial Council in the first decade of the twentieth century show that for vast sections of the working class this remained only an aspiration, historians such as Sonya Rose and Keith Mc-Clelland have shown that apart from its economic rationale, considerable emotional investment was placed in the equation between notions of 'respectable masculinity' and status as family provider.[27]

It is impossible to assess exactly how widespread was acceptance of these ideas, but they certainly found ready expression among the trade union respondents to the Royal Commission on Labour of 1891–4. Thomas Homer, the president of the Cradley Heath and District Branch of the National Amalgamation of Chain-Makers' and Chain-Strikers' Associations, lamented that his was the only part of the country where women worked alongside the men in the trade, and as a result

> everything is being neglected at home, all little domestic duties are neglected, and when the man goes in his little place, his little castle as it should be, there is nothing clean and tidy. It drives him off to the public-house and all that kind of thing in our country, which would not be if the women were better domesticated.

Even more significant, perhaps, was the view expressed by William Mullin, the representative of the Amalgamated Society of Card and Blowing Room Operatives. Despite the fact that the majority of his society's membership consisted of women, with 18,500 against 6,500 men, he stated that his union was actively working to obtain 'a man's wage for the men', so that they would be able to support a family on their own earnings.[28] Thus, ideally, men and women's roles were clearly distinguished: '[Men] have no more right poking [their] . . . nose into the kitchen than [women] . . . to walk into . . . [the men's] place of business and give them directions.'[29]

Understandably, contributors to *The Workman's Times* considered women's competition in what was perceived as 'men's work' to be particularly obnoxious. As Harriet Bradley has shown, although by the 1890s the masculine nature of trades such as fishing was firmly established, others like hosiery and pottery were experiencing feminization and shifting gender divisions. She considers the 1880s and 1890s to have been central decades in the redefinition of gender roles in the workplace, causing a widespread sense of crisis among many sections of the male workforce, presumably including the readership of *The Workman's Times*.[30] The paper clearly reflected such concerns, although an attempt was made to soften the condemnation by emphasizing that the objection was to the 'unfairness' of women's competition:

> By all means let the ladies have a chance. But . . . no woman ought to take work previously done by a man at less wages than the man was wont to receive. If she does . . . she is neither more nor less than a blackleg.[31]

And yet there was a clear distaste for what was perceived as a reversal of proper gender roles, which resulted in men standing idle while women were engaged as cheap labour to the benefit of the employer and detriment of the family. Thus it was suggested that if women were excluded from chain-making there would have been more work and higher wages for men. It was largely because of female competition that this was the 'worst paid skilled industry in the world'.[32]

Such an ambivalent attitude towards women's work was often bound up with (and possibly at the same time rationalized by) an emphasis on the 'unsuitability' for women of certain types of employment. *The Workman's Times* tended to place particular importance on the strength necessary to perform tasks such as chain-making, a strength which men, but not women, were considered to possess.

This issue was raised in an article by a J. W. Gardner, dealing with the problem of unemployment in the mining industry. Among the various suggested solutions, such as reducing hours of work or abolishing royalties, can be found the abolition of the work of women on the pit brow. Although the author's central concern was clearly to increase male employment opportunities, he still felt the necessity of rationalizing his demand for the exclusion of women from surface work by emphasizing the unsuitability for women of work which involved using heavy hammers, wheeling barrows and pushing wagons full of coal.[33]

Only a little more than a month after the appearance of Gardner's article, *The Workman's Times* published a rather startling challenge to such ideas in a piece whose aim was to refute the 'physical force' argument against women's suffrage. This stated that men such as the Prime Minister, William Gladstone, had obviously never

> seen the women in the white-lead works carrying great loads up and down ladders on their heads, nor the poor girls cleansing the dirt out of their lordships' garments in damp cellars; nor the girls in countless factories, warehouses and shops preserving the divine ideal of the politicians' 'woman' at high pressure through a 60 or 70 hours week.

If political representation were a case of physical force, women could hold their own.[34] A note of pride in the strength of working-class women can certainly be detected here, but none the less the work itself was hardly portrayed as a possible source of pride. Furthermore, this piece was unique: women's employment in 'unsuitable' trades, especially those requiring masculine attributes of physical strength, was otherwise always seen as both degrading to women and a threat to men.[35]

It is also interesting to note the extent to which neither women's trade unionism nor equal wages were advocated exclusively (or in some cases even primarily) in order to improve the well-being of the women themselves, but rather to minimize their competitiveness towards men.[36]

A good deal was written about women's role and responsibilities as wives and mothers. They were supposed to be confidantes, advisers and makers of a 'little domestic sphere so bright and cheerful that . . . [the] husband and children will not want to spend their evenings away from it'.[37] Although a contributor writing under the *nom de plume* of 'Proletarian' looked forward to a time when women would no longer be 'domestic drudges', and motherhood and domestic work received a state payment, he did not question the association of women with these activities.[38] Burgess chose to emphasize the power wielded by women in their capacity as house-keepers and consumers. He pointed out that no co-operative venture could be successful without enlisting the support of those in charge of buying household goods. He himself had taken great pains to explain to his wife Sarah why, on coming home in the evening, he did not wish to see 'certain articles' on the tea table. It seems clear that the Burgess household also operated on the basis that the husband's role was to provide financial support, that of the wife to care for house and numerous offspring.[39]

Nevertheless marriage and motherhood were not always seen as the only future open to women, although it is doubtful whether many of the paper's readers would have gone as far as the correspondent who advocated birth control in order to safeguard women's health.[40] For those who did not meet the 'right man', earning their own livelihood was emphasized as a perfectly acceptable alternative. The useful and fulfilling nature of 'old maids'' lives was stressed, whilst most of the court cases reported in the paper's columns and describing incidents of violence between spouses, must effectively have subverted any idyllic image of domestic life, especially among the poorer sections of the population.[41]

On the whole, though, the image of womanhood represented by *The Workman's Times* was connected only in a very limited sense to waged work: a woman was by no means always also a 'worker'. Women's work was accepted, or even commended in the case of single women, although even here only so long as it was considered 'suitable' and did not interfere with men's employment, while married women's domestic role, at least as an ideal, if not always a reality, was emphasized.

It is necessary now to consider the ways in which independent labour representation was advocated and the gender assumptions expressed, particularly in relation to the use of the term 'workers'. Was the latter gender-neutral in its meaning, thereby including both men and women?

With very few exceptions, the tone of the language used when advocating independent labour representation was uncompromisingly masculine. It was the election of 'working men' that was almost invariably sought.[42] This may well have been the result of linguistic convention, whereby the feminine was simply implied within the masculine: the use of 'working men' may have been a convenient short-hand for 'working men and women'. 'Frances' certainly thought so: she started her regular feature on women workers in the belief that the paper's editor and contributors wished *The Workman's Times*'s title to be 'parsed "common gender" and understood *Workers' Times*'.[43] Nevertheless, it is my contention that we are dealing not with linguistic convention, but with the construction of a notion of 'worker' associated with a masculine identity, the latter contributing an essential characteristic to the 'labour' whose independent representation was being sought.

In many cases, the independent representation of workers was suggestively portrayed as a masculine affair. A particularly interesting symbolism was proposed, for example, by John Trevor, who compared capitalists and their parties to a bad mother who tried to control Labour, her son, first by kicking and then by 'wooing' him, until eventually the latter achieved his 'manhood' by starting to despise her and then breaking off relations with her.[44]

The drawing which marked the 1893 Conference of the Independent Labour Party is also revealing, and certainly seems to confirm Eric Hobsbawm's suggestion that by the 1890s a 'masculinization' of socialist and trade union imagery was taking place, with the naked muscular male torso now taking centre stage. The drawing was provided by an artist working under the pseudonym of 'Leon Caryll', and obviously sympathetic to the cause of independent labour representation. He portrayed the insurgent Labour as a male, muscular and bearded figure, reminiscent of a Saxon warrior (Plate 1).[45] Most often, though, the masculine nature of labour was suggested by the use of the ambiguous term 'working man'. While women were seen only in a very limited sense as 'workers', the image of the male worker was generally much more positive, despite some deprecation of the excessive identification of the working-class man with the 'worker'. This may have reflected the shift away from an exclusively work-centred masculine culture, observed by some historians, as even well-paid manual workers tended to find less satisfaction in their work. Writing about Salford in the first quarter of the twentieth century, Robert Roberts scorned the romanticization of men's attachment to their work. As he succinctly put it, 'they

Plate 1 Leon Caryll's commemorative drawing of the first conference of the ILP, *The Workman's Times*, 1893. By permission of the British Library

toiled on through mortal fear of getting the sack'.[46] It was stated in *The Workman's Times* that the labour movement stood not only for improvements in workplace conditions. As a contributor writing under the *nom de plume* of 'Bronterre' pointed out: 'the toiler has discovered that he is also a man, and demands a man's necessities: health, clothing, housing, culture.'[47] The emphasis placed by some commentators on the importance of 'honest toil' was considered to be a mockery under the present system, seeing that all the advantages of labour went to the capitalists. The drudgery of workers such as alkali operatives was stressed.[48]

Nevertheless, in general, waged work was considered to hold a distinctively positive role in a man's life, to the extent that it could be stated that 'not only, in the case of most men, does daily work get daily bread, but the daily work is as necessary for health and happiness as daily food'. Conversely, unemployment was almost invariably portrayed as a masculine calamity. Thus, although 'Jean Val-Jean' emphasized the right not only of men but also of women and children to live by their labour, he saw unemployment, pauperism and the consequent disfranchisement as making 'the man . . . an outsider; he has no place among his fellows except such as they choose to accord him'.[49]

The drawings of workers provided for the paper from May 1892 by 'Leon Caryll' are also revealing. Not only were the workers portrayed invariably male, but their 'maleness' was also greatly emphasized. Although some effort was made to depict these as intelligent men (for example, two agricultural labourers were portrayed as reading the paper), greater stress was placed on their muscular arms and bodies and the fact that they were obviously engaged in hard, manual labour (Plate 2).[50] By the end of the century the performance of physically demanding work was a central route to the achievement of a successful working-class masculinity within the workplace, and one more easily realizable than the ability to support a family, especially by unskilled/casual workers. In his autobiography, Will Thorne remembered the pride in their physical strength common among navvies. Being called 'thick leg' was the highest accolade a man could receive. 'I have known them to wrap pieces of calico around their calves to make them bulge and give them a "thick-legged" appearance.' There are very interesting parallels with the imagery used in the United States in the early years of the twentieth century by the International Workers of the World (the 'wobblies'), which focused on the male workers' 'brute

Plate 2 Leon Caryll's representation of labour, *The Workman's Times*,
1893. By permission of The British Library

strength'. The aim was to emphasize the union's inclusive policies and desire to represent a broader constituency than that of skilled workers. Nevertheless, one of the consequences was to ignore (mostly female) workers such as domestic servants and textile operatives. Equally, within *The Workman's Times*, labour requiring physical strength was portrayed as a masculine prerogative only occasionally usurped by women, such as in the case of the Cradley Heath chain-makers.[51]

Efforts to broaden the ranks of Labour did not include women, but rather those men who did not conform to such images of muscular, manual labour. This can be seen in a number of different instances: for example, in the need felt to justify the inclusion of those who laboured not only by hand, but also by brain, and in the calls made to clerical and shop workers to abandon their pretensions to gentility, recognize that 'they are no better off than unskilled labourers' and join the ranks of labour. Very little importance was placed on the notion of 'respectability' and excessive attachment to it among workers was condemned.[52]

In some ways, therefore, *The Workman's Times*'s 'worker' seems to have been quite different from Keith McClelland's 'independent' and 'respectable' artisan of the third quarter of the nineteenth century, as the earlier language of respectability was rejected and the importance of physical strength given greater prominence. Sonya Rose has located a shift in definitions of masculinity among organized workers in the 1880s, with the rise of 'new unionism'. Nevertheless, the continuities were just as significant: the sexual division of labour and the family wage, themselves central gender components of earlier working-class 'respectability', remained unchallenged. Thus, when white-collar workers' 'respectability' was being condemned, the reference was not to its basis in family arrangements, but rather to its manifestations within the workplace: the deferential attitude and the aping of middle-class habits, symbolized by the wearing of the black coat.[53]

It is possible to conclude that *The Workman's Times*'s advocacy of independent labour representation for 'working men' was no simple linguistic short-hand, but rather represented a more or less conscious association with masculinity of workers for wages outside the home: this was often a new type of uncompromising, 'muscular' masculinity, although still based upon domestic authority. Both the paper's male readership and contributors would have been able to identify with this.

It is clear that the terminology used to advocate the independent representation of labour was a class-bound one, serving to emphasize the opposition between the 'workers' and the 'non-workers' who controlled the main political parties. It was also a gendered one. Women were perceived primarily *not* as workers, but rather as domestic beings (although the distinction was never quite so clear-cut). They could thus be ignored when advocating independent labour representation because their role within society was seen as different from that of the masculine worker: women's claim to political empowerment was a separate, if equally just, cause.[54] Once obtained, this would lead to their separate interests being represented on political bodies, although at least one contributor to the paper felt there were limits beyond which women's separate interests should not be allowed: he condemned the situation where both husbands and wives could be enfranchised while holding different political opinions.[55] He, though, was a lone voice. As 'Cunctator' pointed out, enfranchised women would be able to look after the interests of all women and to legislate for working women in particular. The latter did not necessarily imply a recognition of women's role as 'workers'. Burgess, for example, considered that one of the first acts of politically powerful women to safeguard the interests of working women would have been to prohibit their employment in chain-making.[56]

It was also emphasized that women's own brand of 'domestic' expertise and distinctive 'female' character could be made use of in the political sphere. As 'C. G.' pointed out, home certainly was the proper sphere for women, but the conception of the home had to be widened to encompass the whole world: 'and here, in her own home, amongst her own children, shall woman, the mother of the race, exercise those qualities of heart and mind that shall raise man from a grovelling savage to a God.'[57]

A pamphlet of 1892 by Mrs Fawcett, later to become president of the National Union of Women's Suffrage Societies, provides an interesting counterpart to these ideas. She shared the view of 'Cunctator' that votes for women would serve to safeguard their interests, but made scant reference to women's domestic expertise. She believed that women's industrial position would improve with the vote, by enabling them to end male trade unionists' restrictive practices, which kept women relegated to the worst paid and least skilled trades, an argument to which she returned frequently. Although Mrs Fawcett and *The Workman's Times* were both supportive of women's suffrage, their positions had clearly little else in common.[58]

The nature of women's participation in the early Independent Labour Party was obviously influenced by notions of their 'special role'. In 1894 a number of women's sections were formed. Sarah Burgess was elected president of the Hightown Branch of the North Salford women's section of the Independent Labour Party. In her branch the women, 'almost in every case the wives, sisters, sweethearts and friends of the members of the North Salford Independent Labour Party', had decided to organize separately and to exclude men from their meetings, as they found that men had a tendency to dominate all discussion. Unfortunately *The Workman's Times* gives little information about this or other similar bodies, and yet it is difficult not to consider them a product of the conflict in the early days of the party between those men and women who genuinely wished for the participation of women within the movement and the women who had reservations about its relentlessly masculine tone. Sarah Burgess's own experiences may serve to indicate the difficulties encountered by a woman burdened with domestic responsibilities, who nevertheless desired to participate actively in the movement: Joseph vividly described her excitement on returning from the Women's Party's weekly meetings. Eventually, though, her growing domestic and family responsibilities meant that she had to give up political activism. There was nothing within *The Workman's Times* which challenged the assumption that it would have to be she who gave up her political work to dedicate herself to the care of her family.[59]

Not all were happy with the establishment of separate groups for women. Marion Coates of the Middlesbrough ILP (and later active in the Women's Freedom League) wrote to express her concern at the establishment of a separate women's organization in Newcastle:

> Should [women] . . . not join hands with their brothers and work together for a common cause? Have not the women been long enough separated in public matters from the men? No party, in my estimation, can succeed which excludes men or women. Each needs the other's presence to refine and inspire.

The reply by Florence Nightingale L. Harrison, secretary of the Newcastle Women's Labour Association, is particularly revealing of the obstacles in the way of women's integration within the Independent Labour Party and of its essentially masculine nature. Although her intention was to deny any desire or need to form an organization separate from the masculine party, she none the less admitted to being the only woman member of the Newcastle Independent Labour Party and remarked on the fact that the latter's headquarters were not a suitable place for women (presumably a public-house).[60]

A further example of the tension resulting from the desire to include women within the Independent Labour Party, but only on very specific terms, was evident in the modification to the design of a party banner presented in the autumn of 1893 by 'Leon Caryll'. The first version was dominated by the figures of two male workers holding their work-implements.[61] Their bearded faces, large, muscular bodies and grim features, all pointed to the expression of a masculinity based on the undertaking of physically demanding, manual toil, whether within the context of industry or agriculture. In the background were further figures of masculine workers and the products of their labour. Together with the lettering, the design served to emphasize further the experience of 'masculine' work as a distinguishing feature of Independent Labour Party adherents (Plate 3).

A week after the publication of the design for the banner, though, Burgess published a letter by a B. Walter, whom he presumed to be a woman, protesting against the absence of female figures from the banner.[62] The result was a modified version, in which two female figures sitting at the feet of the central male figures were introduced (Plate 4).[63] The artist had made an effort to portray these women as 'workers': the rolled up sleeves of one figure further suggested that such work need not always have been of a delicate character. Yet, these figures were much smaller and daintier than the male ones. Particularly notable is the much reduced emphasis on the size of arms and feet. The impression is that although the women may also have been 'workers', the nature of their work would have been different from the men's, and would not have required the same amount of physical strength: the sewing performed by one of the female figures would thus have been an example of 'suitable' work. Despite these reservations, the second banner shows that it would not have been impossible to elaborate a notion of 'labour' and of 'workers' without the masculine undertones to be found in *The Workman's Times* and thus possibly opening the way for women's fuller integration within the party.[64]

Among the male contributors to *The Workman's Times* the only radically different position on the subject of women's political power was that taken by H. Halliday Sparling, at the time a member of the

Plate 3 Leon Caryll's design for an ILP banner (first version), *The Workman's Times*, 1893. By permission of The British Library

Plate 4 Leon Caryll's design for an ILP banner (final version), *The Workman's Times*, 1893. By permission of The British Library

Fabian executive. He did not emphasize the distinctiveness of the position of women within society. Sparling considered it a duty on the part of socialists to aim for the extinction of all privileges of sex, just as much as those of class, women's emancipation lying at the very heart of the labour movement, where it could not be dismissed with excuses about expediency. He concluded by stating that 'there must be no whittling away of the Democratic claim of equal political power, as a step towards equal economic freedom'. Of course, it is only too easy to read too much in one phrase, and yet it is possible that H. Halliday Sparling may not have been too enamoured of the 'domestic' argument in favour of women's political empowerment, and may have favoured a greater integration of 'women' within the ranks of 'workers'. If carried to its logical conclusion, this would then have subverted the notion of independent labour representation as a masculine entity.[65]

Nevertheless, the different rhetoric used by *The Workman's Times* throughout the period under consideration when advocating independent representation and women's suffrage, also lends weight to the argument that most of its male contributors continued to view the emancipation of women and of workers as separate causes. In the latter case, the two most commonly recurrent images were those of war and of slavery. The labour movement was on the one hand portrayed as engaged in battle, and a plethora of related images utilized: banners, marches, armours, strongholds and soldiers all served to lend vividness to the picture. On the other hand, workers were portrayed as slaves who would finally be able to throw off the chains of bondage only through the labour movement. 'Jean Val-Jean' combined both forms of imagery when he called upon the 'Spirit of liberty':

> Rouse thou the toiler's bands.
> Strengthen the toiler's hands
> For victory.
> Freedom our battle cry
> Rending the vaulted sky
> Hark! hear the dying sigh
> Of slavery.[66]

These images need not necessarily imply gendered overtones, although the language of war may have been more or less consciously associated with masculinity, since, very simply, slavery had never been the exclusively male institution which the army has been in the western world. None the less, this rhetoric emphasized once more the masculinity of the workers whose independent representation was being sought. Thus 'The errand boy' stated that he would march under the banner of the 'sons of toil [and] . . . my brothers, my comrades shall march behind it . . . [against Capital]', and workers would escape from the condition of slavery into which they had fallen and regain their 'manhood' only through participation in the labour movement. 'Elihu' accused the landowning classes of having used the power derived from their monopoly of high office and possession of the land '. . . to crush these men into helpless servitude . . . generation by generation you have brutalised and destroyed their manhood'.[67]

These images were not used when the political empowerment of women was advocated. No significant generalization is, however, possible about the rhetoric used when advocating women's suffrage; often the articles dealing with the issue were quite short, while the longer ones differed widely in the arguments used. One only has to think of Halliday Sparling's emphasis on women's suffrage as a democratic right and the arguments of C.G. about women's distinctive contribution to political life. Yet it is clear that women were not appealed to as slaves of Capital and were not called upon to prepare themselves for battle.[68]

Nevertheless, the image of slavery was not completely absent when women's suffrage was advocated though such imagery was used to condemn contemporary relations between the sexes, rather than between employers and employees. Women were seen to have become 'the slaves of slaves', the latter often being identified with the figure of the husband. The development of a new type of relationship was advocated, whereby men and women would be 'free comrade(s)', rather than the woman being treated as a 'chattel'. 'C. G.', though, went further and emphasized how contemporary relations between the sexes were affecting political life, by ensuring the dominance of the masculine element:

> Individualism . . . with its every man for himself maxims . . . its worship of strength and brutal contempt of weakness, is the natural outcome of an extreme development of the male principle in human affairs . . . never 'til man vacates his usurped powers . . . will the din of battle and confusion of strife cease.[69]

The rhetoric employed by the (male) contributors to *The Workman's Times* thus not only emphasized the masculine nature of independent labour representation, but also showed the way in which women were perceived to suffer from distinctive problems characteristic of their sex, particularly in their relations with men. Suffrage was thus often seen as part of a wider need to reform the unequal relations between the sexes.

Ultimately, the challenge presented to the latter by *The Workman's Times* was only limited. First of all, it did not lead to a critique of the male-dominated nature of the workplace. Furthermore, it did not lead to the theorization of a sphere of power centred in the home, despite women's identification with the 'domestic'. The emphasis placed on the desirability of a 'family wage' is symptomatic of how a family's economic dependence remained central to workers' masculinity. In practice, male power was never effectively challenged, neither in home nor workplace, the two remaining inextricably linked.[70]

The conclusion must be that on the one hand women's suffrage was seen by male contributors to the paper as enabling women to contribute their particular brand of expertise to political life and to look after their own interests, while on the other hand it was a means of emancipating themselves from the position of slavery to the other sex. There was an awareness that the desired domestic idyll did not always correspond to reality. Nevertheless, the challenge to masculine power and the potential for change in the relations between the sexes were both limited. *The Workman's Times* continued both to construct a masculine identity for the 'independent labour' whose cause it championed and to identify men as 'workers' and as family providers.

NOTES

1 D. Hopkin, 'The Newspapers of the Independent Labour Party', University of Wales, College of Aberystwyth, PhD, 1981, pp. 11–12.
2 D. Howell, *British Workers and the Independent Labour Party, 1888–1906*, Manchester, Manchester University Press, 1983, pp. 283–300; H. Pelling, *The Origins of the Labour Party, 1880–1900*, Oxford, Oxford University Press, 1966, pp. 99–124.
3 J. Burgess, *A Potential Poet? His Autobiography and Verse*, Ilford, Burgess Publications, 1927, especially pp. 143–9; J. Burgess, *John Burns. The Rise and Progress of a Right Honourable*, Glasgow, Reformers' Bookstall, 1911, especially pp. 1–4.
4 The tone of the paper did become increasingly outspoken, although it is impossible to pinpoint precisely a date marking the beginning of this shift.

5   By way of comparison the *Clarion*'s early circulation of around 30,000 seems to have established the paper as a 'reasonably high-selling weekly'. See C. Steedman, *Childhood, Culture and Class in Britain: Margaret McMillan, 1860–1931*, New Brunswick, NJ, Rutgers University Press, 1990, p. 147.

6   *The Workman's Times* (hereafter *W.T.*), 19 June 1891; 19 December 1891; 17 September 1892; 24 September 1892.

7   *W.T.*, 5 November 1892; 12 August 1893. See also D. Hopkin, 'The Socialist Press in Britain, 1890–1910', in G. Boyce, J. Curran and P. Wingate (eds), *Newspaper History from the Seventeenth Century to the Present Day*, London, Constable, 1978, p. 297; Hopkin, 'The Newspapers', p. 13.

8   E. S. Pankhurst, *The Suffragette Movement*, London, Longman, Green, 1931; R. Strachey, *The Cause. A Short History of the Women's Movement in Great Britain* (1928), London, Virago Press, 1978.

9   J. Liddington and J. Norris, *One Hand Tied Behind Us. The Rise of the Women's Suffrage Movement*, London, Virago Press, 1978; S. Holton, *Feminism and Democracy. Women's Suffrage and Reform Politics in Britain, 1900–18*, Cambridge, Cambridge University Press, 1986; J. Hannam, *Isabella Ford*, Oxford, Basil Blackwell, 1989.

10 Class is another obvious factor: this has been explored in relation to the debate over adult versus equal suffrage. See, for example, Holton, *Feminism and Democracy*, pp. 53–75. The influence of race, ethnicity, age and so on has, though, still to be studied.

11 For a lucid discussion of the role of gender in culture formation and its influence in economic relations see S. O. Rose, *Limited Livelihoods. Gender and Class in Nineteenth-century England*, London, Routledge, 1992, pp. 7–11.

12 C. Rover, *Women's Suffrage and Party Politics in Britain, 1866–1944*, London, Routledge & Kegan Paul, 1967, p. 220; *W.T.*, 10 April 1891; 24 April 1891; 8 May 1891; 11 February 1893; 18 February 1893; 20 January 1894. In a fictional piece, a 'female agitator', for example, was described as a 'queer woman', and the suspicion was left to hang in the air that she might intend to steal the money collected at the end of the meeting. See *W.T.*, 28 November 1891.

13 *W.T.*, 11 March 1893. See also, for example, 9 October 1891.

14 *W.T.*, 24 July 1891; 8 October 1892; 11 March 1893; 29 April 1893; 3 June 1893; 5 August 1893.

15 *W.T.*, 10 July 1891; 15 July 1893.

16 *W.T.*, 6 January 1894.

17 *W.T.*, 2 January 1892. See also 3 April 1891; 8 May 1891; 26 June 1891; 2 April 1892; 30 April 1892; 3 September 1892.

18 N. Blewett, 'The Franchise in the United Kingdom 1885–1918', *Past and Present*, 32 (1965), pp. 27–56. Although excluded from the parliamentary franchise, by the late 1880s unmarried women ratepayers represented between 12 and 25 per cent of the municipal electorate, and could both vote for and be elected to school boards and boards of guardians. In 1894 this eligibility was extended also to the newly established parish and district councils. See P. Hollis, 'Women in

Council: Separate Spheres, Public Space', in J. Rendall (ed.), *Equal or Different. Women's Politics 1800–1914*, Oxford, Basil Blackwell, 1989, pp. 192–213.

19 *W.T.*, 8 May 1891. See also 31 December 1892; 6 May 1893; 16 September 1893.

20 *W.T.*, 3 December 1892.

21 *W.T.*, 6 February 1892.

22 H. Bradley, *Men's Work, Women's Work. A Sociological History of the Sexual Division of Labour in Employment*, Cambridge, Polity Press, 1989, pp. 175–87.

23 S. Meacham, *A Life Apart. The English Working Class, 1890–1914*, London, Thames & Hudson, 1977, p. 97; *W.T.*, 23 April 1892; 30 April 1892; 18 June 1892.

24 *W.T.*, 19 December 1891. See B. Drake, *Women in Trade Unions* (1921), London, Virago Press, 1984, pp. 26–43.

25 For a positive attitude towards women's work, see *W.T.*, 5 June 1891; 11 September 1891; 7 May 1892; 10 September 1892.

26 For the 'family wage' see, for example, W. Seccombe, 'Patriarchy Stabilized: the Construction of the Male Bread-Winner Norm in Nineteenth-Century Britain', *Social History* 11, 1 (1986), pp. 53–76.

27 C. Black, *Married Women's Work*, (1915), London, Virago Press, 1983; Rose, *Limited Livelihoods*, pp. 126–53; K. McClelland, 'Masculinity and the "Representative Artisan" in Britain, 1850–80', in M. Roper and J. Tosh (eds), *Manful Assertions. Masculinities in Britain since 1800*, London, Routledge, 1991, pp. 74–81.

28 Royal Commission on Labour, XXVIII (1892); XXVII (1891). See also Meacham's description of the segregation of roles within the family in this period, in A Life Apart, pp. 64, 72–3.

29 *W.T.*, 6 February 1892. See also 1 May 1891; 17 July 1891; 10 September 1892; 18 March 1893.

30 Bradley, *Men's Work*.

31 *W.T.*, 1 May 1891.

32 *W.T.*, 3 April 1891. See also 20 February 1891; 5 June 1891.

33 *W.T.*, 18 March 1893.

34 *W.T.*, 30 April 1893.

35 *W.T.*, 15 May 1891; 14 August 1891; 2 April 1892.

36 *W.T.*, 5 June 1891; 21 August 1891; 5 November 1892.

37 *W.T.*, 19 December 1891.

38 *W.T.*, 27 February 1892. See also 20 February 1891; 12 December 1891; 10 September 1892; 17 March 1894.

39 *W.T.*, 19 December 1891.

40 *W.T.*, 13 February 1892.

41 *W.T.*, 30 January 1891; 24 July 1891; 4 September 1891; 8 October 1892; 19 August 1893.

42 See, for example, *W.T.*, 28 August 1891; 4 November 1893; 25 November 1893. An example of such language is Will Sprow's use of the term 'horny-handed sons of toil'; *W.T.*, 21 October 1893. Possibly as a counter to its overwhelmingly masculine tone, on 21 May 1892 the subtitle 'Everybody's paper' started to appear on the paper's front page.

43 *W.T.*, 13 February 1892.
44 *W.T.*, 5 December 1891.
45 See Plate 1. *W.T.*, 4 February 1893. E. Hobsbawm, 'Man and Woman in Socialist Iconography', *History Workshop Journal* 6 (1978), pp. 121–38. For the use of masculine imagery and rhetoric, see also *W.T.*, 31 July 1891; 3 September 1892; 31 December 1892; 10 March 1894. Joseph Burgess seems to have become aware of such a masculine bias. In an editorial in which he stated that the Labour movement 'is a movement in which the man asserts the dignity of man, and of labour as man's most divine attribute', he took pains to add that the movement at its best also embraced women and children. *W.T.*, 20 January 1894.
46 G. Stedman Jones, 'Working-Class Culture and Working-Class Politics in London, 1870–1900; Some Notes on the Remaking of a Working-Class', *Journal of Social History* 7, 4 (1974), pp. 485–6 (pp. 460–508); R. Roberts, *The Classic Slum. Salford in the First Quarter of the Century*, Harmondsworth, Penguin, 1974, p. 88.
47 *W.T.*, 19 December 1891.
48 *W.T.*, 14 November 1891; 26 March 1892; 10 December 1892.
49 *W.T.*, 28 October 1893. See also 12 December 1891; 27 February 1892; 21 May 1892; 1 April 1893; 30 September 1893.
50 See Plate 2. *W.T.*, 1 April 1893.
51 Rose, *Limited Livelihoods*, p.130; W. Thorne, *My Life's Battles*, London, George Newnes, 1925, pp. 32–3; E. Faue, '"The Dynamo of Change": Gender and Solidarity in the American Labour Movement of the 1930s', *Gender & History* 1, 2 (1989), pp. 150–1 (pp. 138–58). For other 'Leon Caryll' drawings, see, for example, *W.T.*, 29 May 1892; 7 January 1893.
52 *W.T.*, 31 October 1891; 26 March 1892; 3 September 1892; 12 August 1893.
53 McClelland, 'Masculinity and the "Representative Artisan"', pp. 74–81; S. O. Rose, 'Gender and Labor History, the Nineteenth Century Legacy', *International Review of Social History* 38 (1993), p. 155 (pp. 145–62).
54 Such views were not necessarily common to the Independent Labour Party as a whole. Nevertheless, in her study of the West Riding Independent Labour Party, J. Hannam has observed a reluctance, similar to that of *The Workman's Times*, to recognize women's role as workers and a tendency to sentimentalize home life. '"In the Comradeship of the Sexes lies the Hope of Progress and Social Regeneration". Women in the West Riding ILP circa 1890–1914', in Rendall (ed.), *Equal or Different*, pp. 214–38.
55 *W.T.*, 23 April 1892.
56 *W.T.*, 10 April 1891; 1 May 1891.
57 *W.T.*, 12 December 1891; 31 October 1891.
58 M. Garrett Fawcett, 'A Reply to the Letter by Mr. Samuel Smith, MP, on Women's Suffrage', quoted in J. Lewis, (ed.), *Before the Vote Was Won; Arguments for and against Women's Suffrage*, London, Routledge & Kegan Paul, 1987, pp. 434–42.
59 *W.T.*, 10 February 1894; 3 March 1894. Sarah Burgess, née Wild, had

met Joseph when in 1888 he had joined the staff of the *Oldham Express*, where she herself worked. She was the daughter of the proprietor, William Wild. Burgess, *A Potential Poet?*, p. 143; Burgess, *John Burns*, p. 91. The 'special commissioner' employed by *The Workman's Times* to tour the country (and plug the paper) in 1893 was particularly keen on the idea of a 'National Guild of Women', both to encourage women's participation in the Independent Labour Party and to involve them in activities suited to them. For example, he singled out for praise the Leeds women who had been feeding the families of striking miners. *W.T.*, 25 November 1893.

60 *W.T.*, 16 September 1893; 23 September 1893.

61 See Plate 3. *W.T.*, 4 November 1893.

62 *W.T.*, 11 November 1893.

63 See Plate 4. *W.T.*, 30 December 1893.

64 It is worth noting here that there was no inevitability about waged work as central to the development of a working-class masculinity either. For the development of a different type of masculinity see, for example, P. J. Walker, '"I Live But Not Yet I for Christ Liveth in Me". Men and Masculinity in the Salvation Army, 1865–90', in Roper and Tosh, *Manful Assertions*, pp. 92–112.

65 *W.T.*, 18 February 1893. 'R.B.C.' also suggested that men and women should work together, in this case in the forthcoming municipal elections, and protect their own interests 'against all would-be representatives of merely class interests'. *W.T.*, 28 October 1893.

66 *W.T.*, 7 October 1893. For images of war, see also 9 July 1892; 7 October 1893. For images of slavery, see 12 December 1891; 4 February 1893; 10 March 1894.

67 *W.T.*, 9 July 1892; 4 February 1893. The use of a romanticized and 'heroic' rhetoric of violence by the American labour movement, and in particular by the Section 574 of the Minneapolis General Drivers' Union in the 1930s, provides an interesting comparison. Faue, '"The Dynamo of Change"', pp. 142–7. As Faue points out, there was no space for women within this rhetoric.

68 *W.T.*, 18 February 1893; 12 December 1891.

69 *W.T.*, 31 October 1891; 10 April 1891; 18 February 1893. Lucy Bland has observed how in the 1890s feminist debates were dominated by the issue of married women, their right to control their bodies and to change male sexual practices. It is possible that *The Workman's Times* was reflecting at least an echo of these debates. L. Bland, 'The Married Woman, the "New Woman" and the Feminist: Sexual Politics of the 1890s', in Rendall (ed.), *Equal or Different*, pp. 141–64.

70 *W.T.*, 10 April 1891; 31 October 1891; 12 December 1891; 13 February 1892; 3 December 1892; 18 February 1893. A number of historians have observed the connection between status as male breadwinner and power within the family. See, for example, J. M. Bennett, 'Misogyny, Popular Culture and Women's Work', *History Workshop Journal* 31 (1991), pp. 166–88.

Chapter 3

Men, manners and militancy
Literary men and women's suffrage

Angela V. John

In December 1907 the writer Israel Zangwill declared at a London demonstration for women's suffrage: 'The petticoat no longer makes the Suffragette. We are suffragettes – suffragettes in trousers.'[1] The 'We' referred specifically to those men who had declared their suffrage sympathies via the Men's League for Women's Suffrage (MLWS) founded nine months earlier. It was the league's first major public demonstration and the audience at the Queen's Hall, Langham Place chiefly consisted of the converted. The term 'suffragette' had been invented the previous year by a hostile press deliberately deploying a feminine diminutive though the Women's Social and Political Union (WSPU) then successfully invested it with a positive meaning. The press caricatured suffragettes as unwomanly and depicted male support as emasculating. During the 1908 Newcastle by-election, for example, suffragettes were described as hysterical wild women and, a newspaper warned, 'wherever women have become virile, there men have become effeminate'.[2] *Manhood* suffrage, in contrast, was often adduced as a worthwhile cause.

Unused to having to examine *and* uphold their own meanings of what constituted a manly man, the male advocates of votes for women on the same terms as men, found themselves on the defensive. They used various tactics to validate their position. In contrast to their traducers, the pro-suffrage men carefully sought to represent themselves as the progressives, the ones who had left Victorian society behind. Zangwill boasted that they had cast off the prejudices of the ages and done their best to rid themselves of their inherent sense of male superiority. This was not a battle of the sexes: it was 'no duel but a duet'. They also countered potential opposition by reappropriating the language and claims made by those who attacked them. Thus the smug statement by the opponents of women's suffrage that they were the chivalrous protectors of the female sex was subverted by the male supporters who stressed that it was *they* who really cared for women.

Women suffragists also utilized the notion of female dependence on male protection as a strategy for gaining support. Yet they trod a fine line since they also wanted to retain control over how policy was directed and deployed, thus relegating the men to the back seat. An appeal to old-fashioned manners was not intended to signify that men were in charge. The intensification of militancy around 1912 brought to a head issues about control and power. A number of women argued that men could not, and as voters should not, attempt to be militant activists.

Male supporters of women's suffrage included a considerable number who mainly earned their living by their pen: scholars, novelists, playwrights and poets. A survey of the first 300 members of the MLWS revealed 10 per cent to be scholars, 16 per cent clergy and authors and 13 per cent journalists.[3] The tension between manners and militancy was exemplified by a small group of influential 'wordsmiths' who knew and corresponded with the suffragette Elizabeth Robins: Gilbert Murray, William Archer, John Masefield, H. G. Wells, Laurence Housman, John Galsworthy and Henry Nevinson. Eminent, influential names, though not best remembered today for their championing of women's suffrage, they played an active, if equivocal, role in upholding women's rights. They shared close friendships with each other,[4] a commitment to serious writing and a love of the theatre. They were Liberal or Fabian in politics and they espoused causes. For example, Nevinson, Murray, Wells and Galsworthy were all involved in the public outcry against the slave-system Nevinson had witnessed in Portuguese Angola. After the First World War several of them became interested in furthering internationalism through organizations such as the League of Nations Union. They also acted as constructive critics of each other's work in private and in print. All, except for Masefield who was born in 1878, had been born between the mid-1850s and mid-1860s.

The Victorian liberal intelligentsia in post-Victorian society inevitably carried with them values from their formative years which they could not simply reject.[5] This united the group as did their belief that what they said mattered and could command attention, a belief which arose from their class assurance and from their position as writers, as author/ity. Significantly, the least privileged of this group,

H. G. Wells, was the one whose relationship with the suffragettes was the most problematic.

There were a number of experiences the seven men shared. A majority had some sort of connection with the legal profession. Four had fathers who were solicitors whilst Galsworthy and Archer trained at the Bar before becoming writers. Over half the group had lost or no longer lived with one of their parents before the age of 7 and three of them had lived in Australia for part of their youth. Three had highly intelligent, politicized sisters. Most of them had been to public school and three had Oxford degrees. They had connections with Kensington and Hampstead in London and with Oxfordshire and the Cotswolds. Several of them were active members of men's societies for women's suffrage and spoke at suffrage events. A number of their books and propaganda pamphlets were available through the feminist Woman's Press.

Unlike most men, they tended not to go *out* to work. Artistic, intellectual, liminal figures whose workplace was, like so many women's, synonymous with the home, they were perceived as creative, unconventional individuals and were both courted by and dependent on, the public. Though they perhaps lacked the manly status of those in jobs seen as strenuous, visible, or linked to empire, Thomas Carlyle's inclusion of the man of letters in his conception of fit heroes had helped their sense of worth.[6] Henry Nevinson's career suggests an extreme form of the paradox of the professional male writer. He was a war correspondent but, according to Gilbert Murray, was 'too gentle, too passionate, revolted by scenes of violence and cruelty, to be mixed up in such things as wars or great oppressions'.[7] In 1909 Nevinson and H. N. Brailsford resigned positions as leader-writers on the *Daily News* because of their suffrage convictions, declaring 'we cannot denounce torture in Russia and support it in England'.[8]

Elizabeth Robins was American-born but had lived in England since 1888.[9] She had introduced the English-speaking world to Ibsen's *Hedda Gabler* and *The Master Builder*. Indeed, Ibsen had influenced most of this group. In addition to acting, producing and managing Ibsen's prose dramas in the 1890s, Robins had become a respected Edwardian novelist. Her quest tale about the search for gold in the Klondike, *The Magnetic North* (1904), was a best-seller, lent veracity by the author's having made a perilous journey to Alaska at the turn of the century. By 1907 Robins had also gained fame as a playwright, the production of her *Votes For Women!* at the

Court Theatre having inaugurated suffrage drama. The following year she wrote an eight-page speech for its producer Granville Barker to deliver at a WSPU 'At Home'.[10] She turned her play into a powerful novel called *The Convert* (1907). Immediately after the split in the WSPU and a month before her novel was published, Mrs Pankhurst persuaded Robins to join the national committee.

In a talk at the Albert Hall in March 1912 Robins paid tribute to the imprisoned Frederick Pethick Lawrence and the WSPU's pride in its support from men, asking what other body of women could boast men friends 'ready to give up their personal ambition, ready to sacrifice money, peace of mind, to risk life and limb'?[11] Robins had been tragically widowed in America in her mid-twenties. Men appear to have found her both intellectually stimulating and sexually alluring, an enigmatic figure who fascinated yet whose independence and seriousness could appear threatening. It seems that they could never really divorce her from her position as an actress and, most notably and notoriously, as Hedda. Their difficulty in reconciling her evident femininity and beauty with her feminism was summed up by her diplomat friend Sir Ian Hamilton who referred to her 'Masculine sentiments' and 'yet a femininity which would *almost* (but never quite) persuade me to do whatever you wished'.[12] Examining the reactions of the seven writers to Robins's involvement in women's suffrage and to the movement more generally via their correspondence with her, helps reveal the disjuncture between their private and public (non-fictional) utterances as well as suggesting something of the dilemma and contradictions these men faced. It is particularly illuminating in terms of understanding the kind of threats that militancy by women appeared to pose to them as gentle men.

Gilbert Murray was the most scholarly of this group.[13] A distinguished academic, known for his translations of Euripides, he had a chair at Glasgow at the age of 23 and became Regius Professor of Greek at Oxford in 1908. In his capacity as a playwright he had corresponded with Robins since the 1890s when she was on the management committee of the New Century Theatre. He called himself 'an old suffragist'. Married to Lady Mary Murray, daughter of the Women's Liberal Association president, the Countess of Carlisle (Shaw drew heavily on the Murrays in *Major Barbara*), he sat on the committee of the Men's Liberal Society for the parliamentary Enfranchisement of Women and was on the council of the Women's Franchise League from 1889. He was president of the Oxford Women's Suffrage Society for a number of years and of the

Oxford University branch of the MLWS from its inception in 1911. He also worked to further the rights of women students, particularly at Somerville. He did, however, on his own admission, feel that dons, himself included, sought to protect and women students to please.

As a Liberal, Murray found himself in an awkward position. He was wary of his party's prevarication over suffrage. On a deputation to Lloyd George at Christ Church Deanery in 1913, where Nevinson was a representative for the Men's Political Union (MPU), Murray stressed that he could not give his full support to a government that did not endorse women's suffrage. Yet he added that he was also critical of the WSPU's policy of opposing Liberal parliamentary candidates, however progressive the latter's views. He told Robins that this policy 'makes me sick. It seems like egotism run to lunacy'. He was vehemently anti-Conservative and feared a reactionary government most of all. Counteracting the oppression of the poor was, he felt, a more urgent priority than the oppression of women by men.

Robins admired the Murrays and in 1909 sent them a draft version of her long article entitled 'Why?'. Published in both Britain and the States, it posed ten questions about why women were banding together for the vote.[14] In his detailed response Murray stressed that he was 'rather out of sympathy' with militant perspectives though, unlike some, was not 'in a state of violent irritation' against the WSPU. He painstakingly took Robins's arguments to pieces. Whilst he agreed that the divorce laws were currently unjust, he had qualms about simply equalizing them. He believed that marriage was currently in a transitional state, that 'in ordinary circumstances' (Robins queried what this might mean) the woman slightly oppressed the man but that in really hard circumstances or when the man was roused, he could tyrannize (Robins added the word 'cruelly') over the woman. When she adduced examples of ill-treatment by men, he countered by arguing that men too could be victims. He believed that she was 'searching in all corners' for something she could call a grievance and feared that she was simply attacking man-made laws for the sake of it. Robins's frustration at Murray's focus on a rational, logical approach that failed to question and analyse the basis of male power, produced some indignant marginalia.

Several months before this correspondence with Robins, Murray had delivered an inaugural lecture at University College, Aberystwyth. Entitled 'Wherewith Shall It Be Salted?',[15] it argued that the new universities (Aberystwyth had been founded in 1872 so, compared with Oxford, was very modern) were producing a new class of intellectuals, men *and* women with important tasks to fulfil. They should act as bulwarks against the dangers of judging everything by a monetary value. They should be better informed about politics, caring for the public interest, which intellectuals had often failed to do. And they should accustom themselves to regard women as fellow citizens, not as property. Conceding that this was a controversial issue, he then alluded to the second Married Women's Property Act, the problems of prostitution, of women's employment and even lack of opportunities for middle-aged wives. He stressed that his concern ranged wider than suffrage, involving 'the whole question of a better adjustment of the relations between men and women'.

It was a powerful lecture delivered to a 'partially hostile audience'. In his opening remarks Murray drew attention to the 'ideal of gentlemanliness'. He had spent his childhood in the Australian bush and explained how he was touched by the sense of gentlemanly behaviour which he interpreted as one of the better results of the English love of emulating the ruling class, this insistence on 'the sense of honour, on chivalry, on truthfulness'. The spread of courtesy was one of the great virtues of the nation.

Murray's conception of women's rights grew out of his study of Greek civilization and from his sense of 'fair play'. His antipathy towards militancy emanated from a belief in achieving change through constitutional, incrementalist methods and may also have been fuelled by his concern for his half-sister Eveline who was a suffragette. Like a number of women for whom the cause really mattered, she was a gentle soul who had to force herself to commit militant acts. Murray could not comprehend her compulsion to do what was clearly reprehensible to her, so instead blamed those who urged such action.

Murray's friends included the poet John Masefield.[16]At the end of 1909 Masefield and Nevinson, both living in Hampstead, considered writing a propaganda play about women's suffrage though Murray dissuaded them. Masefield did, however, read some of his verse at a reception held by Britain's first professional organization of women writers, the Women Writers' Suffrage League (WWSL), at the Waldorf Hotel, London. Robins read a short story about Alaska. Masefield and Robins were at this time involved in an intense, largely epistolary relationship – he wrote her over 260 letters during a six-month period. He also collaborated with her in the early stages of what would become her popular story of white slavery, *Where Are You Going To . . .?*

Masefield delivered a speech, 'My Faith in Woman Suffrage', at the Queen's Hall in 1910.[17] Here he demonstrated how present-day society was outmoded. He quoted Ibsen and the kind of barbarism lauded in the press; for example, 'A manly Briton spat at some unsexed women who were asking for the vote'. Having been deeply unhappy at boarding school, he attacked the way that public school-boys were socialized into learning how to deal only with certain kinds of men, to make empty verses in dead tongues and be contemptuous of their sisters. Modern Britain was not an attractive place for this sensitive poet who regretted that 'John Bull has long supplanted the St George who rescued women'.Yet the suffrage cause offered new hope, having 'flung into the world a blazing torch of beauty'. He proclaimed that 'the old rule of sex is dead. And that the new rule of human beings, of comrades may begin'.

It was a well-crafted, romantic talk and it went down well. Emmeline Pethick Lawrence declared that it 'held us all spell-bound'.[18] Nevinson pronounced it 'extraordinarily good, lifting the whole question into a higher realm'.[19] Yet that, in a sense, was its problem as well as its strength. Masefield was not concerned with practical suggestions for suffrage action. The thrust of his speech – and indeed of his letters to Robins – was that men go wrong, lacking the 'great reverence' they should have for women.They needed to make reparations. The young man whose mother had died when he was 6 and who had spent a miserable youth at sea, felt guilty and repulsed by the sexual excesses he had witnessed then. His written conversations with Robins and his fantasizing of a mother–son relationship show him trying to expiate what he saw as former sins. He wanted to make sense not only of his past but also of his own masculinity. Here he was confronting himself in a way that most other men were not prepared to do. His celebration of female difference was less progressive. He idolized and idealized the role of motherhood and much of his language in his letters to Robins is concerned with the service he wanted to perform for women. Here was another chivalrous knight.

Masefield had been a last-minute replacement at the WWSL reception. The original speaker was to have been H. G. Wells but Robins (who was president of the society) had objected. Hardy, Shaw and Henry James all declined to speak and although Wells protested that he believed in women's suffrage (though not in militancy which he thought to be 'ridiculous and irritating'), Robins had her way. She had once seen Wells as a kindred spirit and had written to congratulate him on *Mankind in the Making* (1903), stressing how well he understood American men.[20] She soon decided, however, that this could not be extended to British women. In *The Convert* she criticized what she called his 'dolly' view of women and was infuriated by *Ann Veronica* (1909) for drawing so unashamedly on his personal life and selfishly advocating a man's view of free love. Although she conceded that Wells was a 'profoundly interesting man and a genius', she resented the way he ridiculed women's suffrage and its workers.

The situation was exacerbated by Wells's fascination with Robins and belief that there was 'a sort of freemasonry between us people of the imaginative life'. She was incensed by his treatment of Amber Reeves, discussed the situation with Amber's mother Maud Pember Reeves, had Amber and her baby to stay and found them accommodation. Her exculpation of Amber Reeves from any responsibility appears to have been a little one-sided (and influenced by Robins's own tricky friendship with Masefield). As Jane Lewis has pointed out, Reeves was not exactly a victim whilst Wells seems to have combined what Robins called 'old-fashioned prejudices' with also anticipating, through his and Reeves's views, future, more open attitudes towards sexual morality. Nevertheless, Wells does appear to have conflated sexual freedom with women's rights. Robins particularly deplored his desire for others to take sex as lightly as he could and tried to explain her perspective as a woman: 'as your southern lady said, you must be one of us to understand.' But he, in return, chose to simplify Robins's position, accusing her of being bitter towards men. By the early 1920s they were hurling insults at each other across the printed page.

In Wells's novel *The Wife of Isaac Harman* (1914), Lady Harman briefly emulates the suffragettes and breaks a window.[21] This emanates from her personal desperation and also frustration at a 'do gooder's' inability to understand that she has not left her antediluvian husband for another man. It does not suggest action prompted by suffrage conviction, so encourages readers to question the motives of militants. Yet, leaving her unhappy marriage has helped Lady Harman to change her approach to social issues. Wells signals this by having her read new kinds of books, several socialist and feminist tomes, including a novel by Elizabeth Robins!

Robins's own fictional characters alarmed some of her men

friends. Her erstwhile lover, the Scotsman William Archer, theatre critic and translator of Ibsen, uncharacteristically ran out of words when describing Vida Levering's bargaining at the end of *The Convert*.[22] Wells, Henry James and J. M. Barrie had already suggested alterations to drafts of her suffrage play, some of which she had resisted. Now Archer expressed wariness of the 'ferocious Vida of the close. Oh Lord! Oh Lord!'

Archer had worked for many years with Robins, stage-managing Ibsen's plays, founding the New Century Theatre and writing plays and stories with her. They both actively resisted stage censorship and cherished hopes for a national theatre, which also found support from, amongst others, Granville Barker, Masefield, Shaw and Murray. Murray described his friendship with Archer as 'one of the most intimate of his life'.[23]

Archer had long been prepared to elucidate his criticisms of Robins's writing. He now extended this to her suffrage activities and to suffragette policies more generally. In 1908 after Asquith had become Prime Minister, Archer's annual birthday letter to Robins tried to dissuade her from working for the WSPU, emphasizing that there were plenty who could break stones and make 'stump speeches' but not so many who could write *The Convert*. He conceded that her 'party' had given 'ample proof of courage and conviction' but felt that this approach had exhausted itself:

> Without slackening their propaganda let them show now, for a year or two, that they can, when they like 'play the game'. By encouraging the opposite opinion, they have been for some time (it seems to me) merely putting backbone into the opposition. Monomaniac tactics are useful at a time *for* a time; they may even snatch a signal victory; but since they have failed to do so in this case, I think that wise generalships would not rely on them for a long campaign, but would keep them in reserve for a possible juncture to which they may be specifically adapted ... it is clear that however good and wise the man – I mean the militant tactics may be, there must be other means as well by which the cause can be advanced, and means for which you are better suited.

With his gendered conceptions of fair play and warfare, Archer failed to appreciate that it was precisely because women had been told what to do for so long that many of them were now determined to go their own way.

Three days later he wrote from the National Liberal Club (where windows would be smashed by suffragettes in 1911). He suggested that Robins's friends ought seriously to consider '*How they can most quickly gain their ends*'. The vote would '*not* be yielded at the parasol's point. . . . There is a great deal of human nature in men, and they will never *openly* capitulate to violence'. They would insist on a 'period of calm to save appearances' during which time attempts would be made to solve the problem. This would involve 'active agitation according to the *rules of the game as men understand it*' (my emphasis). His emphatic language now shifted into a series of commands:

> Hold meetings and let the other side do the breaking up. Heckle candidates in due time and season. Keep yourselves technically in the right instead of technically in the wrong. Rowdyism and anti-feminist fanaticism will play into your hands fast enough.

The rowdies who interrupted meetings were thus contrasted with 'real men' with their strategies and control. Archer suggested that Liberals could hardly object to tax resistance, adding that if in future they endorsed only strictly constitutional propaganda, the next Tory government might carry the day!

We do not have Robins's replies to these letters. She did not meet Archer much in these years though her diary records dining with him on St Valentine's Day the following year and quarrelling over suffrage policy. His advocacy of 'patience and postponement' and his predisposition to preach at suffragettes were, however, roundly condemned by Christabel Pankhurst in June 1913 in an editorial in *The Suffragette*.[24] Archer had denounced militancy as 'War upon society at large'. Its intensification in the context of the 'Cat and Mouse' Act and a three-year sentence for Mrs Pankhurst, led him to see 'ultra militant' tactics as a negation of the fundamental principles of democracy.

Militancy meant different things to different people at different times.[25] For the WSPU it had at least three identifiable stages, the first of which involved interrupting Liberal speakers and attending deputations. Robins did not involve herself in the former and although, as a WSPU representative, she somewhat reluctantly attended the deputation of suffrage groups to Lloyd George in November 1911 in the wake of the manhood suffrage bill and torpedoing of the Conciliation bill, she stipulated that she would not speak.

Nor was she prepared to engage in the second level of militant action which involved smashing glass. She witnessed, from a distance, several clashes with the police including Black Friday but never sought to be or got arrested, or participated in the final stages of arson. She preferred to persuade with the pen. She adopted what might be seen as a problematic position: inciting militancy through talks and the press but not risking her own life or health. This was appreciated by the WSPU leadership who understood where her skills lay and also knew that she was not a British citizen. She exposed the irony of men bent on militarism yet aghast at the breaking of windows, distinguishing between, on the one hand, the suffragettes' symbolic acts which (in contrast to Archer) she presented as the only means left to secure their rights and, on the other hand, the violence of the authorities. Her influential speeches and writings caused a stir. They appeared in suffrage pamphlets and newspapers and as a book called *Way Stations* (1913) on both sides of the Atlantic. Moreover, Robins became a major apologist for militant WSPU tactics in *The Times*, introducing many who might not otherwise have read such views to the arguments of the militants and, in the process, making Archer even more exasperated.

Another writer who expressed concern about militancy was the artist and writer, Laurence Housman.[26] When his play *Pains and Penalties: The Defence of Queen Caroline* was refused a licence, the Pioneer Players staged it privately at the Savoy in November 1911. During the interval at the first performance a protest meeting was held on stage against the appointment of a new censor the previous day. Robins was one of the speakers.

With a 'hot Tory' father and a mother who died when he was small, and always in the shadow of his more famous academic brother Alfred the poet (an anti-suffragist), Housman nevertheless had one family member who espoused radical beliefs. His sister Clemence was a talented wood engraver and suffragette with whom he lived in Kensington. Both were founder members of the artists' Suffrage Atelier – Housman chaired its inaugural meeting at Caxton Hall in 1909 – and its headquarters were in his studio. Brother and sister were involved in designing and making suffrage banners and Laurence designed the MLWS banner and a badge. He sat on the league's committee from 1909, speaking frequently at their meetings and debates. In 1912 he attended the International Suffrage Alliance conference, representing the WWSL and the Women's Tax Resistance League. Much of his written work concerned women's suffrage, directly or indirectly.

Housman was attracted to the romance of the struggle for women's suffrage. His first commercial success had been a book published anonymously from the assumed viewpoint of a woman, *An Englishwoman's Love-Letters* (1900). As a homosexual who became involved in organizations campaigning to change the law and aiding individual victims, he welcomed a movement which appeared to challenge the accepted definitions of masculinity. Whereas Wells hoped that women's suffrage would lead to greater freedom between the sexes but in the process found himself criticized, these years enabled Housman to explore his own sexuality and question gender roles. At a suffrage garden party he stressed that as a man, he could hardly condemn the militants who were acting as they did because men had refused them justice for so long. In a Women's Freedom League (WFL) pamphlet called *What Is Womanly?* he discussed the male code of honour in relation to duelling, suggesting that *refusal* to fight showed more courage than consent and 'a very true manliness'. By manly he meant the 'pick and polish' of qualities which enabled a man to possess himself and develop all his faculties. He applauded those men courageous and manly enough to 'dare to be thought unmanly and cowardly'[27] and deplored the self-sacrificing qualities usually associated with true womanliness. Full womanliness, in his view, emanated from education and must begin in self-possession, though, like Masefield, he felt that it was motherhood which decided 'the social order of things' and made women superior to men.

Over time he developed a number of misgivings about the effectiveness of militancy as the WSPU appeared to be shaping it. He expressed his concerns to Robins in a less confrontational manner than Archer, his gender awareness marking him out from Robins's other pro-suffrage writer correspondents. This male elector once more supplied a disclaimer about his right to disapprove of acts of revolt. He questioned whether shock tactics were succeeding, adding that 'if the WSPU has not the power to make the shock greater and greater till it becomes irresistible, I shall feel bound to think the "tactics" a mistake'. His sympathy with the 'revolting spirit' would remain but he would question the 'generalship'. Understanding that militancy entails an inexorable escalation of activity, he felt it essential that shock tactics constituted but one part of a carefully worked-out programme with different sequences. Hoping that he would be proved wrong, he admitted qualms lest the WSPU had over-estimated the strength of its approach. He also voiced concern lest

his anxiety reached unfriendly ears and admitted that he had no easy
solutions and was not privy to certain knowledges:

> Now a man cannot write *inciting* the women to go further, or even
> stating as *a fact* what he believes to be the only logical justification
> of the present development from the *generalship* point of view:
> and I am for the present mentally held up, being in the dark.

Elsewhere he stated that men could not understand women. Admiring
the courage of the women, he told Robins, 'I only wish that – just for
the time – I could be a woman too.'

Housman advocated what has been called 'constitutional militancy'.[28] His sister was a founder and committee member of the
Women's Tax Resistance League. He refused to serve on a jury in
cases with a female defendant and encouraged boycotting the census,
an activity which enabled large numbers of people to feel they were
doing something (see Chapter 4). It provoked dismissive remarks
from one census enumerator who told the press that its success was
over-estimated by 'a few conceited, hysterical women and their
effeminate supporters'.[29] Such passive resistance tactics were endorsed by the WFL. Housman's relations with the WSPU, however,
deteriorated over time and the man who would become a pacifist and
Quaker wrote (at a later date) that the union's recourse to 'more wild
and extreme measures' spelt suicide.

Robins also participated in passive resistance, refusing to complete her census form in 1911. When Mrs Pankhurst was imprisoned
she undertook in May 1912 to draft, sign and send circular letters to
'men of distinction and of widely varying pursuits' to press for First
Division treatment of suffrage prisoners.[30] She stressed the hardships
involved in political prisoners being treated as common criminals
and, bearing in mind epistolary advice she had already received,
she added:

> The Suffragist who has not broken windows is constantly being
> told that there are more effectual ways of drawing attention to
> unfair discrimination, and of enlisting help to right a miscarriage
> of justice. I am addressing you in the hope that you will do
> something to encourage this view.

The responses she received were illuminating: 'A curious and
unexpected window opened upon "Opinion".' Some were genuinely
helpful and the majority who were supportive were prepared to sign
petitions or write to the press. There were others ready to condemn

and mock. Some were free with advice and warnings. Stanley
Weyman (who did not know Robins personally) dismissed window-
breaking as 'stupid and mistaken', not comparable in any sense to
the rick-breaking of the early 1830s.[31] Having recently written a
historical romance set at the time of the 1832 Reform Act, he could
judge militancy only in the light of the male political struggles that
he felt really mattered. Failing to understand the women's motives,
he stated that it was 'very unheroic' of them to break the law and
then complain when it was enforced. They should take control of
boards of guardians rather than national matters, concentrating on
issues which were relevant and important to them as a sex.

Another reply came from the successful writer and dramatist John
Galsworthy.[32] Close to Masefield and Murray, he had been an early
adultist, joining the People's Suffrage Federation, but he also
supplied autographed copies of his work to raise money for the
WSPU. Writing in the *Daily News*, he distinguished himself from the
militants but argued that it was the silence of the press which was
largely responsible for their policies. By fair and full reporting,
'militant suffragism might still be helped towards a natural death'.[33]

He espoused a number of causes, including opposition to the
censorship of plays, the docking of horses' tails and the caging of
wild birds. He advocated reform of the divorce laws and the
minimum wage. Barrie claimed that Galsworthy would 'go to the
stake for his opinions' though he would go 'courteously raising his
hat'. This aspect of Galsworthy the Gent. is evident in two articles
he wrote for *The Nation* in March 1910 where this former lawyer
made a plea for women's suffrage on the basis of equity. He began
by defining the essential characteristics of a gentleman: putting
yourself in the place of others, not forcing people to do what you
don't want to do yourself, having the power to do what is right. He
then related this to the position of women, arguing that their full
emancipation would be a symbol that the nation 'was still serving
humanity, still trying to be gentle and just'.

In his 1912 letter to Robins he claimed that such pronouncements
via the press had produced 'not a particle of result' so feared he could
not usefully offer much now. He did, however, stress that women's
suffrage would not progress until constitutionalists and militants
worked together on non-militant lines and an appeal was made to the
'sympathies of the multitude'. He suggested that bodies of professional nurses might show what could be done. Processions and
pageantry were especially valuable and 'singing, if beautiful, might

have an enormous effect in arousing people to some kind of emotional interest'. The suggestion of drawing on processions, pageants and music was hardly novel for a movement so alive to the symbol and potency of spectacle. They had been widely utilized in recent years. In the context of the brutality of treatment faced by suffrage prisoners, such solutions seemed especially flippant and inadequate from a man who had recently been passionately concerned about reducing the hours of solitary confinement for prisoners. Galsworthy's powerful play of 1910, *Justice*, had helped stimulate the subsequent amendment of the law in this respect.

Never one to waste an opportunity, Robins recognized that such letters were more helpful than their authors supposed, revealing in effect 'how successful were those representatives of the sex that legislate for us, in looking at our questions from our point of view'. And without being so disloyal as to name names or publications, she promptly used some of the contents of these letters for a speech at the Albert Hall in mid-June. She described Galsworthy as a man 'so eloquent, so resourceful in attacking abuses other than the root one of women's disenfranchisement', adding cynically, 'We are not even to sing unless we "do it beautifully"' (a quote from her role in *Hedda Gabler*). She speculated on the effects of singing to the Prime Minister or playing the harp to Lloyd George!

Although he would support women's suffrage in a letter to *The Times* in 1916 and become first president of the international writers' club PEN (Poets, Essayists, Novelists) in 1921, Galsworthy became increasingly an establishment figure. In 1918 he wrote to Robins about her proposal for honouring Nevinson's 'many-sided public services' as war correspondent, suffrage supporter and man of letters. Limited women's suffrage had just been granted. Galsworthy explained that he would be happier not to be formally associated with the dinner, not least because Nevinson was likely to break out into 'violent pacifism' or commit some worse indiscretion. He did, however, attend the meal (for over 200 people) which Robins organized. She chaired the speeches and spoke on suffrage.

Henry W. Nevinson had long espoused radical causes.[34] He has been described as 'the last and noblest of the Victorian war correspondents', though the first of his many distinguished assignments was only in 1897 (covering the Greek and Turkish war). Friendly with the other six writers under discussion, he was particularly close to Murray with whom he shared a love of Greek and he greatly admired Masefield's intellect. Nevinson was a founder member of the MLWS, sat on its committee and edited its journal for more than a year and a half. Critical of its somewhat legalistic focus, he helped found the more radical MPU in 1910 and chaired this. He described 6 February 1918, when the Representation of the People Act received the Royal Assent, as the happiest day of his life. During the years before the war he had expended a vast amount of energy on speaking and writing about women's suffrage, working with the WSPU. His estranged first wife Margaret Wynne Nevinson was a member of the WFL and Cymric Suffrage Union and his second wife, whom he eventually married in 1933, was the suffrage militant and writer, Evelyn Sharp.

He had been influenced by Christian Socialism at Oxford and was an early member of the Social Democratic Federation. He had lived and worked in London's East End where he commanded the first working-class cadet corps. Described as 'a knight, giving to the cause of freedom and to the wrongs of men and women, wherever he found them, his combination of gifts',[35] he was, however, critical of what currently passed as chivalry: men springing up to surrender their tube seats to pretty women yet burying themselves in their newspapers when it was a worn-out woman standing with her baby. Yet although his diaries and, indeed, innumerable articles and letters in the suffrage and Liberal press, are testimony to the enormous amount of time he invested in suffrage, his accounts of suffragists are unwittingly revealing. When recounting meetings with male supporters, it is words like 'diplomacy' which predominate whilst mention of the women is almost invariably accompanied by physical descriptions. He persisted in seeing Christabel Pankhurst as 'that brilliant, smiling girl'. Robins emerges as 'a strange and mysterious figure, very capable of love'.

Nevinson's and Robins's approaches to militancy were not dissimilar since both acted as verbal catalysts for others. In 1912 he wrote to Robins after reading her article 'Sermons in Stones'.[36] Here she explained why stone-throwing had become necessary. Breaking glass was the preliminary to warning people of a danger that threatened the community. The stone was not to injure people 'but by way of sounding an alarm'. Nevinson was in broad agreement with her but felt that her point about stones being thrown into empty offices and not hurting anyone now needed to be extended. He believed that 'serious and fatal violence was imminent – from both sides'. The fact that no lives of non-activists were actually lost as a result of militancy should not detract from the very real fear of the time that this was likely to happen, just as many genuinely believed that Mrs Pankhurst might become a martyr and so trigger a massive reaction.

In the wake of the secret arson attack on Nuneham Courtney House in July, Sir Edward Grey and twenty-five eminent figures, including Murray, published a letter in *The Times* deploring the WSPU's 'provocative and bellicose' position, arguing that, with a majority currently pledged to support suffrage and an amended franchise bill, it was foolish to alienate support.[37] Those persisting in militant methods were now cast as the most serious enemies of women's suffrage. Four days later a lengthy reply appeared from Robins in which she argued that women cared about suffrage more than they cared about 'peace or praise'. For the first time she publicly attacked Grey, a personal friend.

Yet, within a few months she had broken with the Pankhursts. Like her writer correspondents, even Housman and Nevinson, she found the recent turn of militant events troubling. In the famous 'Peth–Pank' split in the autumn she sided with the Pethick Lawrences, shocked by the way they were jettisoned and wary of the increasingly autocratic leadership (as she now informed Christabel Pankhurst in long letters to France). Yet, she maintained, along with the Pethick Lawrences, that she was still a militant in spirit, seeing militancy as much more than direct breaches of the law but opposing incitement to violence.

In 1914 the Pethick Lawrences turned their energies to setting up the United Suffragists, bringing together men and women working for the suffrage in a way not permitted by the single-sex WSPU. They aimed 'to interpret militancy to the average woman and man'.[38] Vice-presidents included Nevinson who played a key role in the society's founding and Housman who designed their banner.

During her five years on the WSPU executive, Robins had received advice, both solicited and unsolicited, from her fellow writers. As leaders in shaping opinions and as liberal thinkers, they liked to see themselves as naturally opposed to those who were not modern in outlook. The diaries of Arnold Bennett (another solicitor's son who abandoned the legal profession to become a writer) exemplify such a viewpoint.[39] In Switzerland in 1908 he got into conversation with two 'antis', an Anglo-Indian major's wife and a Yorkshire woman, noting in his diary that 'It is incredible how people still talk . . . their whole talk and all the phrases they used were too marvellously stupid'. When Evelyn Sharp later asked him if he would sign a suffrage testimonial, he was anxious to prove his credentials, de-claring in exaggerated language: 'I am an out-and-out Radical of the most ferocious description', adding, 'Of course I am a suffragist.'[40] Readers of his tongue-in-cheek novel about suffragettes, *The Lion's Share* (1916), might, however, be forgiven for not automatically assuming this and it is interesting to note that in 1911 he criticized the behaviour of 'certain husbands of martyrs'.[41]

The intensification of militant action, especially from the end of 1911, caused many to rethink their views about the WSPU – the socialist F. J. Gould argued that it associated women's votes with 'the idea of disorder and rough manners'.[42] This view, of course, was not gender-specific and there were many more constitutionalists than militants. Mrs Fawcett's umbrella National Union of Women's Suffrage Societies far exceeded other suffrage organizations in size. In contrast, a small group of MPU men like Hugh Franklin were prepared to take militant, even incendiary, action and face its consequences. Yet the writers examined above tended towards cau-tion, a caution which befitted their image as successful, creative artists and as gentlemen. They defined the latter not so much in terms of social class as in relation to enlightened, thoughtful, caring and well-mannered individuals. Whereas opponents described suffrage supporters as hysterical women and effeminate men, pro-suffragists deployed positive adjectives. An advertisement for the suffrage pages in *The Standard* declared that 'Every thinking woman and every chivalrous man will want to read, and to keep, "Woman's Platform"'.[43]

Mark Girouard begins his study of chivalry and the English gentleman by evoking for 1912, not the spectacle of suffrage but another potent kind of imagery: 'Knights in armour, St George, the Empire, knights rescuing maidens in distress, chivalry and gallant gentlemen, dying like gentlemen, women and children first'.[44] Here was a society alive to the thrills of the Earls Court Tournament and the terrors of a sinking *Titanic*. The seven pro-suffrage writers were Victorians who had imbibed the carefully constructed notions of the chivalric gentleman and the adaptation of the medieval code of chivalry to the modern day and empire with its ideals and sense of service now extended to produce chivalry for the people. Murray and Galsworthy both turned down actual knighthoods in 1912 and 1917 respectively but they were keen to perpetuate their own definitions of the well-mannered courteous gentleman and relate this to their own worlds. Even Housman, who showed sensitivity towards men dictating to women, was still caught up in the romance of chivalry. He too was concerned about good manners and good form though he articulated this in relation to women's behaviour. Although he did not mention it to Robins, in his autobiography written in the 1930s, he admitted his reservations about the suffragettes: 'What chiefly annoyed me was the exceedingly bad manners which some of them displayed – quite away from militancy – when good manners would have been such a much better policy.'[45] He recalled a lecture at a social club chaired by Zangwill. It was billed as being about the women of Shakespeare, but the eminent suffragette lecturer actually gave instead 'a violent and aggressive address on woman suffrage'. It produced a protest and Housman departed, humiliated by what he perceived to be the speaker's rude and gratuitous arousal of her audience's resentment.

Girouard's evocation of the chivalric ethos of 1912 needs to be matched by the expressions of militancy in that same year, whether in bellicose actions in the wider world such as the Turkish suppression of Albania and the Italian invasion of Tripoli or, closer to home, in the actions of striking miners and intensification of demands for Irish Home Rule. The more such protest manifested itself, the greater the concern of Christabel Pankhurst that it must be organized and articulated by women alone. Yet pro-suffrage men believed in generating support, not disparagement.

The pro-suffrage writers saw women's suffrage as one important issue amongst a number of causes. They were well aware of the necessity of votes for women in a society that liked to see itself as free, just and civilized. Nevinson was prone to quote Mazzini when writing about women's suffrage. Slightly tongue in cheek, Housman tried to reconcile male courtesy with political propaganda, suggesting that when men gave up seats to women in public they should carry suitcases from which they could give them suffrage literature. This might help remove scorn since the ladies would have received courtesy, so justice towards women would not deprive men of 'the lighter and more easy practised instincts of chivalry'.[46]

Protecting the women against the young male hooligans who attacked them, enabled the men to keep intact their sense of worth. Nevinson's flooring of a steward after attempts to manhandle a woman interrupting Lloyd George, enhanced his reputation with male supporters. Holton has observed that Housman's concerns about militancy were partly prompted by its potential to encourage the worst aspects of the male sex.[47] Zangwill's claim that they were not involved in a battle of the sexes but a duet, requires refining: at times it was a battle *between* men, *for* the protection of women.

Yet, metaphorically or almost literally, slaying the enemy became difficult when the subjects at the heart of the chivalric quest resisted having things done for them and being told what was in their best interests. The increase in militancy made it more and more difficult to square the women's intentions and actions with the notions of fair play and good manners on which these men had been nurtured. It also enhanced the temptation to give advice, thus reappropriating control through words. Although far more enlightened than the majority of their gender and even many fellow writers, there remained something of the knight in these men, still caught up in the seductive old story of riding to the rescue of the maiden in distress. And when the maiden rewrote the script, it did not go down so well. The old stories had no room for militant maidens on their own.

NOTES

1 Suffragette Fellowship Collection, Museum of London, Unaccessioned.
2 *Newcastle Daily Journal*, 18 September 1906.
3 *Women's Franchise*, 27 June 1907.
4 See, for example, Nevinson's descriptions of Galsworthy and Masefield in H.W. Nevinson, *More Changes, More Chances*, London, Nisbet, 1925, pp. 291–4.
5 See S. Pedersen and P. Mandler (eds), *After the Victorians. Private Conscience and Public Duty in Modern Britain*, London, Routledge, 1994, Introduction.
6 N. Clarke, 'Thomas Carlyle and the Man of Letters as Hero', in M. Roper and J. Tosh, *Manful Assertions. Masculinities in Britain since 1800*, London, Routledge, 1991, pp. 25–43.
7 Murray in H. W. Nevinson, *Visions and Memories*, London, Oxford University Press, 1944, pp. 1–2.
8 *The Times*, 5 October 1909.
9 For Elizabeth Robins (ER) see A.V. John, *Elizabeth Robins. Staging a Life*, London, Routledge, 1995.
10 Elizabeth Robins Papers (ERP), the Fales Library, New York University Library, 2 February 1909.
11 ER, *Way Stations*, London, Hodder & Stoughton, 1913, p. 289.
12 ERP Series 2B, Box 16, Folder 88, 7 December 1907.
13 For Murray see F. West, *Gilbert Murray. A Life*, London, Croom Helm, 1984; D.Wilson, *Gilbert Murray OM*, Oxford, Clarendon Press, 1987; J. Smith and A. Toynbee (eds), *Gilbert Murray. An Unfinished Adventure*, London, Allen & Unwin, 1960; and my correspondence with Alexander Murray.
14 ER, *Way Stations*, pp. 130–83; A. V. John, 'Radical Reflections?

Elizabeth Robins, the Making of Suffragette History and the Representation of Working-Class Women', in O. Ashton, R. Fyson and S. Roberts (eds), *The Duty of Discontent. Essays in Honour of Dorothy Thompson*, London, Mansell, 1995, pp. 76–98; Harry Ransom Humanities Research Center (HRHRC), the University of Texas at Austin, Murray to Robins, 14 and 21 September 1909 and Gilbert Murray Papers 16, the Bodleian Library, Oxford, f.54–9, 9 September 1909.

15 *Sociological Review*, 11 (July 1909), pp. 260–73.

16 For Masefield see John, *Staging a Life*, Ch. 8 and the diaries of Henry Nevinson, Bodleian Library, Oxford, MS Eng. Misc., e615/4, 15 and 21 November 1909, 9 March 1910.

17 J. Masefield, 'My Faith in Woman Suffrage', Letchworth City, Garden Press, 1909.

18 HRHRC, Mrs Pethick Lawrence to ER, 16 February 1910.

19 Nevinson Diaries, e615/4, 14 February 1910.

20 For Wells see D. Smith, *H. G. Wells. Desperately Mortal*, New Haven, CT, Yale University Press, 1986; J. Lewis, 'Intimate Relations between Men and Women: the Case of H. G. Wells and Amber Pember Reeves', *History Workshop Journal* 37 (1994), pp. 76–98; H. G. Wells Papers, University of Illinois, Urbana-Champagne, R–179–1, 24 August 1905 and R–179, n.d.; HRHRC, Wells to ER, 26 May 1909 and January 1910, copy of letter, ER to Wells, 8 January 1910, ER to Bessie Hatton, 8 January 1910; ERP, Diary, 6 November 1918; H.Carter (ed.), *Women's Suffrage and Militancy*, London, Frank Palmer, [1911?], p. 68 and ER, *The Convert*, London, Macmillan, 1907, p. 108.

21 H. G. Wells, *The Wife of Isaac Harman*, London, Odhams Press, 1914.

22 For Archer see P. Whitebrook, *William Archer*, London, Methuen, 1993; ERP, Diary, 6 August 1908 and 14 February 1909, and HRHRC, Archer to ER, n.d. (1907), 5 August 1908, 16 February 1909.

23 Smith and Toynbee, *Gilbert Murray*, p. 109.

24 *The Suffragette*, 27 June 1913.

25 For discussions of militancy, see John, *Staging a Life*, Ch. 7 and C. Eustance, 'Meanings of Militancy: the Ideas and Practice of Political Resistance in the Women's Freedom League 1907–1914', in J. Purvis and M. Joannou, (eds), *The Women's Suffrage Movement. New Feminist Perspectives*, Manchester, Manchester University Press, forthcoming.

26 For Housman see L. Housman, *The Unexpected Years*, London, Jonathan Cape, 1937; L. Housman, 'The "Physical Force" Fallacy', Suffragette Fellowship Collection, Museum of London, 50.82/173; J. Woodfield, *English Theatre in Transition*, London, Croom Helm, 1978, p.127; L. Tickner, *The Spectacle of Women. Imagery of the Suffrage Campaign 1907–14*, London, Chatto & Windus, 1987; S. S. Holton, *Suffrage Days. Stories from the Women's Suffrage Movement*, London, Routledge, 1996, pp. 138–60, 183–204 and 230–2; HRHRC, Housman to ER, 8 March 1912 and correspondence with H. Stephen Housman.

27 See also his 'Militancy and No Mistake' article in *Votes For Women*, 15 March 1912.

28 I am grateful to Sandra Holton for letting me read her unpublished paper

'Militancy, Masculinity and Militarism in relation to Women's Suffrage' given to the University of Greenwich Research Project Seminar.

29 *Brighton Herald*, 15 April 1911. I am grateful to Claire Eustance for this reference.

30 ER, Diary, 22–9 May 1912.

31 HRHRC,Weyman to ER, 27 May 1912.

32 For Galsworthy see HRHRC, Galsworthy to ER, 25 May 1912, 15 February 1918; C. Dupré, *John Galsworthy*, London, Collins, 1976; *The Nation*, 19 and 26 March 1910; and ER, *Way Stations*, pp. 322–5.

33 Fawcett Library, 396 11.B.

34 For Nevinson see his papers in the Bodleian Library, MS Eng. misc., c496–7, d663 and e610–28 (his diaries), especially e616/1, 28 May 1910; H. W. Nevinson, *Words and Deeds*, Harmondsworth, Pelican, 1944; Nevinson, *More Changes*; HRHRC, Nevinson to ER, 19 September 1912; and *Woman's Franchise*, 10 June 1909.

35 J. L. Hammond in Nevinson, *Words and Deeds*, p. 158.

36 It appeared in the *Contemporary Review* in April 1912. See ER, *Way Stations*, pp. 219–313.

37 *The Times*, 23 July 1912. See 27 July 1912 for ER's reply.

38 HRHRC, Mrs Pethick Lawrence to ER, 14 April 1913.

39 N. Flower (ed.), *The Journals of Arnold Bennett 1896–1910*, London, Cassell, 1932, p. 303.

40 Evelyn Sharp Letters, Bodleian Library, Oxford, MS. Eng. Lett. d.277, Arnold Bennett to Evelyn Sharp, 10 June 1910.

41 Carter, *Women's Suffrage*, p. 7.

42 ibid., p. 19.

43 *The Standard*, 20 October 1911. I am grateful to Sowon Park for this reference.

44 M. Girouard, *The Return to Camelot. Chivalry and the English Gentleman*, New Haven, CT, Yale University Press, 1981, p. 7. See, too, J. A. Mangan and J. Walvin (eds), *Manliness and Morality: Middle-class Masculinity in Britain and America 1800–1940*, Manchester, Manchester University Press, 1987.

45 Housman, *Unexpected Years*, pp. 275–6.

46 MLWS *Monthly*, October 1909.

47 Holton, 'Militancy, Masculinity and Militarism'.

Chapter 4

Manliness and militancy

The political protest of male suffragists and the gendering of the 'suffragette' identity

Sandra Stanley Holton

INTRODUCTION

> Women must grow their own backbone before they are going to
> be any use to themselves or to humanity as a whole. It is helpful
> and good for men themselves when they try to promote women's
> emancipation; but they have to do it from the outside and the really
> important thing is that women are working for their own salvation,
> and are able to do it even if not a living man takes any part in
> bringing it about.
>
> (Christabel Pankhurst to Henry Harben[1])

With the above advice, Christabel Pankhurst signalled her determination to exclude men from the activities and deliberations of the
Women's Social and Political Union (WSPU). This was a determination which had grown during 1912, and it marked a significant shift,
for previously there had always been a few men among the inner
circles of the WSPU. This chapter will argue that such exclusion
served to recognize, for the first time fully, the gendered nature of
the figure of the 'suffragette', a figure which, by this time, had come
to stand for the political militancy specifically of women.[2] The
suffragette identity was one built around a feminine heroic, and a
rhetoric of female rebellion which the presence of men continually
threatened to undermine. The exclusion of men became essential,
then, if the legitimacy of militant methods of the WSPU were to be
maintained, and the figure of the suffragette were to continue to
represent, unblurred, new ways of being womanly.[3]

Men in sympathy with the WSPU had earlier on sought to define
themselves as 'suffragettes in trousers', but such a definition became
increasingly difficult to sustain from 1909, as the nature of militant
methods underwent significant change.[4] That year saw the adoption

of the hunger strike by militants serving prison sentences, as a protest at the refusal of the authorities to give them political prisoner status.[5] The government responded to this militant tactic with forcible feeding, a practice which became increasingly commonplace in the years that followed, despite the protests of leading members of the medical profession, and the intense suffering it clearly brought to some who underwent it. Forcible feeding was both experienced and represented as instrumental rape by the suffragettes.[6] From 1913, such suffering might be prolonged under the provisions of the 'Cat and Mouse' Act, a measure which allowed the government to release militant prisoners for short periods to recuperate, and then required their return to prison, where the whole sorry cycle might begin again.

It was in these years that the uncertain standing of the 'suffragette in trousers' began to produce among the women leaders of the WSPU a growing ambivalence about some of the activities of their male sympathizers. The rhetoric of militancy had served to establish a clearly gendered identity for the suffragette, creating a new 'type' of femininity while simultaneously appealing to long-established ideals of chivalrous masculinity. While male sympathizers restricted their militant activism to non-violent protest, and to the role of auxiliaries, their presence around the WSPU was relatively un-problematic. But, from late 1909 on, some male champions began to make their own independent protests, protests which occasionally included violence towards the persons of members of the government. Some also sought to emulate militant martyrdom through imprisonment, hunger strike and forcible feeding. Such actions were at odds with the specifically female heroic established by the rhetoric of militancy. And they often brought about, also, the symbolic unmanning of the male militant by the authorities, throwing into doubt whatever value he might have had as a champion of women.

MILITANCY AND THE 'SUFFRAGETTE' IDENTITY

A pathological model of militancy has dominated conventional historical narratives of the suffrage campaigns since the publication of George Dangerfield's powerfully written *The Strange Death of Liberal England* in 1935.[7] Here, the suffrage militant is presented as a sign equally of the decay of a passing political system, and of personal psychological deviancy among women in this period, most especially in terms of a retreat into a lesbian community apart from the world of men. Presently, the historiography of the suffrage movement is under extensive scrutiny from feminist researchers.[8] Fresh accounts of the meaning of militant action are emerging in terms, for example, of women's spirituality and moral community, their pursuit of autonomy, the claims they were making to enter new public spaces, and in suffrage militancy as the acting-out of Romantic theories of social change.[9]

The feminine diminutive form of 'suffragette' may have been intended to mock or demean. But the term was quickly taken up by the WSPU to good effect, and so transformed as to stand for a new type of femininity, an alternative model that emphasized strength, courage, daring, alongside enterprise, ardour and wit, to challenge conventional stereotypes of what it was to be womanly. Christabel Pankhurst, in an editorial in *The Suffragette*, insisted: 'Militancy is not unwomanly as those admit who reverence the memory of Joan of Arc, and are prepared to applaud the women who fight side by side with their fathers, their brothers and husbands in every war.' Similarly, she argued that militancy was not immoral 'as those people admit who rejoice in the Chinese revolution, and rejoice, despite all its horrors, in the Balkan War'. In sum, she concluded, all that could be said against militancy was that it was 'not quite in accordance with last century ideals of gentility'.[10]

Yet if the meaning of militancy lay principally in showing new ways of being a woman, its rhetoric also appealed to long-standing notions of masculine chivalry.[11] Men were called on to defend, to protect and to champion the militant woman as the embodiment of social, political and spiritual progress. The appeal was to a conception of manliness which harked back to the idealism and altruism of Arthurian romance, and which defined the mission of Englishmen, most especially in terms of their historic role in a staunch and unbending resistance to the forces of repression and barbarism.[12] Militant representations of prominent anti-suffragists often portrayed them as unchivalrous, or, more sardonically, as representing the 'New Chivalry', the banner headline above a cartoon that formed a front page of *The Suffragette*. This shows a suffragette, with a distinctly Pre-Raphaelite cast of features, being bludgeoned by the Prime Minister, Herbert Asquith, with a cosh labelled 'LAW'.[13] (See Plate 5.)

Male sympathizers with militancy readily responded to such appeals, and themselves took up the rhetoric of the old chivalry. 'Pointz Wright', a member of the Men's Political Union (MPU), rejected the argument that suffragettes brought down upon them-

THE NEW CHIVALRY.

ASQUITH (Guardian of Law and Order) to Mr. Bonar Law and Sir Edward Carson:
"As for you, sirs! Your sex protects you."

Plate 5 Cartoon of 'The New Chivalry', *The Suffragette*, 1913. By permission of The British Library

selves the violence of crowds and of the authorities: 'it is men's lack of chivalry which drives them to militancy, and men alone are to blame . . . the shame is with the men who deliberately cause women to suffer and drive the courageous to desperation.'[14] Reporting on an incidence of such harassment on Wimbledon Common, one militant sympathizer asked: 'Can men be so lost to reason, to say nothing of sportsmanlike feeling, and still less of chivalry, to take part in this women baiting?'[15] Every so often, the old chivalry of the male militant sympathizer scored a decided hit. Laurence Housman, the writer and a WSPU sympathizer, recounted how, on one occasion, Jack Hobbs 'startled the clubs of Piccadilly' when he joined the men's section of a suffrage procession. He recalled: 'When the hated cause had enlisted the support of a famous cricketer, matters were becoming serious.'[16]

Clearly, the advent of suffrage militancy served to throw into contention competing claims among men to represent upright, stalwart English manliness. For some men the verbal and physical harassment of suffrage demonstrators and speakers, both militant and constitutional, appears to have provided an opportunity for asserting one particular sense of manhood. It often also entailed deriding male suffrage sympathizers as effeminate weaklings and degenerates. For 'suffragettes in trousers' like Charles Gray, organizer of the MPU, support for and defence of the militant suffragist entailed the assertion of a competing masculinity, one he summarized as quite simply 'a question of whether we are gentlemen or cads'.[17] Reflecting on the harassment of women militant speakers in Hyde Park, a 'Citizen of New South Wales' went further still and suggested that the ill-treatment of militant suffragists threw into question the masculinity of all Englishmen, while laying claim to a superior quality in colonial manhood. He upheld the reported comments of another Australian present that his countrymen 'would never allow their women to be treated like this'. For himself, he reported:

> I was shocked and disgusted at what I saw on Sunday. I had often been told that Englishmen at bottom are cowards, but I never believed it until last Sunday . . . I do not know what is coming to our Mother Country, but it seems to me that as long as there are women who care enough for her to stand up and speak, a few against thousands, and receive clods of earth in their faces for their pains, all is not lost for her. We Australians wish them 'Good Luck', and a speedy victory over the powers of evil that are against them.[18]

The rhetoric of the WSPU also produced, however, an account of militant protest, heroism and martyrdom that was so gendered, and so feminized, as to subordinate to a secondary, auxiliary role men's impulse towards chivalry. To begin with, the very adoption of militant methods, initially revolving around civil disobedience and passive resistance and gradually extending to window-breaking, was justified in terms of women's exclusion from constitutional means of political protest.[19] One WSPU supporter argued, in the columns of the *Daily Herald*: 'Violence is demanded of women as it was from men before justice is granted.'[20] The same claim to legitimacy could not be made by the middle-class men who were most prominent among male sympathizers, however. They, after all, had the vote and were within the constitution. Similarly, the later violence of women militants was often justified in terms of a 'sex war' which it was claimed men were waging against the other sex – in the courts, in Parliament, in prisons, in the home. Militancy became, then, the self-defence of women against the violence of men and the social institutions that men controlled. Here, again, was a justification for militancy which excluded the participation of men.[21]

Moreover, the rhetoric of suffragette protest defined militant actions in terms of 'symbolic violence', in contrast to the violence of earlier generations of men protesting their own exclusion from the constitution. So, it was argued, a woman militant might lightly tap a policeman on the cheek in protest, or heckle and harass a male speaker.[22] Men, in contrast, had killed and rioted over the matter of the franchise. Similarly, women's militancy was directed against material objects, not persons – the suffragette broke windows, not heads. Women's militancy was rightful, men's was fearful. This was an account of militancy that most male sympathizers accepted and promoted. Laurence Housman was close to the WSPU leadership until the last year or so of the prewar campaign, and insisted that it was generally forgotten that 'the illegal use of violence began with the police', and with the over-ruling of 'the constitutional right of the voteless to go in petition to Parliament'. He explained his own continuing 'warm sympathy', a sympathy which surmounted personal slight and alienation, by the violence he had seen women experience at the hands of police and the crowd on 'Black Friday' in 1910. He also consistently sought to legitimize the 'symbolic militancy' of the early years by arguing 'that glass windows must be taken as a symbol of the governed, and . . . if consent was withdrawn on a large scale, glass would become an expensive luxury and shutters a necessary substitute'.[23]

The specifically feminine definition of suffrage militancy is made explicit by the character of the references to the militancy of men found in statements from the WSPU leadership. These never refer to the male supporters of the WSPU, but focus instead on the wrongful violence of other men, past and present, in pursuit of political ends. In her apologia for militancy, *My Own Story*, Emmeline Pankhurst, for example, argued thus:

> The militancy of men, through all the centuries, has drenched the world with blood, and for these deeds of horror and destruction men have been rewarded with monuments, with great sagas and epics. The militancy of women has harmed no human life save the lives of those who fought the battle of righteousness.

She went on to explain how she herself 'had to get a close-hand view of the misery and unhappiness of a man-made world, before I reached the point where I could successfully revolt against it'.[24]

Equally, there were frequent accounts of the actions of 'male militants' in *The Suffragette*, but, again, it is noteworthy that such references never relate to the male sympathizers of the WSPU. Instead, the WSPU most often identified male militants with Sir Edward Carson and his followers among the Ulster Unionists. Their hallmark was treason, subversion and physical violence. The 'mild militancy' of the suffrage militants was contrasted by its supporters with the 'ultra-militant' stance of Carson and his supporters in the government.[25] The government's failure to act against Ulster Unionists with the same savagery with which it moved against suffrage militants was often drawn attention to in the columns of *The Suffragette*.[26] In all these ways, then, representations of the militant suffragist were exclusively feminine. Male militants there might be, but by this characterization, they were not to be counted among the men who lent their sympathy to the suffragettes. Clearly, any role for the male supporter of the WSPU was severely circumscribed by such representations of militancy.

MALE SYMPATHIZERS AND MILITANT CAMPAIGNING

Those men attracted to the stance of the militant wing of the movement took on a variety of roles. These included promoting among men the relatively unproblematic activities of 'constitutional militancy'. As we have seen, it was far harder to legitimize the participation of men in even symbolic violence, for they had not, as a group, been placed absolutely outside the constitution. Laurence Housman expressed his frustration that a man could not give 'testimony in the same way, seeing that he has a vote. It seems to confuse the issue.'[27] However, there remained a certain scope for emulating the female militant, for some of the early methods of militancy entailed no violence, symbolic or otherwise. What was often termed 'constitutional militancy' depended rather upon acts of civil disobedience and passive resistance. And these did not raise the same issues of principle, it seems, for many male sympathizers like Laurence Housman, who pursued a number of 'constitutional milit-ant' tactics throughout the campaign. He anyway 'wished greatly that a less headlong and more constitutional form of opposition to unrepresentative government' had been pursued by the WSPU: 'I believed that tax-resistance, so organized that the government would be forced to seize not the goods but the persons of the resisters was the best and most constitutional line for militants to adopt.' Hence, he dedicated a great deal of his time and energies to the work of the Women's Tax Resistance League, while acknowledging that such methods required far more time to take effect.[28]

One of the earliest and best-publicized instances of tax resistance by a male militant sympathizer was that of Mark Wilks. He was a relatively low-paid LCC schoolmaster, married to a woman doctor and suffragist who had refused to pay her taxes. When he, in his turn, refused a demand by the authorities to pay these taxes for her, he found himself in Brixton prison. Mark Wilks was a member of the Men's League for Women's Suffrage, and his colleagues organized a protest march to the prison, and joined with the Women's Freedom League and the Women's Tax Resistance League in planning a major demonstration in Trafalgar Square. The *Daily Herald* sent a reporter to interview Dr Wilks who supported her husband's actions, and reported that he was presently under medical care in the prison, and passing the time in reading Kropotkin's *History of the Great French Revolution*. While another protest meeting was under way outside the prison, Mark Wilks was unexpectedly released, receiving 'a tremendous ovation' as he approached the platform. Addressing the crowd, 'Mr Wilks said he could hardly thank them enough for their loyalty and devotion. Every night he had heard the cheering and singing, and it had had a stimulating effect on him.' Subsequently, the Women's Tax Resistance League held a meeting at the Caxton Hall to honour Dr Wilks and her husband.[29]

In pursuit of further 'constitutional militant' options, Laurence Housman thought up a scheme whereby suffragists might refuse to participate in the collection of the 1911 census. Initially, his scheme was rejected by the WSPU leadership, though the 'restiveness of its own rank and file' on the question eventually forced its participation. The Women's Freedom League, as well as some within the National Union, supported the plan from the beginning. He explained: 'Census-resistance was well-suited to the mentality of the non-heroic many; thus it ensured numbers. It was also good principle, and as such could not be despised by the heroic ones who preferred to get their shock of battle in more active form.' Laurence Housman so arranged things that he had no way of knowing how many women slept in his own house on census night, for he had it barred against himself by his women guests. When he returned in the morning, they had all decamped, 'leaving by way of recompense a nicely-prepared breakfast'. When the census official called, Laurence Housman dutifully reported that his house had been full the previous night with 'a quantity of females, names, numbers, and ages unknown'. His assessment of this particular protest was that 'It was a useful bit of peaceful penetration of skulls which had hitherto remained offensively impervious to argument, while heartening the suffrage movement itself with a sense of its numbers and solidarity'.[30]

Constitutional militancy provided male sympathizers, then, with a number of tactics that allowed them perhaps the fullest sense of participation in militant protest. Their part as auxiliaries to the women's campaigns was altogether more marginal, and also increasingly vexed. Male sympathizers were welcomed as polemicists and apologists on behalf of women militants. Bohemians and intellectuals like Laurence Housman and George Bernard Shaw gave a certain avant-garde cachet to the WSPU when they defended its methods, or attacked the introduction of forcible feeding of its prisoners as an abuse of state powers. Similarly, women militants welcomed the lobbying of prominent male professionals, like the group of leading medical men who also protested forcible feeding. The WSPU depended also on the advice and support of radical lawyers, like Frederick Pethick Lawrence, in calculating the effect of certain kinds of protest, and possible government retaliation.[31] Men suffragists and their organizations also provided a useful channel of communication between the women leaders of the various suffrage societies, whose relations with each other sometimes suffered from conflicts of strategy and temperament. It was the Men's League, for example, which organized a demonstration to welcome the leading Australian suffragist, Vida Goldstein, in 1911, when Millicent Garrett Fawcett, Christabel Pankhurst, Emmeline

Pethick Lawrence and Charlotte Despard all appeared on a platform presided over by Laurence Housman. It is difficult to imagine any other venue in which these leading women suffragists might otherwise have come together by this stage of the campaigns.[32]

Men also acted as 'auxiliaries' to the suffrage movement – providing speakers, polemicists, aid with fund-raising, and go-betweens for discussion with the government or the various branches of the movement itself. Problems arose, however, when male auxiliaries moved beyond the role of intermediaries to intervene in policy-making, and in negotiations with male politicians. These problems intensified over the period between 1910 and 1912. A suspension of militant protest was secured in these years by the introduction of a series of Conciliation bills. These measures had been drafted by a committee established by two men close to the inner circles of the WSPU, Henry Brailsford, whose wife, Jane, was a militant, and Lord Lytton, brother of Lady Constance Lytton who had endured a notorious episode of imprisonment and forcible feeding in 1909. This committee was an all-party body, and the Conciliation bills represented a compromise between all the varying shades of suffragist opinion within the House of Commons. It was hoped that a successful second reading of such a measure must force the hand of the Liberal government to act on the issue.

The diaries of Brailsford's close colleague and friend Henry Nevinson record the deterioration of relations between male sympathizers and the leadership of the WSPU in 1910–12, as tensions over the negotiations between male sympathizers and government members grew.[33] Initially, the Liberal leadership was forced into promising to provide government facilities for a further such Conciliation bill. But the strategy began to founder late in 1911 when the government undermined the worth of this promise by announcing its intention of introducing a new manhood suffrage measure. Although this was to be open to a women's suffrage amendment, the announcement was seen by all suffragists as a betrayal of the original undertaking. The National Union's response was to seek greater co-operation with the Labour Party and the People's Suffrage Federation, an organization committed to securing universal suffrage. The WSPU leadership, however, retaliated with more ferocious militancy than ever before, and the first mass window-smashing raids in London's West End were organized.

The price of this failure of a men's initiative was a loss of credibility within the inner councils of the WSPU for male sympathizers like Brailsford, Nevinson and others. But success might equally produce alienation and suspicion. After WSPU leaders failed to secure for themselves a deputation to the Prime Minister, some of their male sympathizers succeeded. Asquith agreed, following the men's request, to receive a deputation made up of representatives from *all* the women's suffrage societies, something the WSPU had not intended. Laurence Housman recalled how he realized only afterwards that 'we, poor innocents, had entirely spoiled their pitch for them'. The WSPU leadership looked for total and unequivocal support from its male sympathizers. The neutral stance of the Men's League towards militants and constitutionalists, and the independent policies it pursued, eventually brought it into increasing tensions with the WSPU leaders. So, when Laurence Housman lent his support to the National Union's efforts to work with Labour from 1912 on, in policies which were contrary to those of the WSPU, he found himself out of favour with the militant leadership: 'my letters ceased to be answered and presently I was no longer allowed to speak at WSPU meetings.'[34]

The Men's Political Union, and another group with a degree of overlapping membership, the Men's Society for Women's Rights, which was formed at the end of 1911, identified one less problematic form of independent action.[35] They used their forums very often to expose the sexual wrongs perpetrated on women and children by men. And it was in these circles of men suffragists that the issue of venereal disease, and its implications for women's decisions about marriage, seems to have been raised. It was these questions which Christabel Pankhurst subsequently pursued in her notorious pamphlet 'The Great Scourge'.[36] The Men's Society for Women's Rights sought to publicize cases where it thought the courts were dealing too leniently with men who harmed women and children. It even appears to have attempted some reparation for such wrongs in rescuing individual women from sexually hazardous situations by finding more respectable situations for them.[37]

Men might also usefully put their physical powers to the defence of militant speakers and demonstrators, for example, as stewards and bodyguards. The East End prize-fighter Kosher Hunt provided such protection for Sylvia Pankhurst, for example. More generally, the members of local Daily Herald Leagues and Independent Labour Party branches often helped to maintain order or to fend off hooligans attracted to militant meetings.[38] Far more problematic, however, was the adoption of violence against persons by a number of members of the MPU, together with their emulation of the martyrdom of women.

From 1910, male sympathizers became increasingly anguished by the suffering of women friends and colleagues undergoing repeated hunger strikes and forcible feeding. Henry Nevinson, for example, who belonged to both the Men's League and the MPU, recorded in February 1911 that among his associates 'a sense of growing wrath, a novel rage, has arisen lately'.[39] Such despair only grew with the introduction of the 'Cat and Mouse' Act in 1913, and the potential for further extension of this barely disguised torture. The introduction of the thirst strike alongside the hunger strike in 1912 also increased the ordeal of those militants who chose this resort to defy the courts and prison authorities. After a lengthy prison sentence in 1913, Emmeline Pankhurst was repeatedly in and out of jail, following a succession of hunger and thirst strikes which seriously undermined her health. Despite his alienation from the WSPU leadership, Laurence Housman, for one, declared: 'if Mrs Pankhurst dies I shall find it hard not to go to prison to relieve my conscience.' Though Emmeline Pankhurst held on to life through this ordeal, Laurence Housman none the less eventually felt moved to make his protest. But, like other men, he found that arrest and imprisonment were not to be so easily achieved as by the female militant. Once arrested, he was simply kept in the cells for a few hours, and then released without charge for an offence for which women were regularly receiving three-month prison sentences.[40] So simply ignoring the actions of these 'suffragettes in trousers' was one way by which the authorities negated their presence among the militants.

Some men began from this time to turn to offences which the authorities could not ignore – setting fire to railway carriages, leaving bombs in railway stations, and assaulting leading figures in the government. In so doing, they threatened to disturb the delicate balance on which rested the female heroic of the suffragette, and to undermine the rhetoric by which the WSPU sought to legitimize its methods. This female heroic consistently sought to provoke in the authorities a far greater punitive response than might appear legitimate to the wider community. Hence violence against persons was consistently eschewed by the WSPU, except in symbolic form or for purposes of self-defence, while the authorities and anti-suffragists were drawn into ever-increasing violence against the persons of suffragettes. In this way the WSPU sought to undermine the credibility of a government supposedly committed to radical reform and liberal principles, while arousing in men the chivalrous impulse to defend the outraged bodies of women. But when men attempted to emulate the suffragette heroic they found it simply brought about their own unmanning, and hence their value as militant champions.

THE UNMANNING OF THE MALE MILITANT

A number of male sympathizers underwent horrifying episodes of imprisonment, hunger strike and forcible feeding.[41] *The Suffragette* commented on 'the special vindictive harshness which the Government shows to men who champion the women's cause', again comparing this with the indulgence shown towards Sir Edward Carson.[42] But both at the time and subsequently, such cases did not receive the same intense degree of reporting and protest as the sufferings of women militants. For example, at one point in 1913, the WSPU's 'Prisoners List' includes the name of Donald McEwan, sentenced to nine months in Carlton gaol, Edinburgh, but there is no coverage of his trial, no details of his offence, and no evidence of protest on his behalf by either the men's or the women's groups. Similarly, Harry Johnson, a Doncaster journalist, received twelve months' hard labour after being convicted of breaking into a house for unlawful purpose, but was released after five days of hunger striking. No details are recorded of his offence, or his affiliations with the suffrage movement, and thereafter he disappears from view.[43] From 1911 on, and more especially after Christabel and Emmeline Pankhurst ousted Emmeline and Frederick Pethick Lawrence from its leadership late in 1912, there is evidence of an increasing distancing of the WSPU from its male sympathizers.

In part, this reflected the intensifying suspicion of any male meddling after the failure of the Conciliation bills. But the growing resort to physical violence and clandestine acts of destruction by the WSPU also rendered the participation of men unwelcome. For these tactics remained precisely calculated so as to attempt to maintain some distinction between the symbolic violence of women and the brute force of the other sex. Empty buildings were fired, the paintings of old masters vandalized, but there appear to have been no serious attempts at violence against the person, or genuinely disruptive sabotage – except by male sympathizers. Christabel Pankhurst recalled an attack on Lloyd George by two members of the MPU, and insisted that this was an 'unpremeditated and independent act' in which the WSPU had no part. She commented: 'Men are more inclined, as history shows, to attack their opponents, and it was harder for them than it was for the Suffragettes themselves to observe our rule of not using force against persons.' It was also her opinion that, but for her mother's restraining influence, 'men champions of women's cause would assuredly have taken far more drastic measures'.[44]

Hugh Franklin, for example, attacked Winston Churchill with a dog whip, after the extreme violence experienced by suffragette demonstrators during Black Friday in November 1910, when he had been among the many arrested. Born in 1889, Hugh Franklin was the son of one of the senior partners of the bankers A. Keyser & Co. At Cambridge, where he studied engineering, economics and sociology, he had joined the Fabian Society, the Independent Labour Party and the Cambridge Men's League for Women's Suffrage. In 1910 he also joined the MPU and the Young Purple, White and Green Club (the colours of the WSPU), having come down from university without a degree. His uncle Sir Herbert Samuel was Postmaster-General, and Hugh Franklin reluctantly accepted a position found for him as private secretary to the Secretary of the Post Office. At the time when he attacked Winston Churchill, he had recently also become the honorary assistant organizer of the MPU, and had resigned from the altogether more moderate and restrained Men's League. He received a six-week prison sentence for this offence. A woman militant wrote to him afterwards to express her gratitude towards himself and the MPU: 'If it were not for you I should begin to be afraid that it was nearly impossible for men to think and act as they should with regard to this question.'[45]

The following year, in the spring of 1911, he was back, throwing stones at Winston Churchill's house. This was a protest at the prison treatment, including forcible feeding, of one of his male suffragist colleagues – Churchill was at this time Home Secretary – and he wrote to the minister in these terms: 'seeing what your actions have been, you at least will have no right to blame me if I am once again sufficiently courteous to fight you with your own weapon of "Might is Right".' He explained to the secretary of the MPU, Victor Duval, that he had undertaken this protest 'in order to show that outlawry is a game that two can play'. He may have thought that his family connections might save him from any severe sentence, thinking back to the differential treatment that Lady Constance Lytton had experienced on her first arrest fifteen months before: 'I expect an Uncle is as good as an Earl any day of the week.' This time he received

one month in gaol, underwent the hunger strike, and was forcibly
fed. On his release, he was welcomed with a warm letter of thanks
from Christabel Pankhurst.[46] The WSPU response to his subsequent
actions, and those of some other male militant sympathizers, became,
however, increasingly restrained in the months that followed.

In the autumn of 1912, Hugh Franklin set fire to a railway carriage
approaching Harrow station, and then ignored the consequent sum-
mons to appear in court. At the hearing, Victor Duval read this
statement from him:

> As Suffragist rebels we consider that under present circumstances
> certain definite forms of action must be taken in order that the
> Government may be forced to give Votes for Women – one of them
> being to cause the authorities as much trouble as we can.

Hugh Franklin challenged the court to issue a warrant for his arrest,
which it did. Some weeks later he was finally arrested, went on trial,
and was given a nine-month prison sentence. He had undertaken the
hunger strike and been forcibly fed while yet on remand. Now he
resorted to the hunger strike once more, securing his release on a
'Cat and Mouse' licence only after having been forcibly fed 114
times.[47]

During his ordeal, the Men's Political Union kept up its protests
outside the prison, and provided a band to play 'rousing tunes', just
as the WSPU did for its prisoners in Holloway. The Men's League
also held some of its defence-of-free-speech meetings outside the
gaol during his imprisonment.[48] His case was followed by both the
Daily Herald and *The Suffragette*, and some of this interest undoubtedly followed from his relationship to a member of the
government. But on his release, he found an unwillingness to pursue
his case, and advice that only by refraining from advocating or
practising acts of violence might he ensure his freedom from
rearrest.[49] He also found that the committee of the MPU was not
prepared to help him with the legal costs he had incurred during his
trial. Several months before his imprisonment, some among the
WSPU leadership were already attempting to call a halt to the
escalating violence of its male sympathizers and imitators. Emmeline
Pethick Lawrence had advised Henry Nevinson against the MPU
'doing anything violent on its own'. Significantly, she had also
added: 'Men in prison only embarrass us.'[50]

Hugh Franklin felt bitter about the lack of support he found on his
release. In his view one of the objects of the union should be 'to

enable those who are not in a position to do active fighting to support
and help those who can, for very few soldiers can fight and provide
their support as well'.[51] Writing of the ill-health that kept him in his
'mouse-trap' for some time after his release, he declared to the
readers of *The Suffragette*:

> I intend to ignore the licence completely, as I consider I have
> already suffered far more than nine months' imprisonment (espe-
> cially as I had been offered the first division if I ceased the hunger
> strike, and was led to expect a reduction in the length of my
> sentence). Therefore I shall consider that, if any further imprison-
> ment be inflicted on me, there would be just one little item lacking
> – namely an offence.[52]

The image of Hugh Franklin, put out by the authorities when he
failed to return to prison, served to suggest both his un-Englishness,
and his puniness: 'Age 21 [he was actually 23 or 24 by this time],
height 5' 8", pale complexion, dark moustache; wears spectacles;
Jewish appearance'.[53] Subsequently, he fled to France so as to escape
further arrest. But his flight, of course, also removed him from the
field of action. In all these ways, the government dragon repeatedly
secured the effective unmanning of those militant sympathizers who
sought to act as knights of old, championing and defending the
rebellious suffragette. Such defeats demonstrated their relative
powerlessness against the might of the state, and might bring the
further subjection of the symbolic rape of forcible feeding. In sum,
they served to support the image of the 'suffragette in trousers' as
an unmanly, un-English weakling.

The case of William Ball illustrates even more clearly the way the
government was able to turn the chivalrous impulse of the male
sympathizer into his own unmanning. William Ball was 'a working-
class comrade', according to Sylvia Pankhurst, a Birmingham
member of the National Transport Workers' Federation and the
MPU. He broke windows at the Home Office in protest at the prison
treatment of another member of the MPU who had assaulted a
Cabinet Minister, David Lloyd George. Conducting his own defence
in court, William Ball explained that his family comprised both
daughters and sons, and that 'he wanted as much protection for his
girls as he did for his boys'. He was sentenced to two months' hard
labour on 22 December 1911, and declined to take food in prison
unless he was allowed to order in his own. This privilege was given
only to first-class prisoners, and was one which had been accorded

Hugh Franklin on his first imprisonment, when he did not hunger strike. On refusing to wear prison clothes or take prison food, William Ball was stripped by his warders, and then forcibly fed twice a day, for something over five weeks. On 25 January he was recorded by prison officials as 'restless and talking wildly'. By 29 January he began to take his food voluntarily. On 9 February he was declared insane, but a letter to his wife informing her of his condition was not sent out until 11 February. The next day he was released as a pauper into the care of Colney Hatch lunatic asylum (it would appear, under the Criminal Lunatics Acts) and, of course, before his wife had been able to act on his behalf. No immediate examination by his own doctors had, thus, been possible. When his wife and her advisers arrived at the hospital they were, after some hesitation, allowed to remove him into private care.[54]

On the day of William Ball's release, Hugh Franklin wrote to his Uncle Herbert: 'I wonder what would be said in England if a Russian were treated like this.' Herbert Samuel agreed to forward his protest to the Home Office.[55] Three weeks later, the Home Office appointed Sir George Savage to investigate the case. The subsequent White Paper was seen by suffrage commentators as no more than a whitewash of the prison authorities. The prison doctors reported that William Ball had never behaved unreasonably, never been violent or suicidal, and had co-operated with his own forcible feeding without complaint. Yet they also recorded how subsequently he had begun to show evidence of sensory and auditory hallucinations, and believed himself to be enduring electrical torture. He had become troublesome at night in the prison infirmary, and had had to be confined to a padded cell on one occasion.

The accounts of these medical witnesses were deployed by Sir George Savage to suggest that William Ball's temporary mental illness had nothing to do with his prison experiences. Instead, the victim was blamed for his own sufferings by being declared 'not strong intellectually', 'of feeble intellect', 'defective' in general knowledge, and 'illiterate', a former tailor's presser who had 'drifted into common labourer's work'. His mental breakdown was suggested to be variously the outcome of his 'living in a state of emotional excitement because of his suffrage activities', or the consequence of an accident he had suffered as a dock labourer. The prison officials responsible for his treatment were thus exonerated.[56]

Though the WSPU recorded these events in its paper, protested the treatment of William Ball, and helped organize his subsequent medical care, its silence on his case thereafter is noteworthy. It was left to *The Eye-Opener*, a journal connected with the Men's Society for Women's Rights, to attempt to restore the public image of William Ball by identifying any number of discrepancies and untruths in the Savage report. To begin with, it found that the Home Office had claimed that William Ball had been released at the expiration of his sentence, and was sent to Colney Hatch as 'a criminal pauper' as no friends or family had come forward to receive him. In fact William Ball still had nine days of his sentence to serve, and had earned no remission for 'industry and good conduct', and so remained, properly, the responsibility of Pentonville prison. Indeed, he had refused to do a stroke of work as protest at being treated as a third-class misdemeanant, and had refused voluntarily to replace even his boots with prison clothing. The report was also untruthful about the lack of action by his wife. She had written repeatedly to the governor, anxious about his health, and asking permission to visit him, but had been refused. She had also tried the ploy of saying that she wished to take out insurance on his life, and requesting permission for the insurers' doctor to examine him in prison. This, too, had been refused.

In terms of his physical condition, Sir George Savage's report had concluded that William Ball's weight had been maintained while he was in prison. But this was disputed by the evidence of Mansell Moullin, vice-president of the Royal College of Surgeons and a medical expert opposed to force-feeding, who had seen him the day after his release. No actual figures were provided in the report. Similarly, the report included no details of the sugar levels found in William Ball's urine both immediately before and shortly after his release to Colney Hatch. Nor did the report include the prison medical notes of what kind of food had been administered to William Ball, making it impossible to determine whether 'improper food caused or aggravated the presence of sugar in the urine'. Neither was the origin of the ulcer found in William Ball's throat on his release investigated, nor the date established on which his mental disorder was first noted.

The Eye-Opener also set about dismantling the representation of William Ball as the mentally defective drifter depicted in Sir George Savage's report. It claimed that his general knowledge had been tested only by questions about the British royal court (about which, not surprisingly, he knew little or nothing), and noted that his literacy levels extended at least to the ability to write. It also pointed out that

William Ball shared some of his beliefs with the 'wisest and best' of men, including John Stuart Mill. His suffrage activity was the outcome of an express concern for the future well-being of his daughters. Nor was he an unskilled labourer by choice. In his youth, it seems, William Ball had been a master gardener, and then a master tailor whose business had failed. He had, nevertheless, always managed to maintain a family of five children, the youngest of whom was now 13. He had also been a sprinter of some local renown as a young man. He had suffered an industrial injury in 1911, but this, it seemed, had caused only 'a strained knee, not a strained intellect'. *The Eye-Opener*'s analysis of the Savage report concluded by asking: 'Are we to infer that a sprained knee threw Mr Ball off his mental balance?'[57] In all these ways, then, his defenders attempted to establish an alternative representation of a manly William Ball. It says something for his commitment and courage that the following year William Ball was back in prison, sentenced after another suffrage protest to twenty more days in Pentonville. He again adopted the hunger strike, but was released after two days when his fine was paid for him anonymously.[58]

CONCLUSION

Men who sympathized with suffrage militancy might prove helpful to the cause when they limited their aid to acts of civil disobedience and passive resistance, or when they kept strictly to the role of auxiliaries. When they began to go beyond such methods, however, their support became of increasingly questionable value. In the splits that occurred among the WSPU leadership in October 1912, and subsequently, it was the forms of militancy and the activities of male protesters that were at issue. The question was whether the WSPU should continue on its present path towards becoming a clandestine, underground organization composed of a small group of dedicated militants prepared to undertake the increasingly dangerous exploits which now characterized its efforts. The Pethick Lawrences, like Sylvia Pankhurst, advocated a return to the organization of popular demonstration, and the methods of 'constitutional militancy' at which the WSPU had proved so adept in its early years. This was a form of militancy that unambiguously provided for the active participation of men, which allowed the possibility of the 'suffragette in trousers'. At the same time, they also supported those who sought to rein in the 'young bloods' among male sympathizers.[59]

Sylvia Pankhurst, together with many male sympathizers, also advocated closer co-operation with the 'rebel' sections of the labour movement, a co-operation which, once again, could have served only to enlarge the role of radical men in suffrage campaigning.[60] By the time of the leadership split, however, Christabel Pankhurst was more and more determined to exclude men from WSPU counsels. Frederick Pethick Lawrence believed, for example, that it was his friendship with Henry Brailsford which had made him now suspect in the eyes of women colleagues in the militant leadership. It is not surprising to find no place for men in the last stages of the WSPU's campaigns. The need for such an exclusion was, in fact, intrinsic to the rhetoric of militancy, a rhetoric that confirmed the suffragette identity as essentially feminine, and that explained militant practice in terms of a female heroic distinguished by the 'symbolic violence' of women as against the brute violence of men. In the three years previously, male violence had threatened to undermine this representation of suffrage militancy – it had, from time to time, extended to personal violence, and it had demonstrated how easily the forces of the state might symbolically unman those champions who responded to the militant appeal to the chivalrous male. The 'suffragette in trousers' had always been something of a contradiction in terms. By 1913 he had become an embarrassment whose very presence threatened both the legitimacy of militant protest, and the coherence of the suffragette identity.

NOTES

1 Quoted in D. Mitchell, *Queen Christabel. A Biography of Christabel Pankhurst*, London, Macdonald & Janes, 1977, p. 35.

2 The term 'suffragette' was coined by a *Daily Mail* journalist, Charles E. Hands, and was quickly adopted by the WSPU to distinguish its members from those constitutional suffragists they termed 'non-' or even 'anti-militant', see H. Moyes, *A Woman in a Man's World*, Sydney, Alpha Books, 1971.

3 On the suffragette as an alternative 'type' of womanliness, see L. Tickner, *The Spectacle of Women. Imagery of the Suffrage Campaign 1907–14*, London, Chatto & Windus, 1987.

4 This designation was put forward by a leading male supporter of the WSPU, Israel Zangwill, in 1907. See A. V. John, 'Men, Manners and Militancy' in this volume.

5 On the prison treatment of suffragists see L. Radzinowicz and R. Hood, *The Emergence of Penal Policy in Victorian and Edwardian England*, Oxford, Clarendon Paperbacks, 1990, with my thanks to Angela John

for this reference. See also J. Purvis, 'The Prison Experiences of the Suffragettes in Edwardian Britain', *Women's History Review* 4, 1 (1995), pp. 103–34.

6   And, indeed, in one case there is evidence of sexual assault during forcible feeding by rectum, see L. Leneman, *A Guid Cause. The Women's Suffrage Movement in Scotland*, Aberdeen, Aberdeen University Press, 1991, p. 206.

7   G. Dangerfield, *The Strange Death of Liberal England* (1935), London, Paladin reprint, 1970, and compare, for example, with R. C. K. Ensor, *England 1870–1914*, Oxford, Clarendon Press, 1936, esp. p. 398, and Mitchell, *Queen Christabel*.

8   See, for example, E. Sarah, 'Christabel Pankhurst. Reclaiming her Power', in D. Spender (ed.), *Feminist Theorists. Three Centuries of Women's Intellectual Traditions*, London, Women's Press, 1983, pp. 259–83; J. Marcus's Introduction to J. Marcus (ed.), *Suffrage and the Pankhursts*, London, Routledge & Kegan Paul, 1987; K. Dodd, 'Cultural Politics and Women's History Writing', *Women's Studies International Forum*, 13, (1990), pp. 127–37, and her Introduction to her edited collection, *A Sylvia Pankhurst Reader*, Manchester, Manchester University Press, 1993; H. Keen, 'Searching for the Past in Present Defeat: the Construction of Historical and Political Identity in British Feminism in the 1920s and 30s', *Women's History Review* 3, 1 (1994), pp. 57–80; L. E. N. Mayhall, 'Creating the "Suffragette Spirit": British Feminism and the Historical Imagination', *Women's History Review*, 4, 3 (1995), pp. 319–44.

9   M. Vicinus, *Independent Women. Work and Community for Single Women, 1850–1920*, London, Virago, 1985, esp. pp. 247–80. L. Stanley and A. Morley, *The Life and Death of Emily Wilding Davison*, London, Women's Press, 1988; S. S Holton, '"In Sorrowful Wrath": the Romantic Feminism of Emmeline Pankhurst and Suffrage Militancy', in H. L. Smith (ed.), *British Feminism in the Twentieth Century*, Aldershot, Edward Elgar, 1990, pp. 7–24.

10 C. Pankhurst, 'An Invincible Repugnance to Disorder', *The Suffragette*, 22 November 1912, p. 82. For a discussion of the subsequent patriot identity created for the militant suffragette, see J. de Vries, 'Gendering Patriotism: Emmeline and Christabel Pankhurst and World War One', in S. Oldfield (ed.), *This Working-Day World. Women's Lives and Culture(s) in Britain 1914–1945*, London, Taylor & Francis, 1994, pp. 75–88.

11 See Holton, 'Sorrowful Wrath', pp. 20–2, and compare Tickner, *Spectacle of Women*, pp. 157–8, and A. V. John, 'Men, Manners and Militancy', in this volume.

12 Such rhetoric was almost always couched in terms of *English* qualities and an *English* cultural and political heritage, as P. Joyce notes in his discussion of male subjectivities in *Democratic Subjects. The Self and the Social in Nineteenth-century England*, Cambridge, Cambridge University Press, 1994, esp. pp. 94–5, 127–8, 134–5, 144–5.

13 *The Suffragette*, 5 September 1913.

14 'Pointz Wright', letter to the editor, *Daily Herald*, 3 October 1912, p. 2.

15 'Hooligans on Wimbledon Common', *Daily Herald*, 7 March 1913, p. 1.

16 L. Housman, *The Unexpected Years*, London, Jonathan Cape, 1937, p. 275. On the construction of English manhood around ideals of athleticism, courage and fair play, see J. Walvin, 'Symbols of Moral Superiority: Slavery, Sport and the Changing World Order, 1800–1950', in J. A. Mangan and J. Walvin (eds), *Manliness and Morality. Middle-class Masculinity in Britain and America, 1800–1940*, Manchester, Manchester University Press, 1987, pp. 242–60.

17 C. Gray, Letter to the editor, *Daily Herald*, 17 December 1912, p. 2. For a thoughtful review of the historical literature on masculinity see the Introduction to M. Roper and J. Tosh (eds), *Manful Assertions. Masculinities in Britain since 1800*, London, Routledge, 1991, pp. 1–24.

18 'A Citizen of New South Wales' to the Editor, *Daily Herald*, 10 April 1913, p. 10.

19 See, for example, the defence of militancy on these grounds in 'Review of the Week', *The Suffragette*, 4 March 1913, p. 399 and M. E. Gawthorpe, 'Votes for Men', London, Woman's Press, n. d. [1907].

20 C. I. Vans Agnew Corbett, letter to the editor, *Daily Herald*, 4 October 1912, p. 2.

21 This argument, too, was accepted and promoted by male militant sympathizers. See, for example, L. Housman, 'Sex War and Woman's Suffrage', London, Women's Freedom League, 1912.

22 Even the threatening of the Prime Minister and another member of the Cabinet with a hatchet by the WSPU protester Mary Leigh was explained in terms of the symbolic meaning of the hatchet, while she herself, in her defence, insisted that the hatchet had merely been placed in their carriage, not thrown, claiming that she might easily have assassinated Asquith if such *had* been her intention; see 'The Hatchet Case', *The Suffragette*, 20 December 1912, p. 152.

23 Housman, *Unexpected Years*, pp. 267, 280, 266 recalling the substance of his first suffragist article some thirty years before.

24 E. Pankhurst, Foreword to *My Own Story* (1914), London, Virago reprint, 1979, n. p., and see also, p. 17.

25 C. I. Vans Agnew Corbett, letter, *Daily Herald*, p. 2.

26 In the cartoon shown in Plate 5 and cited in n. 13, for example, Sir Edward Carson appears in the background, carrying a bucket marked 'ABUSE', accompanied by Arthur Bonar Law firing a pistol. See also 'The Militancy of Men', 'The Treatment of Militant Men', 'Compliment and Conciliation for Militant Men', in, respectively, *The Suffragette*, 25 July 1913, p. 691; 12 December 1913, p. 209; 26 December 1913, p. 243. When it was announced that its editor, George Lansbury, might be tried for treason for a speech upholding suffrage militancy, the front page headline of the *Daily Herald*, 15 April 1913, asked 'What about King Carson?' Occasionally, the syndicalist strikers leading much of the industrial unrest of these years are also presented as examples of the lawlessness and violence of 'male militancy'.

27 Housman Papers (henceforth HP), Street Public Library, Street, Somerset, L. Housman to S. B. Clark, 28 June 1913.

28 Housman, *Unexpected Years*, pp. 280, 284. He took great glee in the imprisonment of his sister, Clemence Housman, for two weeks in 1911, when she refused to pay rates on a house rented in her name, having circumvented the option of distraint by borrowing from friends all the furniture in the house. See also the photo of brother and sister outside Holloway, from *The Standard*, 30 September 1911, reproduced in S. Housman, 'The Housman Banners', *Housman Society Journal* 18, (1992), pp. 39–47.
29 *Daily Herald*, 20 September 1912, p. 2; 26 September 1912, p. 2; 28 September 1912, p. 3 (which also carries a photograph of Dr and Mark Wilks); 2 October 1912, p. 2; 3 October 1912, p. 12; *The Suffragette*, 15 November 1912, p. 64.
30 Housman, *Unexpected Years*, pp. 286–90.
31 See, for example, the text of G. B. Shaw's speech on forcible feeding, reprinted in *The Suffragette*, 18 April 1913, p. 457 from *New Statesman*, 12 April 1913; the text of the speech by C. W. Mansell Moullin, MD, FRCS, 'Artificial v. "Forcible" Feeding', *The Suffragette*, 4 April 1913, p. 405; 'Torture. Medical Protest to the Home Secretary', *Daily Herald*, 5 July 1912.
32 For a report of this event see *Men's League for Women's Suffrage Monthly* 21 (June 1911).
33 See, for example, Henry Woodd Nevinson Papers, Bodleian Library, Oxford, MS Eng. Misc. (henceforth, Nevinson Diaries), e612/2; 8 November 1910; 29 November 1910; 1 December 1910; 3 December 1910; 2 January 1911; e616/3: 20 January 1911; 8 February 1911; e616/4: 24 October 1911; e617/1: 8 November 1911.
34 Housman, *Unexpected Years*, pp. 279, 282. The Men's League claimed its policy of co-operation with Labour led the way with regard to similar changes in National Union and Women's Freedom League policies, see *Men's League for Women's Suffrage Monthly* 33 (June 1912).
35 On the latter group, see the report in *The Eye-Opener*, 1 June 1912, p. 7. It began to publish its own *Men's Society for Women's Rights Monthly Paper* in November 1913. My thanks to David Doughan, Fawcett Library, London Guildhall University, for bringing this material to my attention.
36 See, for example, G. Rayne, 'A Duty towards our Daughters' and J. Stenson Hooker, MD, 'The Immorality of Certain Marriages', in *The Eye-Opener*, 22 June 1912, p. 5, and 1 February 1913, p. 9 respectively. Christabel Pankhurst ran a campaign around this issue the following year.
37 See 'A Pathetic Case', 'Brothels', and case reports, *Men's Society for Women's Rights Monthly Paper* 1 (November 1913), pp. 1, 2, 3 respectively.
38 E. S. Pankhurst, *The Suffragette Movement* (1931), London, Virago edition, 1977, p. 498; 'The Heraldites Check Rowdyism', *Daily Herald*, 12 May 1913.
39 Nevinson Diaries, 16 February 1911.
40 Housman, *Unexpected Years*, pp. 282–3. His offence was to join in surrounding the statue of Richard Coeur de Lion with a group of

protesters, men and women. The magistrate initially bound him over for six months, but when he refused to abide by this, sent him to the cells till the court was cleared and then released him unconditionally.

41 See, for example, E. Pankhurst, *My Own Story*, p. 255, which recounts the forcible feeding of Frederick Pethick Lawrence for ten days in 1912, after which he was 'released in a state of complete collapse'; see also, Annie Kenney, *Memories of a Militant*, London, Arnold, 1928, p. 218.

42 *The Suffragette*, 1 August 1913, p. 715, when reporting George Lansbury's three-month prison sentence for refusing to be bound over after a suffrage protest.

43 *The Suffragette*, 30 May 1913, p. 548.

44 C. Pankhurst, *Unshackled. The Story of How We Won the Vote*, London, Hutchinson, 1959, p. 195.

45 Franklin Papers (henceforth FP), the Fawcett Library, London Guildhall University, B. Brewster to Mr Franklin, 24 December 1910.

46 FP, H. A. Franklin to W. Churchill, 8 March 1911, FP; C. Pankhurst to Mr Franklin, 7 April 1911, FP; H. A. Franklin to V. Duval, 8 March 1911.

47 *The Suffragette*, 20 December 1912, pp. 148–9; 29 April 1913, p. 3; C. Gray, 'The Case of Mr Hugh Franklin', *Daily Herald*, 18 April 1913.

48 ibid., 11 April 1912, p. 438. By this time WSPU speakers had been banned from Hyde Park, and the Men's League, alongside the National Union, mounted a series of Sunday meetings to defend the principle of free speech.

49 FP, K. Hardie to Mr Franklyn [*sic*], 29 April 1913. When he did receive moral support, it might take the dubious form of advising him that there was 'a friendly suffragette' living in the house abutting the back of his own, who not only was prepared to help him escape his 'Blue Cat', the policeman keeping him under surveillance, but also was within easy range of his uncle's house. She suggested that it might be possible to cause the minister some annoyance with an air gun. FP, D. W. Evans to 'Dear Sir', 4 May 1913.

50 Nevinson Diaries, e617/1: 19 January 1912.

51 FP, H. A. Franklin to Mr Harben (treasurer of the MPU), 9 November 1913.

52 'A Hero's Letter', letter from Hugh Franklin in *The Suffragette*, 2 May 1913.

53 Reported in 'Where, Oh Where Can He Be', *Daily Herald*, 15 May 1913, p. 5.

54 This summary is based on reports of the case in *The Eye-Opener*, 1 June 1912, pp. 5–6 and 'The Pentonville Atrocity', *Votes for Women*, 16 February 1912, pp. 302, 303; and see also G. Aldred, 'Our Prison System', *The Freewoman*, 22 February 1912, p. 275, and Mary Gawthorpe's account of her own protest at William Ball's treatment, *The Freewoman*, 29 February 1913, p. 283.

55 FP, H. A. Franklin to 'Uncle Herbert', 12 February 1912; H. Samuel to 'Dear Hugh', 13 February 1912.

56 United Kingdom Parliamentary Papers. 'Case of William Ball. Report by Sir George Savage, MD, FRCP', 23 April 1912, Cd 6175.

57 *The Eye-Opener*, 1 June 1912, pp. 5–6.
58 *The Suffragette*, 10 October 1913, p. 910; 17 October 1913, p. 15, which provides, however, no account of his protest or his court hearing.
59 Nevinson Diaries, e617/3: 31 January 1913.
60 E. S. Pankhurst, *The Suffragette Movement*, pp. 502–3, 516–20.

Chapter 5

Sharing the burden

The Pethick Lawrences and women's suffrage

June Balshaw

The late nineteenth and early twentieth centuries produced a number of political partnerships such as the Webbs and the Bruce Glasiers. The specific cause of women's suffrage also attracted some notable names, including the Pankhursts and the Fawcetts. And yet, there is one partnership that has to be seen as foremost in terms of its crucial role in the women's suffrage movement: that of Emmeline and Frederick Pethick Lawrence. However, despite the importance of their contribution, very little has been written about this partnership[1] although their involvement in the Women's Social and Political Union (WSPU) has been well documented in other histories. This chapter focuses on the uniqueness of their political partnership in the context of gendered support.

Emmeline Pethick Lawrence (1867–1954) and Frederick Pethick Lawrence (1871–1961) were married for more than fifty years and during that time fought for many causes. However, it is their combined commitment to the single issue of women's suffrage when it was at its most militant, for which they are best remembered. An examination of their partnership with particular emphasis on how, as a couple, they both challenged and reinforced the gendered nature of political work, will raise questions about the ways in which Fred Pethick Lawrence both used and dealt with his masculinity and the reactions to this. Moreover, it will enable their political partnership to be explored by seeing how it functioned and developed during their involvement with women's suffrage, and how their ideas and actions were understood and represented through existing meanings of gender roles in both a political and a familial context.

Emmeline Pethick Lawrence's background and upbringing were typical of one born into a comfortable middle-class family in the mid-nineteenth century. She had a good relationship with her father and when she was first arrested for her suffrage activities he reacted with pride:

> he was met by one of his colleagues on the Bench with expressions of sympathy. 'Sympathy, my dear fellow,' he replied, 'I don't need sympathy. Give me your congratulations! I'm the proudest man in England!'[2]

Like other privileged Victorian women, Emmeline wanted to experience and contribute to the lives of those less fortunate than herself. In 1891 she became a 'sister' at the West London Mission, founded by Mark Guy Pearse whom she had known since childhood. Here her Liberal ideas realigned themselves in a move towards socialism and she met Frederick Pethick Lawrence.

Frederick Lawrence was born in 1871, the youngest of five children. His father, Alfred Lawrence, son of a self-made carpenter, died when Fred was 3 and his Uncle Edwin took over a parental role. Like Emmeline, Fred was sent to boarding school, an experience he did not enjoy and at 13 he went to Eton. Mathematics was Fred's forte and from Eton he went to Cambridge where he took a double first and was president of the Union. In 1897 he won a fellowship at Trinity College but rather than settle into a life of academia, he spent two years travelling around the world. This desire to see how others lived stemmed, in part, from the influence of the economist Alfred Marshall, of whom Fred later said, 'He really cared passionately that a knowledge of economics should be applied to bettering the lot of humanity and in particular of the underdog.'[3]

A further influence was Percy Alden who was warden of Mansfield House University Settlement of which Fred became treasurer whilst reading for the Bar. In addition to this fairly heavy workload, Fred also became a Liberal-Unionist parliamentary candidate at the suggestion of his uncle, Sir Edwin Durning-Lawrence. Thus far, Fred's experiences were framed by exclusively male institutions and one of his contemporaries at Cambridge, Dr G. P. Gooch, believed 'he might have succeeded in half a dozen spheres, at the Bar, in the City, in journalism, as Professor of Mathematics or Political Economy no less as a Cabinet Minister'.[4] Yet instead, he channelled his energies into supporting the 'underdog'. Vera Brittain attributed this to the combined influence of Alfred Lawrence, Percy Alden and Emmeline Pethick.

From their initial meeting in 1899, until their marriage, both Fred and Emmeline spent a considerable time contemplating their individual and mutual futures. Like other couples of their generation, they were initially divided over the Boer War. It was not, however, this issue alone that made Emmeline refuse Fred's initial marriage proposal, for she had no intention of embarking upon a conventional Victorian marriage that accorded her only a secondary role.

Fred determined to see the Boer situation for himself. He returned to England a pro-Boer, no longer harbouring thoughts of being a Liberal-Unionist MP but instead on the verge of converting to socialism. He became owner of the *Echo* newspaper in a bid to put forward the pro-Boer viewpoint, inviting Emmeline to sit on the council responsible for the paper's policy.

After a brief engagement, they were married in Canning Town, London on 2 October 1901. As a public statement of how they intended to conduct their marriage, they combined their respective surnames henceforth becoming known as the Pethick Lawrences. Emmeline continued her work as president of the Esperance Social Guild, Fred devoting his time to the *Echo*. If anything, marriage to Fred had, in some ways, created new opportunities for Emmeline because of his wealth, causing her to write:

> now that all this loveliness had fallen into my lap I rejoiced in it, and wanted to share it, as Mary Neal and I had shared all that we had with our working girls and other friends. My husband was ready to encourage all my ideas, and to co-operate with me in carrying them into fulfilment.[5]

In her autobiography, Emmeline makes frequent reference to the 'family' which included friends, colleagues, the working-class girls and children who holidayed at their various properties. In this respect, the Pethick Lawrences as a 'political partnership' perceived themselves to be representing not only their own personal beliefs but also those of a much larger group; they realized that their strength lay in surrounding themselves with others who would work with them, running things on a day-to-day basis, thus enabling them to fulfil the role they had consciously created for themselves.[6]

Their correspondence during the early years of their marriage was romantic, very frequent and often repetitive. On their first wedding anniversary, Fred gave Emmeline her own flat at the top of the Clement's Inn building, effectively giving her a 'room of one's own'. Vera Brittain saw this as a sign that 'already he was learning to be not only efficient, but human'.[7] This indicates a shift in their private life and the development of the equality that they advocated both in public and private. The early letters also indicate a strong combined sense of what they, as an equal couple, stood for. Nowhere is this clearer than in the following extracts from a letter written by Fred to Emmeline in April 1902:

> You and I were born to fight dear; ourselves and all the world and all the powers of darkness. . . . Courage lady, sing a poem beloved that you and I are found worthy to stand up together and fight. Fight for the light against the darkness, for truth against the lie, for life against death.[8]

They both had, prior to meeting, a strong sense of justice but for Fred, in particular, the meeting of their two minds extended this into a spiritual calling to embark upon a mission which together they could accomplish. Such dramatic sentiments had yet to be matched with a specific cause but it indicated the direction in which they were heading.

From 1901 onwards, they became more involved with the labour movement under the influence of Keir Hardie. Fred established links with various trade unions as a result of his involvement with Percy Alden and in 1904, after letting the *Echo* cease publication, they went to Egypt, followed by a visit to South Africa in 1905. There, they spent time with Olive Schreiner whose writings had impressed them and she remained a strong influence. Christabel Pankhurst and Annie Kenney were arrested in Manchester whilst the Pethick Lawrences were still in South Africa but the newspaper reports they received aroused their interest sufficiently to make Emmeline, in particular, want to meet these women.

In his autobiography, *Fate Has Been Kind* (1943), Fred admits that at the time of reading about the arrests, he could not see what middle-class women had to complain about, or that they had a specific contribution to make in the world of politics.[9] Nevertheless, his wife's subsequent involvement with the WSPU and Christabel's political prowess altered his view to such an extent that it was to change his life dramatically for several years and remained a strong influence in his subsequent political work.

The Pethick Lawrences were involved with the WSPU for six and a half years and their combined contribution during this time cannot be underestimated. However, although they achieved a high profile in the public sphere, despite or even because of the challenges they now faced, this period also seems to have fulfilled their desire to be brought closer together through shared experiences. As Emmeline Pethick Lawrence later observed:

> It is one of the intriguing facts about the W.S.P.U. that minds and temperaments so fundamentally dissimilar could have remained for so many years in practical working harmony under the inspiration of a great ideal.[10]

In her autobiography, Emmeline makes it clear that the 'franchise question' was not uppermost in either her mind or Fred's at the beginning of 1906 and that 'political interests were subordinate to our fervent desire to bring about an amelioration of the social conditions of the workers'.[11] Nevertheless, the increasing emphasis they gave to feminist rather than labour agendas is evident. Whilst Fred Pethick Lawrence saw socialism encompassing rebellions against the domination of class, sex and colour, it was the rebellion against the domination of sex that they chose to focus upon.[12] It was Annie Kenney who persuaded Emmeline to meet the others involved in what she later described as the WSPU's 'pathetic little committee'.[13] The result of the meeting was that in February 1906, Emmeline Pethick Lawrence and Mary Neal joined the Central London Committee of the WSPU with Emmeline as honorary treasurer.

Why did the Pethick Lawrences become involved with an organization that excluded men, creating an ambivalent position for Fred? To what extent was a role consciously developed for him? Their early involvement suggests that they had not deliberately set out to create a specific role for Fred other than that of a supportive nature. Yet from 1907, as he pointed out:

> the daily executive control of the agitation passed for a time unobtrusively and almost unconsciously into the hands of an unofficial committee of three persons – Christabel, my wife and myself.[14]

The main reason for this was that Mrs Pankhurst trusted Christabel's judgement and preferred to spend her time touring the country. Christabel, in turn, clearly welcomed the combined expertise of the Pethick Lawrences with the result that all three effectively ran the WSPU.

During the years of militancy, however, Mrs Pankhurst and Christabel's attitudes towards the Pethick Lawrences shifted. Mrs Pankhurst was, according to Emmeline, 'distressed by the way in which Christabel consulted us about everything and was influenced by our opinion'.[15] Mrs Pankhurst appears to have become increasingly concerned that the Pethick Lawrences, and Fred in particular, were being publicly perceived as the WSPU's true figureheads.

As treasurer, Emmeline recognized that her dealing with the organization and finance of the WSPU meant the others could effectively carry out what she described as 'the guerrilla method of political warfare'.[16] She had her husband's support and assistance and fully acknowledged that it was his business acumen and financial knowledge that helped the union. However, Emmeline also possessed a high degree of business sense and Roger Fulford's suggestion that 'although Mr Lawrence never obtruded himself, the organisation of the union rested on his aptitude and foresight'[17] seems unfair. Rather, the union's success resulted from their combined skills and team work. Indeed, if any further endorsement of Emmeline's involvement in matters of business and finance both within the union and elsewhere were needed, then a letter she wrote to Fred from Holloway prison in 1909 reveals that she was not only consulted by him on their private financial dealings but also appeared to direct them – something usually classed as a male responsibility.[18] In this letter Emmeline also discussed issues connected with her role as treasurer of the WSPU and requested the WSPU financial report and balance sheet which required her signature.

In terms of Fred's involvement with the WSPU, it would seem logical to assume that Emmeline would have utilized his services from the outset but there were key moments, particularly during the first year, that help to explain his developing role within the campaign. On 23 October 1906, Emmeline was one of ten women arrested for taking part in a demonstration in the Central Lobby of the House of Commons and was sentenced to two months in prison after refusing to give an undertaking to keep the peace for six months. Suffering from exhaustion, she was discharged four days later after Mrs Pankhurst had sent a message stating she should give the undertaking.[19] The Pethick Lawrences travelled to Italy then he returned to take her place as treasurer whilst she recuperated.

According to Emmeline, her imprisonment 'was the incident that brought him finally to devote all his manifold powers to a cause which needed the help that a trained mind like his could give'.[20] The personal impact of seeing his wife suffer for the cause motivated him into dedicating himself to that same cause, and the most effective way to do this was to use his legal and business knowledge, although it was not long before his contribution extended into other areas. With the increase in militancy, Fred assumed an essential role, ensuring that those who had been arrested were properly instructed upon how to deal with their defence. Additionally, he also took responsibility for arranging bail, dealing with worried relatives and liaising with the police as well as helping to keep the union running.

Plate 6 The Pethick Lawrences going to the lawcourts, 1908

It was whilst representing three suffragettes in court, in July 1906, that Fred felt he first made a real commitment to militancy. He saw that the dock was dirty and wiped it with his handkerchief. Writing about this incident nearly forty years on, he stated:

> Ridiculous as it may seem, this single act, which I performed out of courtesy to my wife's friends, made a greater demand on my courage and resolution than anything I did later in the campaign, not excluding my own prison sentence and forcible feeding. By it I testified that in this matter of the women's revolt I had taken sides with the dock against the bench; and I accepted the full implication of all that that entailed.[21]

His representation of the three suffragettes had, in effect, brought into question conflicting representations of masculinity. Whilst on the one hand the act of wiping the dock could be interpreted as chivalrous, although it could also be seen as effeminate given that cleaning is perceived as women's work, in his position as a barrister defending these women it could be viewed as a threat to the male establishment. This is clearly how Fred himself saw it; he had made a choice about which he wrote, 'C'est le premier pas qui coûte.'[22] The consequences of this action manifested themselves in a number of ways including an unsuccessful attempt to disbar him in 1908, whilst representing a suffragette (Plate 6).

Press coverage initially focused on the support that married suffragettes received from their husbands, although this was soon replaced by stories with headlines such as 'Suffragettes' Neglected Children'[23] challenging the 'manliness' of these husbands through implications of weakness and forced domesticity. The Pethick Lawrences, however, were represented in rather a different way and the press had yet to find the language to express Fred's role in the campaign. He was not a father and had, of course, represented the suffragettes. Emphasis was given to Fred's wealth – he had pledged £10 for every day of Emmeline's imprisonment – and when she was released after four days, one report stated that 'Mr Lawrence, if he chooses, can save quite a considerable sum of money'.[24]

The *Daily Mirror* reported on a statement made by Sir Patteson Nickalls, chairman of the New Reform Club Committee, which stressed that the 'New Reform Club has nothing to do with the Women's Social and Political Union, Mr Pethick Lawrence is not a member of the NRC Committee'.[25] Already, Fred's involvement in women's suffrage was creating waves within other sites of masculine culture, for which he would eventually be punished.

Fred's lack of an official role within the WSPU is deceptive, for he corresponded on WSPU letter-headed notepaper and was the only man to have done this.[26] What is also significant is Emmeline's comment that 'he was the person with whom the police were glad to deal'[27] for in addition to it being a relief to have him organize these 'troublesome' women, the police clearly found security in dealing with a man, a gentleman in fact. It is as though they were temporarily prepared to ignore conflicting masculine relations and focus on conventional ones.

The Pethick Lawrences had been involved with the WSPU for just over a year when their combined threat to the establishment was brought to the notice of the Public Prosecutor in the form of a letter from a Miss Meechan:

> Dear Sir,
>
> May I respectfully ask if it is not possible to break up the Suffragette movement by taking action against Mr and Mrs Pethick Lawrence for conspiring and inciting to serious breaches of the peace. It can very easily be proved that Mr Pethick Lawrence went to East Ham on one occasion and hired a number of women at 2/- per day + expenses and women who carried babies in their arms at 2/6 per day + their expenses. These women were drilled into their work by Mr Lawrence and his assistants and as you will remember took part in very disorderly scenes. . . . These women (& many of the women agitators who are paid £2–5 per week) know nothing of politics or Votes for Women questions and are paid for creating disturbance at command of the leaders . . . [I] like many thousands of women feel it is a dreadful thing to let these cranks bring such discredit on women.[28]

Although the writer suggests taking action against the Pethick Lawrences as a couple, it is Fred who is held responsible for mobilizing the forces. Female opponents of the suffragettes would presumably have viewed Fred's involvement as betraying his own sex. The letter was taken seriously and a CID officer was sent to investigate, subsequently reporting that the writer had retracted much of what had been stated. However, the police were sufficiently interested in the Pethick Lawrences to keep Clement's Inn under 'casual and discreet observation' but found there was no evidence to justify 'that women of the lower order, with or without children, are drilled or receive instruction in connection with any organised procession of the suffragettes'.[29]

Fred's contribution to the WSPU extended far beyond a legalistic position. He wrote articles, including one entitled 'The Opposition of the Liberal Government to Woman Suffrage' (1908), where he stressed that

> It is essential to success in a political fight to discern who are the actual enemies to be fought. In the battle for Woman Suffrage both the teaching of history and of political common sense point to the same conclusion – there is only one enemy, and that is the Government of the day.[30]

It was Christabel Pankhurst who had convinced Fred that this was the way forward and having adopted this position, he explained that

> Some people suppose that the enemy of Woman Suffrage is the men of the country. That is entirely a mistake; Woman Suffrage is not in any sense an anti-man movement, and as such it should not, and does not, rouse the hostility of the men of the country. On the contrary, in the old days, when petitions were being got up in favour of this reform, large numbers of men signed in favour of it. The Women's Social and Political Union find that at great meetings all over the country, and in particular at the bye-elections, the majority of men give a hearty support to the cause whenever it is properly explained, and carry this to the extent of their vote at the polls.[31]

Fred's profile within the women's suffrage movement and his support of WSPU militant tactics, saw him attempt to defuse the 'sex war' issue by firmly implicating government. The concluding words of the pamphlet are unequivocal about the militant policy adopted:

> women will know that it is the Government of the day who stand between them and their enfranchisement, and they will accordingly waste no powder upon any other section of the community who may appear to be unfriendly, but will strike directly at the Government of the day, conscious that in so doing they are fighting the battle against their real enemy.[32]

Now that the 'enemy' had been located, the opportunity existed to turn the dramatic words Fred wrote to Emmeline in 1902 into deeds.

Emmeline and Fred were coeditors of *Votes for Women*, first published in 1907 and in line with the other aspects of their lives they both contributed. Fifty years later Fulford described the paper as 'occasionally rabid' but conceded that it was 'conducted with force and judgment by Mr Pethick Lawrence'.[33] This is just one example of how Fulford wanted to portray Fred Pethick Lawrence's role in the Women's Suffrage campaign; there was a niche for Fred amongst all this unsavoury militancy and that was to promote his gentlemanly qualities. This way it was easy for him to be perceived as the 'Prince Consort of militancy' and not just Mrs Pethick Lawrence's husband.[34] Perhaps, Lord Pethick Lawrence was happy by this stage to be written about in this way for, when Fulford's book was published in 1957, it was Christabel and Sylvia Pankhurst who were furious about their misrepresentation. Interestingly though, it was to Fred they individually wrote about their concerns and it was Fred who attempted to 'smooth' things over.

On 5 March 1912, the Pethick Lawrences, Christabel, Mrs Pankhurst and Mrs Tuke were charged with 'conspiracy to damage the property of liege subjects of the King'.[35] Christabel had recently escaped to France, Mrs Pankhurst and Mrs Tuke were already in prison. Emmeline and Fred were refused bail and so, for the first time, Fred experienced prison. On 28 March they were released on bail and the trial was held at the Old Bailey in May. Fred conducted his own defence which, as Brittain has pointed out, finally introduced a statement on his own position. He said:

> I am a man and I cannot take part in this women's agitation, but I intend to stand by the women who are fighting . . . . I think it is a battle waged for the good of the people of this country, waged by one half of the community whose deeds are valuable to the other part of the country and should not be excluded.[36]

Here it is admirably stated that women need to fight their own battles and that, whilst as a man he could offer support, he could not join them. Clearly, this contradicted his practice but perhaps Fred was choosing to focus on his position as one half of a partnership rather than as a man. By removing gender from the equation, he could participate. And yet, it was precisely because of his gender that he was able to contribute in many areas. Moreover, there were men who were actively engaged in acts of militancy and who paid for it by suffering physical violence. Was it a calculated decision that Fred would be better served to distance himself from direct action and use his legal expertise, or was it perhaps the case that there remained in him a natural aversion to behaving in an 'ungentlemanly fashion', which brings concepts of class as well as masculinity into play? Even the charge of conspiracy was a step removed from actually damaging something though that is not to alleviate its seriousness (particularly for a lawyer).

The defendants were found guilty and sentenced to nine months' imprisonment as well as having to pay the full cost of the trial, a decision that was met with public indignation. An interesting outcome was that the daughters of Judge Coleridge, who presided over the trial, immediately applied for membership of the WSPU, a good example of how women's suffrage impacted on family politics. However, for the Pethick Lawrences, prison meant something rather different. Fred described the elation of not being 'shut off in General Headquarters, but right up in the front line, sharing its dangers and excitements with the rank and file of my women comrades',[37] highlighting the military element and revealing through those last few words that he was actually an integral part of the movement despite his claims in court. In a letter to Fred sent from Holloway prison on 18 June 1912, Emmeline wrote:

> the purpose to which we were born and for which we were mated is accomplished. . . . It is enough . . . . I think we two are the happiest and luckiest people in all the world.[38]

This suggests that the Pethick Lawrences had achieved a private, as well as a public, position in terms of their partnership.

Whilst in prison, Emmeline, Fred and Mrs Pankhurst went on hunger strike; Emmeline was force-fed once and then released but Fred was subjected to forcible feeding which he described as an unpleasant and painful process over a period of several days before his release on 27 June 1912. He also commented on the visible distress of the head doctor, 'a most sensitive man', concluding that prison reminded him of 'prep' school.[39] Two days prior to his release, Emmeline wrote to him explaining, 'I was privileged to share what our brave comrades had experienced. I never had a moment's fear or a moment's hunger. I should have felt it bitterly had I been released without going through all.'[40] Although the Pethick Lawrences both experienced prison and forcible feeding, their individual interpretations of these events demonstrate that for Fred it was bound up in militarism, whilst Emmeline emphasized the heroic element.

Discussing the meeting that she and Fred had with the Pankhursts in Boulogne shortly after their release, Emmeline's autobiography emphasizes that the Pankhursts' announcement of a new campaign involving widespread attacks upon public and private property came as a shock, 'as our minds had been moving in quite another direction'.[41] Essentially, what the Pethick Lawrences were advocating was to maximize the public awareness created by the trial by organizing popular demonstrations on a scale hitherto unseen.

After the Boulogne meeting, Emmeline received a letter from Mrs Pankhurst. In describing the position of the authorities, she wrote:

> So long as Mr Lawrence can be connected with militant acts involving damage to property, they will make him pay. Nothing but the cessation of militancy, (which of course is unthinkable before the vote is assured) or his complete ruin will stop this action on their part. They see in Mr Lawrence a potent weapon against the militant movement and they mean to use it.[42]

The WSPU leadership now saw Fred as a liability and were not prepared to acknowledge his commitment to women's suffrage.

Emmeline Pethick Lawrence's response could be construed as contradicting her earlier sentiments. However, it is important to recognize how the Pethick Lawrences broadly defined militancy. In her reply to Mrs Pankhurst Emmeline wrote:

> Our answer today is the same as it has been since we entered the struggle. You will realise directly we state it that there is only one answer possible. It is the answer which you yourself would give if asked to choose between the Movement (which you and we have in so large a measure jointly built up) and any other possession in life however dear and precious. You would not hesitate for a moment. Neither do we. Our answer is that we shall continue to be jointly responsible with you in the future as we have been in the past, and that the more we are menaced the harder we will fight until victory is won. . . . With regard to Militancy – we have never for a single instant allowed our individual interests to stand in the way of any necessary action or policy to be pursued by the Union, and we never shall.[43]

This suggests that she was prepared to condone militancy at any level no matter what the personal cost. It may well have been the case that after a break from WSPU activities, and time to consider their future, the Pethick Lawrences had decided they were prepared to accept Mrs Pankhurst's autocratic leadership for the sake of the cause. Certainly, the solidarity of the Pethick Lawrences' partnership is undisputed in the letter. Nevertheless, upon their return to England, Mrs Pankhurst informed Emmeline that she was severing her connection with her. Neither Emmeline nor Fred was prepared to accept this and they felt sure that Christabel would not have been a party to this decision but at a further WSPU meeting on 14 October at which Christabel was present, they were left in no doubt as to their situation.

We need to consider Fred's position in this. Although never a member of the WSPU, his gender automatically excluding him, his contribution was outstanding. Yet Mrs Pankhurst never addressed him personally in this matter until forced to during the second meeting. Elizabeth Robins, who was also present at the second meeting, recorded in her diary how Mrs Pankhurst was opposed to Fred reading a statement after she had made hers and noted that 'we all feel he should be allowed. He does. Mrs P. interrupts. He calls for a quiet hearing. "We listened to you".'[44] The result of the meeting was that a statement was signed by all parties (the Pethick Lawrences, Mrs Pankhurst and Christabel) and printed in the next issue of *Votes for Women*, which remained in the hands of the Pethick Lawrences.

It would seem to be the case that neither Emmeline nor Fred really advocated an increase in militancy. Rather they were prepared to agree to it on the basis that they could convince the Pankhursts of a better alternative and perhaps, more importantly, they could remain in the 'family circle' that had been their life for over six years.

A *Punch* cartoon soon after the split asked, 'Are you a Peth or a Pank?', but this was to reduce the issue to its most basic for, as the next few years were to prove, the Pethick Lawrences and the Pankhursts were to become divided on issues that extended far beyond militancy within the WSPU. In this sense, 1912 has to be considered in terms of the development of the Pethick Lawrences' partnership and its changing focus. During their time with the WSPU, the Pethick Lawrences broke new ground in the public sphere. As a couple, they managed to avoid a complete inversion of roles, for although officially outside the WSPU, Fred's individual contribution was of a sufficiently high profile for him to be recognized by many as an equal half of a partnership rather than just a supporter. This view was not, however, shared by the Pankhursts who never gave him the recognition he deserved. The status Emmeline had achieved publicly through her position as treasurer can be seen as an extension of her status within the marriage although their individual and joint public status was to alter as they pursued new interests.

Despite the Pethick Lawrences no longer being connected with the WSPU, the full consequences of their suffrage involvement were still to come. In June 1913, the Government forced the sale of their personal possessions to meet the costs of the 1912 court case (many of the items were bought by friends and returned to them) and civil actions were brought against them by shops that had suffered broken windows. These actions were contested and both Emmeline and Fred conducted their own defence. Although they were not acquitted, the judge was sympathetic and was particularly impressed by Emmeline's address to the jury, describing it as 'a most eloquent speech'.[45] She used it as an opportunity to highlight the problem of infant mortality, citing New Zealand and Australia where women already had the vote as examples of how death rates had been more than halved since the women of these countries had become enfranchised.[46]

Nevertheless, they were held liable for the full costs and payment was taken from Fred's estate. In her autobiography, Emmeline wrote of Fred: 'thus he underwent every variation of the sacrifice demanded for the freedom of women – imprisonment – hunger strike – forcible feeding – bankruptcy – loss of financial substance – expulsion from his club.'[47] She went on to make the point that 'deep as is the love between us he never took up the women's cause for my sake but as a result of our common outlook'.[48] Even if this were the case, it was Emmeline's involvement that drew him in and Fred himself claimed her first prison experience as a key turning-point for him.

Their dissociation from the WSPU did not prevent the Pethick Lawrences from continuing to be influential. From the *Votes for Women* paper which they continued to edit, the Votes for Women Fellowship was formed in early 1913. Emmeline explained in a letter to Elizabeth Robins that it was not intended to compete with the WSPU, writing that 'at the present juncture it is more than ever important to interpret militancy to the average woman and man and this we feel is our little bit of service and is the raison d'être'.[49] However, by May 1913 it was receiving around fifty applications for membership daily[50] at a time when some WSPU members were finding it difficult to live with the autocratic Pankhurst leadership. In 1914, the Pethick Lawrences became founder members of the United Suffragists, a mixed-sex organization committed to the suffrage cause.

With the outbreak of the First World War, however, their energies became focused in different directions. Emmeline was a founder member of the Women's International League (for Peace and Freedom), and was one of only three British women to attend The Hague conference in 1915. She had long-held strong pacifist beliefs and spent the duration of the war campaigning for peace although she never lost sight of the franchise issue.

Brittain has asserted that the war did nothing to advance Fred's political rehabilitation.[51] He became treasurer of the Union of Democratic Control, an organization formed in response, primarily, to the government's foreign policy, whose members included Ramsay MacDonald and H. N. Brailsford, the left-wing suffrage supporter and writer. In 1917, Fred stood as a 'peace by negotiation' candidate in the South Aberdeen by-election but polled only 333 votes. In 1918, when the age for conscription was raised to 50, he became a conscientious objector.

The Pankhursts and the Pethick Lawrences now displayed differing attitudes towards the war but the paradoxical issue of militancy, which was so integral to their relationship, is also worth noting. The latters' militancy during this period helps to explain how, fundamentally, their understandings of it were so different. For the Pankhursts it was tactical action confined to a specific cause, whilst for the Pethick Lawrences it was a type of protest that could be used in varying forms and could affect a whole range of issues. During the war, Fred joined the Society of Authors and both he and Emmeline corresponded with a range of writers including Laurence Housman and Miles Malleson. Vera Brittain has suggested that Fred was looking for 'reinforcement by a respectable professional organisation'[52] after his expulsion by the Reform Club and whilst there may be some truth in this, as his subsequent membership of PEN (Poets, Essayists, Novelists) testifies, this also has to be considered in terms of the balance between work, home and association and how this impacted on socially defining Fred's masculinity. John Tosh has written of the uncertainty of these bases of masculine identification, concluding that men with limited social and economic power were as likely to lose masculine self-respect as they were income.[53] For Fred, however, these three arenas had been solid; he was wealthy, had several homes and membership of a 'decent' club. Being made bankrupt affected all these areas but it was his expulsion from the Reform Club that had the greatest effect on his masculinity. Society, and very likely Fred Pethick Lawrence himself, would have viewed exclusion from such a site of masculine culture as shameful and belittling.

The first general election in which women were allowed to vote took place just four weeks after the end of the war on 14 December 1918. In November 1918, a bill to allow women to stand as Members of Parliament was rushed through and seventeen women stood in the general election, including Emmeline Pethick Lawrence and Christabel Pankhurst. Fred had been adopted as the prospective Labour candidate for Hastings in April 1918, but his decision to become a conscientious objector provoked sufficient disaffection from his supporters for him to withdraw in November 1918, and he was unsuccessful in securing another candidature. In his auto-biography he wrote: 'in these circumstances, my wife felt herself free to accept the invitation of the local Labour Party in the Rusholme division of Manchester to contest that seat in the Labour interest.'[54] Fred appears to have seen himself as the one who should pursue a political career and to have perceived Emmeline's candidature as a secondary consideration. Indeed he pointed out, 'there was little prospect of success'.[55] In her autobiography, Emmeline gave her sole reason for standing as being 'that an opportunity was offered to explain publicly the reasons why I believed that the only chance of permanent peace in Europe lay in a just settlement after the war'.[56] Moreover, she gave the election campaign only one page of coverage in her autobiography but enough to make the point that

> It was a strange experience for one who had given eight years of life as I had, in the endeavour to win votes for women, to watch working-class mothers, with their babies and small children, eagerly going to the poll to record their votes against me. But not more strange after all than that soldiers should vote for a pacifist.[57]

Paradoxically, it was the soldiers' vote that saved her deposit, helping her to poll 2,985 votes and placing her above the Liberal candidate, but her claim that 'working-class mothers' voted against her is perhaps exaggerated given the terms on which the franchise was extended to women in 1918 – there were still a substantial number of women without the vote.

Whether Emmeline would have been really interested in pursuing a political career is difficult to say, for although it would have been an excellent opportunity to act as a voice for women's rights, her disillusionment was strong enough to cause her to write to Elizabeth Robins in 1919: 'I have come to the end of Politics and all they stand for. I see that the only possibility of real reconstruction lies in finding some new principle of life and way of living.'[58] This view did not, however, stop her from supporting Fred in his continuing attempt to get elected as a Labour MP and throughout the 1920s and 1930s she campaigned for many women's issues and actively supported women in the labour movement in areas such as the provision of birth control information to working-class women. She was also president of the Women's Freedom League (WFL) for several years.[59]

In 1923, Fred stood as the prospective Labour candidate for Leicester West against the Liberal, Winston Churchill. With Emmeline's support, which Fred openly acknowledged, they set about creating a suitable image for him that would appeal to the electorate. One of the most successful pieces of propaganda was a song (which according to Fred was written by Emmeline,[60] although she attributes it to Harry Peach[61]) entitled 'Vote, Vote, Vote for Pethick Lawrence'. Part of the lyrics read:

> Once again the party cry, do not let it pass you by!
> Labour's out to win no matter what they say.
> We are sick of promise vain, must we have it all again?
> We want deeds not words to bring the better day.
>
> *Chorus*
> Vote, vote, vote for Pethick Lawrence!
> Work, work, work and do your best!
> If all workers we enrol, he is sure to head the poll,
> And we'll have a Labour man for Leicester West.
>
> So we work to bring the day that will give to all fair play;
> We can do it here in Leicester if we will.
> And you Leicester Women too, Pethick Lawrence worked
>   for you;
> Work for *him* and not for Instone or Churchill.[62]

This was sung at all meetings and undoubtedly helped to instil the name of Pethick Lawrence in the minds of the voters. The lyrics are especially interesting, for they embodied both Fred and Emmeline's political beliefs, as well as serving as a reminder to the electorate, particularly the women, of Fred's involvement in the women's suffrage campaign. 'Deeds not Words' was the phrase originally coined by Christabel Pankhurst when militancy was at its height.

The result of the Leicester West election was that Fred, for the first time, became a Member of Parliament. Whilst supportive of him, Emmeline continued to work for the causes in which they both believed and in that sense, retained her own identity. Harrison has written of Emmeline that 'though childless, she had no career, and left Fred to manage the finances ... she contented herself with running the household', and that she 'rarely commented on politics between the wars'.[63] In fact, she spoke all over the world on a vast range of political issues including the inevitability of another war which she (along with many others) had predicted after the signing of the Treaty of Versailles. Moreover, the WFL annual conference reports show that in her nine years as president, she continued to be heavily involved in feminist campaigns, including the extension of the franchise to all women.

Fred's public status altered as his political career developed and although his involvement in the militant campaign for women's suffrage was not totally forgotten, his immersion in parliamentary concerns soon took over. Nevertheless, his commitment to feminist issues remained because it was, in essence, the basis of their marriage and his *maiden* speech was concerned with the question of widows' pensions.

Emmeline, on the other hand, once so prominent in the public sphere because of her suffrage activism, could never hope to sustain this role, whereas Fred could take advantage of conventional political openings. Now women had the vote the press were keen for other 'news'. Moreover, the government's interest in those issues of concern to Emmeline was negligible.

Nevertheless, throughout their political partnership, they succeeded in pursuing their common goals and appear to have adapted well to the shift in their individual political activity, viewing the changing nature of their respective positions both in the public and private sphere as part of some greater plan. Nowhere is this made clearer than in the preface to Emmeline's autobiography in which she wrote: 'Life is one. Separation is a delusion.'[64]

Towards the end of his life, Fred wrote 'The Men's Share', a reworking of a pamphlet he had first written in 1912. In it he stated:

All down history women have supported men in their fight for liberty. They have toiled with them, suffered with them, died with them. There is nothing surprising therefore in the fact that in the militant struggle of British women for their own emancipation some men stood with them in the fight.[65]

The years between 1906 and 1912 seem to have been a time when the Pethick Lawrences were closer than at any other time in their life. Moreover, the results of their efforts continued to manifest themselves in a variety of ways. As a political partnership, they saw their participation in the suffrage cause epitomizing everything they stood for at a public and a personal level. In effect, it was the culmination of their combined desire to break down the barriers that separated the public and private spheres.

Their prime strength lay in the way in which they complemented each other and in their ability to resolve areas of potential conflict without its appearing to affect their personal relationship or their public image. Additionally, they gave each other the freedom and space necessary for their partnership to be successful. Of course, reading about their lives as written by them, it is difficult to assess to what extent this actually accurately reflects their private relationship as they sought to give the impression that there was little difference between the way they portrayed themselves publicly and the way in which they functioned as a couple privately.

What is interesting is the way in which Fred, after having been involved and thus connected with the women's suffrage movement, was able subsequently to enter into a traditionally male domain, that of parliamentary politics. Nevertheless, as a politician Fred continued his commitment to feminism throughout his parliamentary career. In 1945, he was rewarded for his political work and given a peerage, as well as being appointed Secretary of State for India and Burma.

Sadly, Emmeline's political career after the women's suffrage campaign has gone largely unrecognized other than in the context of being the wife of Fred Pethick Lawrence, the MP. Yet it could be argued that in the interwar period her role was of equal importance though because she was not involved in 'parliamentary politics', she effectively became redundant. Their respective careers are represented in the highly gendered autobiographies they wrote; in Fred's, suffrage is portrayed as a short period in his life, covering four slim chapters, whilst in Emmeline's it is presented as her life's main focus.

The Pethick Lawrences have to be seen as unique in terms of their contribution to women's suffrage and especially during their involvement with the WSPU. Without them, it is difficult to imagine how the organization would have grown in the way it did, such was the importance of their input at so many levels. Nevertheless, they must also be viewed in terms of their broader commitments. Addressing the annual conference of the Women's Freedom League on 13 April 1929, the president, Emmeline Pethick Lawrence, said:

Today we rejoice in the fact that a complete Women's Enfranchisement Act has been placed on the Statute Book, and we meet on
the eve of the General Election, when, for the first time, young
women will be free to exercise their vote.[66]

Whilst women getting the vote was, in part, a realization of all that
the Pethick Lawrences had fought for, it was for Emmeline only a
beginning. There were still many other issues pertinent to women to
be addressed and her belief 'that one in the House and one out of it
make the best team',[67] whilst certainly true in their case, remains
flawed by the gendered location of those roles and the distance of
the house from the House!

NOTES

1 B. Harrison, *Prudent Revolutionaries*, Clarendon Press, Oxford, 1987,
   includes a chapter on the Pethick Lawrences, focusing on the interwar
   period.
2 E. Pethick Lawrence, *My Part in a Changing World*, London, Victor
   Gollancz, 1938, p. 47.
3 Quoted in V. Brittain, *Pethick-Lawrence, A Portrait*, London, Allen &
   Unwin, 1963, p. 21.
4 ibid., p. 20.
5 E. Pethick Lawrence, *My Part*, p. 130.
6 Harrison, *Prudent Revolutionaries*, makes reference to the importance
   of mostly female servants and secretaries in terms of middle-class
   feminist achievement, p. 11.
7 Brittain, *Pethick-Lawrence*, p. 34.
8 Pethick-Lawrence papers, Wren Library, Trinity College, Cambridge
   (hereafter referred to as P-L followed by the number), P-L 6/26, Letter
   from F. Pethick Lawrence to E. Pethick Lawrence, 1 April 1902.
9 F. W. Pethick Lawrence, *Fate Has Been Kind*, London, Hutchinson,
   1943, p. 69.
10 E. Pethick Lawrence, *My Part*, p. 152.
11 ibid. p. 146.
12 Harrison, *Prudent Revolutionaries*, p. 247.
13 E. Pethick Lawrence, *My Part*, p. 148.
14 F. W. Pethick Lawrence, *Fate*, p. 75.
15 E. Pethick Lawrence, *My Part*, p. 283.
16 ibid. p. 152.
17 R. Fulford, *Votes for Women*, London, Faber & Faber, 1957, p. 167.
18 P-L 7/165, Letter from E. Pethick Lawrence in Holloway prison to her
   husband, 4 March 1909.
19 In his autobiography, *Fate Has Been Kind*, Fred wrote that initially Mrs
   Pankhurst did not want Emmeline to give the undertaking, making some
   scornful remark about the attitude of husbands, p. 73.

20 E. Pethick Lawrence, *My Part*, p. 169.
21 F. W. Pethick Lawrence, *Fate*, p. 69.
22 Translated, this means 'it is the first step which costs'.
23 See, for example, the *Daily Mirror*, 5–10 July 1906.
24 *Daily Mirror*, 29 October 1906, p. 3.
25 *Daily Mirror*, 26 October 1906, p. 3.
26 See, for example, Public Record Office (PRO), MEPO 2/1222 XC2585, letter from F. Pethick Lawrence to the police, 13 October 1908, requesting an improvement in conditions at Bow Street cells, etc.
27 E. Pethick Lawrence, *My Part*, p. 169.
28 PRO, MEPO 2/1016 XC2783, pp. 52–3, Letter from Miss A. Meechan to the Public Prosecutor, 23 March 1907.
29 PRO, MEPO 2/1016 XC2783, p. 63, Report from Criminal Investigation Department, New Scotland Yard, 11 April 1907.
30 Suffragette Fellowship Collection, Museum of London, F. W. Pethick Lawrence, 'The Opposition of the Liberal Government to Woman Suffrage' (1908).
31 ibid.
32 ibid.
33 Fulford, *Votes*, p. 167.
34 ibid. p. 139.
35 Quoted in Brittain, *Pethick*, p. 61.
36 ibid. p. 62.
37 F. W. Pethick Lawrence, *Fate*, p. 89.
38 P-L 7/168, Letter from E. Pethick Lawrence to F. Pethick Lawrence, sent from Holloway prison, 18 June 1912.
39 F. W. Pethick Lawrence, *Fate*, p. 89.
40 P-L 7/169, Letter from E. Pethick Lawrence to F. Pethick Lawrence still in prison, 25 June 1912.
41 E. Pethick Lawrence, *My Part*, p. 277.
42 P-L 9/31, p. 2, Letter from Mrs Pankhurst to E. Pethick Lawrence, 8 September 1912.
43 P-L 9/32, pp. 3–4, Letter from E. Pethick Lawrence to Mrs Pankhurst, 22 September 1912.
44 Elizabeth Robins diary extract, October 1912, Fales Library, New York University. Information from Angela V. John.
45 E. Pethick Lawrence, *My Part*, p. 288.
46 P-L 7/170, p. 8, E. Pethick Lawrence, speech to the Jury, June 1913.
47 E. Pethick Lawrence, *My Part*, p. 290.
48 ibid.
49 Harry Ransom Humanities Research Center (HRHRC), University of Texas at Austin, Letter from E. Pethick Lawrence to E. Robins, 14 April 1913. Information from Angela V. John.
50 HRHRC, Letter from E. Pethick Lawrence to E. Robins, 5 May 1913. Information from Angela V. John.
51 Brittain, *Pethick*, p. 76.
52 ibid.
53 J. Tosh, 'What should Historians do with Masculinity?', *History Workshop Journal* 38 (1994), pp. 192–3 (pp. 179–201).

54 F. W. Pethick Lawrence, *Fate*, p. 119.
55 ibid.
56 E. Pethick Lawrence, *My Part*, p. 322.
57 ibid. p. 323.
58 HRHRC, Letter from E. Pethick Lawrence to E. Robins, 14 November 1919.
59 For a detailed history of the WFL, see C. Eustance, '"Daring to be Free": the Evolution of Women's Political Identities in the Women's Freedom League, 1906–1930', DPhil, University of York, 1993.
60 F. W. Pethick Lawrence, *Fate*, p. 128.
61 E. Pethick Lawrence, *My Part*, p. 336.
62 P-L 7/6, West Leicester Elector, 30 November 1923.
63 Harrison, *Prudent Revolutionaries*, pp. 253–4.
64 E. Pethick Lawrence, *My Part*, preface.
65 P-L 5/133, p. 1, F. W. Pethick Lawrence, 'The Men's Share', (*c.* 1960).
66 E. Pethick Lawrence, Address to the Women's Freedom League, Report of the twenty-second annual conference, 13 April 1929. Information from Claire Eustance.
67 E. Pethick Lawrence, *My Part*, p. 337.

Chapter 6

The political platform and the language of support for women's suffrage, 1890–1920

Carolyn Spring

I am not afraid of seeing woman's influence more directly felt in this Assembly and reflected in its legislature. A great statesman is really great because he combines in his nature something of the essential characteristics of woman – her generosity, her enthusiasm, her unselfishness, and her large sympathies.[1]

In this speech in the House of Commons in 1872 Liberal MP John Maguire was advocating the suffrage bill to remove the electoral disabilities of women. It heralded the political rationale of later debate. Early parliamentary pro-suffragists shared the conviction with anti-suffragists that the differences between male and female culture had social and political significance and that the character of the state was coterminous with that of its citizens. Suffrage petitions stressed the benefit to be gained for both the masculine and feminine character from the greater sharing of experiences and sympathies, resulting in civilizing constitutional transformation and balanced state legislation. This accentuation of sex characteristics and the distinctions made between masculinity and femininity were commonplace by 1890. Both demarcated the discursive parameters within which both support for and dissent from women's suffrage were articulated and each remained intact until the First World War disrupted these largely unassailed dichotomies.

Using the Hansard reports of the House of Commons and the published pamphlets of speeches recorded from public halls and meeting-places in Britain, this chapter will focus on the chronology of language and arguments supportive of women's suffrage both within Parliament and through the extra-parliamentary platform. It demonstrates that the discourses of legitimization employed by men revealed both directly and indirectly their construction of masculinity and femininity during the years 1890 to 1920. It is argued that the language of support was primarily concerned with reforming political constructions of masculinity, throughout a period in which the possibility of women's political representation depended enormously on the perception of sex differences. The chapter illustrates how pro-suffragist perceptions of gender shared many similarities with anti-suffragist arguments, and as a consequence of these common conceptions of sex-specific characteristics, pro-suffragist discourse failed to challenge the deeply entrenched political ethnographies of masculinity, obstructing the realization of women's full rights of citizenship. The resulting masculinization of reform, in which men purported to adopt perceived female characteristics to enhance the morality and conscience of the political and legal fraternity, retained the institutionalized political dominance of men. Moreover, the overall orientation of pro-suffragist men actually reproduced deeper assumptions about the natures of men and women.[2]

The impact of linguistic agitation was determined by who was able to move within the public political space, and who possessed legitimate authority to give meaning to key cultural symbols, signs and codes.[3] Pro-suffrage men accessed supportive networks, providing a means of exploiting both formal and informal political platforms to reinforce and confirm their standpoints. The Men's League for Women's Suffrage (MLWS) and the Men's Political Union (MPU) primarily functioned as a platform to voice extra-parliamentary male endorsement. Men also took advantage of the political authority sanctioned by their professional status to utilize platforms within trade unions and social welfare reform movements. The effectiveness of these platforms relied heavily on the established channels of communication instigated by women's suffrage activists. The availability of the feminist press, publishing and printing resources granted male supporters effective political media. Speeches made in halls and at public demonstrations were often translated verbatim into pamphlets for circulation to a wider audience via sympathetic suffragist societies, private clubs and intellectual cliques, and were frequently précised within the columns of suffragist journals.

The agitation for women's suffrage between 1890 and 1920 cohered into a gender drama involving not only the changes in women's roles but also the changes in men's lives and their consequent reactions. To obtain access to the institution of Parliament, women suffragists, as outsiders, negotiated with a group of

UWE LIBRARY SERVICES

men whose accomplishments and experience were vastly different from and bore little resemblance to those of the majority of their sex. Pro-suffragist men were specifically motivated by suffragism, but were perturbed and challenged by feminism more generally, yet both were often simplistically collapsed into 'the woman question' within debate. Representative not only of demands for suffrage, the debates raised many questions concerning the political, economic and social relations between the sexes. Discussions were characterized by constant reiteration of vital reforms needed in the education system, in laws concerning married women's property and child custody, and within employment practices.

Between 1890 and 1920 the deployment of discourses between pro-suffrage and anti-suffrage groups across the political parties involved a linguistic struggle to co-opt or discredit existing systems of representation to establish political credence. Inside Parliament and externally, political platforms hosted discursive battles to prioritize the constituents of 'true manhood' and 'true womanhood'. These processes were played against a changing background of rival conceptions of the political order characterized by competing organizations working towards different and often conflicting social interests. The relevance and priority of arguments of both supporters and opponents of women's suffrage changed significantly throughout the fluctuating impact of the campaign, responding to the divergent political influences generating international and party concern. Across the political spectrum anxieties emanated from the perceived inflation of sex antagonism, anxieties that were articulated through misgivings around broadening democratic representation and in the expression of concerns about the erosion of the strength of empire.

Parliamentary campaigns for women's suffrage both prior to and following 1890 were protracted and arduous. The first suffrage bill introduced in the Commons by the Liberal MP Jacob Bright in 1870 signified a culmination of demands for women's rights over recent years. For the next decade a private member's bill was introduced every year except 1875, prolonged debates customarily concluding in rejection on second reading.[4] The Reform Act of 1884, increasing the male electorate to around two thirds of adult men, heightened the sense of injustice, yet the period 1885 to 1892 was conspicuous by the dearth of women's suffrage debate in Parliament. The increasing mobilization of political activity from external political platforms, revealed by 1905 the determination to secure women's suffrage regardless of consent from the Commons, a resolution evidenced in women's incitation to militant tactics.[5]

From the onset the argument and actions of pro-suffragist coalitions of women and men largely determined the pace and reaction of anti-suffragists to women's enfranchisement proposals. The consolidation of an effective pro-suffragist extra-parliamentary agitation compelled anti-suffragists to instigate a coherent campaign against a distinct series of suffrage demands by forming a coalition between parliamentary and extra-parliamentary conservatives. Reinforcement of parliamentary dissent was deeply entrenched in the world of masculine leisure and recreation. Through the informal political platforms offered by exclusively masculine social clubs, networks of men coalesced in directing counter-ideologies to undermine the dogma expounded in the public meetings, demonstrations and mass processions undertaken by pro-suffragists.[6]

The suffrage debates inside the House of Commons in the 1890s took place within a culture of resistance, regardless of an individual's support or dissent. An unspoken male complicity retained the exclusion of the issue of sexuality from suffrage debate. By disregarding the political vocabulary of sexuality which women recognized, men marginalized the private domain, constituting it as a site of silence.[7] The language of moral outrage employed by agitators for the repeal of the Contagious Diseases Acts had recently operated to de-stabilize formations of manhood by problematizing the relation of the sexual to men's political potency, simultaneously contesting an enshrined moral individualism within the hegemonic narrative of liberal individualism.[8] Not only did parliamentary language in the 1890s function to exclude the issue of an abusive male sexuality, but the complete omission of the issue of women's sexuality and marital sexual relations also characterized suffrage debates. George Bernard Shaw, in an article entitled 'The Unmentionable Case for Women's Suffrage', published in *The Englishwoman* in 1909, remarked: 'I strongly suspect that, though we never mention it, the cry for the vote is often really a cry for the key of one's bedroom.'[9]

Omitting to reflect upon their own *personal* political agency, parliamentarians in favour of women's suffrage generally adhered to a critique of the capitalist transformation of gender relations linked with an account of the moral laxity and disease generated by 'vicious classes' in the disorderly metropolis.[10] In the House of Commons, debates were conducted by the 'pro-' lobby in a manner and atmosphere of gentlemanly respectability. Advocates presented themselves as eloquent negotiators undertaking debate as civilized representatives of an imperial nation, frequently interspersing their argument with references to the classics and evolutionary 'science'. MPs also regularly offered an experiential rationale expressing their convictions of women's political capabilities gained through their own practical experience and observation of women within philanthropic and municipal committees.

Parliamentary suffragists attempted to account for the perpetuation of sexual inequality by focusing upon the experiences available to women in order to form an understanding of women's social inferiority. That pro-suffrage men responded to an unspoken choice was unacknowledged in parliamentary debate. Either women really were different from and inferior to men in some basic and unalterable way, or the structuring principles of state and society were founded upon man-made injustice. The choice men made reflected their political convictions, encompassing conservative appeals concerned with suffrage reform as an end in itself, or demonstrated a more critical approach to, and struggle for, revision of men's management of the state.

Within the Commons debates multiple systems of oppression within society were frequently reduced to an identifiable cause – usually the inadequacy of education – to contest women's perceived intellectual mediocrity, as a necessary precursor to secure reform. Instead of making more radical demands for women's enfranchisement based on the human right to representation, pro-suffrage MPs, in alliance with women's suffrage agitators, attempted to mould women into the existing criteria for male enfranchisement by advocating their political representation on the same basis as men.[11] Clark contends that in initially isolating propertied widows or spinsters as candidates for enfranchisement, they reinforced the prevailing concept that political institutions should be responsive primarily to heads of household.[12] These conservative limitations assisted in the defeat of the early private members' bills. The pro-suffragists weakened their case by including married women in their arguments despite the omission of married women from parliamentary bills. In 1892, Sir A. Rollit, an Independent Conservative, demanded women's need for electoral representation citing the necessity of women's influence in reviews to the laws concerning divorce and breach of the promise of marriage.[13] Anti-suffragists capitalized on the resulting confusion to collapse an argument riddled with contradictions.

The exclusion of married women from women's suffrage bills represented a tactical compromise by parliamentary suffragists, a measure which was indicative of their failure to recognize women's unequal status as a sex. Consciousness of women as a sexual class had limited linguistic currency in the House of Commons. Greater prevalence within speeches of many parliamentary suffragists – both inside and outside the Commons – was granted to the Victorian language of virtue and character, a consolidation which formed an integral part of the most conservative support. George Wyndham, the Conservative MP for Dover, urged that women's philanthropic endeavours in many spheres of life were indicative of their 'higher power than men to transcend the brutalities and degradations of their surroundings' and women's ability 'to sweeten and elevate the atmosphere of political life'.[14]

Commentary on the contested merits and defects of the feminine character was embedded within the machinery of competing parties. MPs on both sides of the Commons professing support for votes for women utilized the issue of women's disfranchisement as a method of castigating the opposition's philosophical and legislative intentions, contrasting their different management of the question and the conflicting commitments of each party. Pugh points out that party motivation was 'an intrinsic feature in the institutional management of the debates', and calculations concerning whether the outcome would be of greater advantage to one or other party informed rhetoric.[15] As a consequence, enormous conflict of opinion existed within the Commons debates regarding what number of women, and what classes of women, should be enfranchised.

The growing support for women's suffrage within the Liberal Party in the early 1890s was checked by the increasing threat posed by socialism, a development which prompted party members to question the wisdom of further franchise extensions. The Labour Party, albeit the most vociferous and unified supporter of women's suffrage, shared with the Liberal Party an awareness that the disadvantage of women's suffrage proposals resided in their duplication of the class distinctions and biases existing within the male franchise.[16] Indeed, it was the prevalence of the view that women would act as a more conservative force, coupled with anxiety over an expanded working-class male electorate, which encouraged a number of Conservative MPs to offer languid support. The appeal of the women's franchise proposals resided in the fact that the measures incorporated would bolster the existing property-based electorate, granting a broader proportion of Conservative female balloters than could be expected from implementing an adult suffrage measure.[17]

Transcribing support into either Conservative or Liberal policy involved a process which meant surmounting divisions not only across party lines but also between disparate factions within parties. Anti-suffragists across parties utilized the art of postponement to thwart women's suffrage proposals through ridicule, laborious mockeries, and outright dismissal as misguided philanthropic endeavours. The parliamentary debates were further circumscribed by tedious repetition of legal, medical and theological impediments to women's citizenship – a stance often insensitive and unresponsive to the nuances of suffragist argument – or to the new social developments impacting upon the question, particularly in the debates of 1917.

The external political platform was subject to a more receptive audience and allowed greater freedom in the agenda of public addresses. Speeches were not uniformly constricted by the necessity to defend claims or refutations of purpose, neither were they subject to habitual filibustering. Women suffragists, in common with the nascent political forces of the left, spoke from a cultural formation which had developed outside Parliament and shared the necessity for greater representation. Yet the political platform of the left was not wholly conducive to women's political participation and the much needed solidarity to strengthen the urgency of reform was only sporadically offered. In the early 1890s the responses of the newly emerging socialist organizations to the demands of the growing women's movement were varied and erratic. There was no common strategy relating to their attitude towards Parliament, neither was there any unity on how reforms conducted within capitalism could accord with the emergence of a socialist society.[18] Conflicting loyalties and expectations existed between socialist organizations which accorded feminist reform low priority and made feminist organizations wary of male-defined socialism.[19]

Outside Parliament only the most 'feminist' of socialist MPs attempted to bridge the struggles of the working-class Labour movement and women suffrage organizations by urging that women needed representation as a sex class. Keir Hardie, leader of the Independent Labour Party, argued in 1907 that since:

women are more and more taking part in the world's work, it surely follows that they ought also to enjoy the chief right of citizenship. Otherwise they will suffer from sex legislation quite as much as men have hitherto suffered from class legislation.[20]

Hardie's tracts epitomized early twentieth-century attempts to reconcile the differences between feminist motivations and class divisions. In articulating women's right to independent political representation as economic agents, Hardie broke with political conventions which recognized women as the economic adjuncts of men, whether through law or blood ties. Hardie's argument implicitly refuted the assumption that no class division existed between the sexes, and correspondingly challenged the contention that no class loyalty endured among women. Despite the enlightened premise of Hardie's argument, the feminist potential of socialist rhetoric was handicapped throughout the period through continued emphasis on sex differences. Anti-suffragist attempts to deny women's political effectiveness by citing their domesticity, pacifism and altruism were inverted by suffragist men who contrasted women's supposedly sex-specific characteristics with those of the masculine government. Maintaining a firm belief in the polarity of the sexes, socialist pro-suffragists suggested that introducing feminine opinion might prevent the gendered partiality arising through the exercise of an exclusively masculine government. In denouncing the political realm as the province of destructive and morally inept males, socialist reformers isolated masculine traits as responsible for social chaos, war, turmoil and poverty.[21] Following these critiques socialists elevated women's ennoblement of the private sphere as the qualification for the office of equal citizenship. Hardie asserted:

> We witness on every hand the effect of unchallenged male dominance, arrogant armaments, harsh and unfeeling administration of law, industrial conditions which are proving fatal to the race. With the incoming of the mother element into politics this would be gradually changed.[22]

Socialists did not elaborate on how change would come about following the incorporation of the 'mother element' in political life. Through emphasis on sex differences, socialist argument incorporated a rationale which had the potential to corrupt its own claims. Locating men's aggression and their drive towards domination as defining masculine traits, designated women's oppression within the social order as a fact of life. Women, deemed less aggressive, were either lesser candidates for political life or else must emulate men to avoid domination. In this rationale equality and liberation for both sexes were not possible. Furthermore, a popular analogy between the body politic and the body corporate was engaged by socialist reformers to denaturalize capitalism by pronouncing the healthy human body as the 'perfect commonwealth' with each part dependent upon the others.[23] The attendant vision of a socialist future was ordained at conception as masculine. In his 'Socialism and Service' (1906) Benson of the Independent Labour Party remarked:

> In declaring the principles of the human body to be the principles of a true society we are simply laying down the principles of socialism. . . . There is in this body a type of true society, and in Genesis this body of man is pronounced by God to be in *His* own image and likeness. [my emphasis][24]

Linked by a common political ontology of mankind and womankind, both pro-suffrage and anti-suffrage men utilized women's altruism in a similar manner for different ends, attributing a similar primary role to women as mothers of the nation. It was the perceived extent of their involvement, influence and power in domestic and political life towards the benefit of the state which differentiated the stance and activism of each alliance. A discursive struggle between different and opposed views of female nature reflected the diverse political complexion of masculine support for women's suffrage, its marginalized socialistic canon and its predominant conservative orthodox tradition.

A minority of liberals applied the language of natural rights to the relationship of the sexes with particular accent on reason. These suffragists proclaimed the need to grant women equal rights before law and the right to economic independence on the premise that there were no natural indelible differences between the sexes in moral and intellectual ability, advancing social factors rather than innate qualities to comprehend the differences between men and women. The liberal writer Joseph Levy, a professor of logic and economics, in a speech at a meeting in St James's Hall in 1892 refuted the supposed biological and physiological impediments to women's full citizenship, maintaining:

> It would be as just and reasonable to deny political rights to men on the grounds of their unfitness for one set of functions [mothering] as it is to deny women the same rights on the grounds of their unfitness – far less absolute – for the other [military service].[25]

With vocabularies which hinged on the concepts of rights, utility and humanitarianism, proponents forged a discursive mechanism which recognized that human nature is subject to a political realm which does not exist merely for the protection of trade and property interests, but is possessed of its own distinctive set of ethics and values. Moreover, by using the language of individual subjective rights, suffragists could make moral assertions that did not necessarily correspond to the moral system concerned largely with duties and sex roles.[26] The Reverend Lloyd Thomas, Vicar of Rhyl, explained in 1909 that

> Women's claim to enfranchisement rests on no one particular qualification ... she is a human being, subject to the laws of the state, and as such has a claim upon the state to be put upon terms of political equality with the male.[27]

The predominant orthodox essentialist tradition existed in conflict with equal rights discourses by sustaining women's primary 'disposition' as wives and mothers, a language of support which emphasized the contrasting natures of men and women. This discursive strand located the crippling of women's reason and conscience, compounded by political exclusion, as a handicap to the rational development of a Christian nation. Proponents argued that women's enfranchisement would afford unique benefits towards the creation of a caring state through social reforms informed by distinctive feminine characteristics. In a Women's Freedom League pamphlet Dr Haden Guest, physician and supporter of the Labour Party, adhered to conservative notions of sex differences by pleading recognition of women's expertise 'on all that has to do with home life and the rearing of children.' Dr Guest linked women's domestic philanthropic qualities with a public function by advising that 'If the Public Health is to be builded [sic] soundly and well, it can only be with the co-operation of women directing the application of legislation to the details of life'.[28] Guest shared with anti-suffragists a belief that women could never transcend their reproductive bodies. His insistence that women are essential to provide domestic knowledge in order that legislation might mediate successfully between need, provision and economy in the administration of public health, adhered to sex-specific categorizations of feminine obligations and roles.

Jewish intellectual and dramatist Israel Zangwill (MLWS) in 'One and One is Two' (1907) incorporated a discursive play on gender which captured the political impasse arising from the persistent dichotomization of the sexes within public discourse and the corresponding masculine domination of the political rostrum. Zangwill, an advocate of women's militancy, observed:

> undoubtedly the best means are not the most ladylike. Ladylike means are all very well if you are dealing with gentlemen; but you are dealing with politicians. Hitherto, I have kept away from political platforms; this is my *maiden* speech.[29] [my emphasis]

The recent commencement of militant activism that Zangwill endorsed signified the creation of a new political platform and the bulldozing of a new path of political intention which meant established procedures and channels no longer dictated the pace. Mass women's suffrage demonstrations existed as the antithesis of disciplined order, exclusivity and solemnity of the parliamentary platform. Discursive dramas played out on external political platforms functioned to connect militant action and group cohesion to political narrative. Gerald Gould, a member of the MPU and an adherent of militancy, remarked in 1911 ('The Democratic Plea'): 'What was it woke the British public from dogmatic slumber and brought the suffrage question from the Egyptian night of absolute indifference, through the wilderness of calumny and derision, to within sight of the promised land?'[30]

Gould's evangelical discourse, infused with martyrdom and deeply embedded in Christian dogma, presented militancy as ennobled and justifiable. Militant agitation undertaken by women inverted, by appropriation, traditional masculine validating behaviour such as forcefulness, assertiveness and the promotion of a code of honour. By presenting militant activism as part of a transcendental movement above force and crude politics, sustained by an undefinable spiritual Christian mysticism, this interpretation of actions undertaken did not conflict with notions of femininity and facilitated militancy as politically palatable within circles of radical men.

Those radicalized by their disenchantment with the parliamentary platform and lacking or rejecting affiliation to parliamentary political parties were in a position to criticize the function and drama of political institutions in entirety, unencumbered by the rhetorical 'rules' of the Commons or the potential loss of electoral confidence. Following his resignation as a Labour MP, George Lansbury cautioned in *Votes for Women*, 15 November 1912:

Many men will come to you and talk of party and principle but
believe me we have been caucus ridden and party ridden for too
long. The House of Commons is dragooned and controlled by a
small handful of men. To vote according to one's conscience is to
be untrue to Party.[31]

Earlier in 1907, Zangwill had expressed a similar conviction that
women must unite to pursue their political interests independently
of political parties. Using the language of the industrial tribunal,
Zangwill depicted the parliamentary platform as a microcosm of the
economy, conflating women's position in the political arena with that
of the wage earner, to demonstrate how women's political subjection
impacts upon their economic subjection. He argued that this position
necessitated women's own rectification through sex representation –
a demand neither party was willing to grant. He pointed to the fact

that both Parties are glad enough to have women's work – the
Tories through the Primrose League, the Liberals through the
Women's Liberal Federation. . . . Their labour has been taken at the
cheapest possible rate. Woman has been sweated by both Parties,
it is time she tried to drive a better bargain.[32]

Anti-parliamentarians sympathetic to women's activism encouraged
the desire to oppose the parliamentary channels available. Self-
proclaimed Communist and 'Freethinker', Guy Aldred opposed
ideologies embedded within parliamentary socialism.[33] His de-
parture from the left was demonstrated by his disdain for those who
maintained the necessity of 'capturing the parliamentary machine'
deeming this an illusory prelude for the inevitable social revolution.[34] An advocate of the atheistic basis of all social progress,
Aldred propounded a language of comradeship which broke with the
assumptions informing liberal discourse by failing to distinguish
explicitly between the natures of women and men. Extolling both
sexes as instrumental to reforming democracy through direct action,
Aldred upheld the incorporation of women within the constitution
on the grounds that a broader electorate body would expose the
intrinsic corruption of Parliament and state – the 'basic rottenness of
capitalist society [and] bring about the downfall of its Empire'.[35]
Few other extra-parliamentary pro-suffragists shared Aldred's communist convictions or revolutionary zeal, instead directing their
propaganda to secure the suffrage constitutionally.

In promoting a bi-social world of politics men challenged a

framework of doctrines emphasizing masculine power – men's supposed intellectual and physical superiority – and male domination in sexual, social and political life. None the less, the revolutionary potential offered by socialist discourse was impeded because of the narrow focus on reforming the masculine personality. Concentrating predominantly on a radical revision of men's material and social relationships with other men, socialist thinkers largely failed to instigate a redefinition of the domestic division of labour and revision to the characterization of the sex roles. Critiques of the unacceptable face of the capitalist system focused overwhelmingly on the negative manifestations men experienced. Of those who attempted a political critique of the relationship of the sexes few depicted women as workers or activists, more commonly presenting them as passive victims. The nonconformist minister J. R. Campbell's tract 'Women's Suffrage and the Social Evil' (1907), though revolutionary for its time, used the issue of women's suffrage as a pledge to circumvent damage to the masculine character. Campbell proclaimed that sexual inequality within the economic nexus of the marriage contract had placed men in the dishonourable and shameful position of pimp and slave-holder. Retaining women within material dependency produced a parasitism conducive to prostitution – whether sanctioned within marriage or conducted illicitly outside the home:

> Broadly speaking, the man owns all there is to own; he used to own the woman out and out; now he owns her indirectly as it were. Man is woman's Capitalist. . . . Women sell themselves to men because men have control of the sources of wealth. The stronger sex has a practical monopoly in the field of politics and industry. . . . We may as well recognize that to give women political power is the best way to secure to them in the long run such an economic status as will lift them out of their present position of reputable and disreputable dependence upon men.[36]

Campbell's use of the language of commerce and business brought what was commonly perceived as private concerns into the public domain. His conviction that men were corrupted by their dominance over women implied that men were no longer allowed to claim that their relationships with their wives were beyond analysis and reform. Nevertheless, in emphasizing the importance of sex attraction by speaking of the necessity to reform marriage he imputed unnatural-ness to those men and women who opposed marriage. In using the family as the metaphor for political order, Campbell cohered with a patriarchal tradition which conceived all normative relations in social, economic and political life to correspond to the relations of men.[37]

Although the majority of pro-suffragist men advanced innately conservative familial discourses, the advocacy of women's suffrage did offer men a platform on which to express the contradiction between the dominant notions of masculinity and individuals' reluctance to pursue that notion. Oratorical attempts to renovate masculinity embedded in a critique of the state not only functioned to promote a public distance from hegemonic ideologies of manliness but also operated to re-establish men's self-affirmation. Thomas Haslam protested in 1906 that 'The appeal to the arbitrament of colossal slaughter for the settlement of international controversies, in these Nineteenth and Twentieth Centuries of our Christian Era, reflects infinite discredit upon our masculine statesmanship'.[38] Members of the MLWS and the MPU also cultivated ideals of manliness within political oratory as a way of reaffirming their precarious stability by promoting a sense of solidarity with like-minded men. Political treatises promoted a new scripting of masculinity within the vacuum arising from the displacement of normative masculinities. In a speech at the Queen's Hall, John Masefield (MLWS) conveyed a sense of betrayal of his sex in pronouncing: 'I come neither to bury *Caesar* nor to praise him.'[39] He imagined a future voice speaking of the dark age of masculinity, remarking: 'I blush for what our grandchildren will say of the men of my generation.'[40] Masefield inquired: 'Were they sane in those days? Were they human beings? Were they not crazy and blinded?'[41]

Although promoting the women's suffrage cause offered men a stage on which to articulate their own subjective dissatisfactions, it is questionable whether men used political rhetoric only to articulate their personal convictions. Some resolved to convert audiences estimated to be sceptical of women's suffrage. Campbell's tract appealed to men's self-interest, not their noble sentiments, suggesting that rather than observing the conditions of women, men were driven to political resolution by basing their analysis on their own position in the labour market. Campbell warned his audience: 'You can no more prevent the *intrusion* of women into fields of activity hitherto reserved for men, than labour was able to prevent the invention of machinery' [my emphasis].[42] The analogy warns that unless their entry is regulated, women workers may also come to replace male labour. Campbell added:

> you will have to ask whether it is good for the body politic, or even possible to prohibit such labour – if it cannot be prohibited, it will have to be represented in Parliament like all other labour. . . . There is no need for sex competition. Enlightened self-interest ought to bid us welcome every improvement in the status of women.[43]

The pledging of commitment to women's enfranchisement was commonly a detached response to a demand which was manifestly personal. Although politics was increasingly being brought home to men, a public examination of the impact of feminism on their own lives was wanting. Isabella Ford, a prominent member of the Independent Labour Party, observed that 'The question of fatherhood . . . receives no consideration at all'.[44] It remained exceptional for men to discuss private roles in a political context, an omission which curbed articulation of the possibilities of manliness available within their cultural moment.[45]

Fears concerning the decay of the national character, the intermingling of social classes and the erosion of the superior race were prominent tenets in vindicating support for women's enfranchisement. Allegiance to imperial nationalism managed to effect some semblance of accord across class and party lines[46] by providing a framework to uphold women suffragist aspirations within a culture in which women were perceived as other than subjects. Antoinette Burton argues that 'where political subjectivity was by definition masculine, subjectivity itself functioned by asserting authority over Others'.[47] Noting that the public and the national were held to be synonymous within feminist discourse, Burton identifies how imperialism offered a means of realizing women's political subjectivity by identifying feminism and feminists with the political and economic strength of nation through the historical context of empire.

Tracts published by suffragist men's societies interspersed argument with a pernicious imperial rationale in their attempts to relieve white male suffragists of the guilt of chauvinism. Speeches implied that the roots and perpetuation of women's social and political subordination resided in the colonized demographies where British authorities had become corrupted. Irish suffragist Thomas Haslam speaking in 1906 presented British imperialists as the necessary Christian arbitrators of barbarous oriental men, remarking: 'If the more civilized Hindoos [*sic*] have never eaten their wives they sometimes insisted that widows should immolate themselves on the funeral pyre of their husbands until the British Government put an end to that practice.'[48]

Exposing the villainy of oriental men by mythologizing their inhumane treatment of women, was a crucial tenet in distinguishing between the civilized superior western male and the inferiority and primitiveness of the eastern male.[49] In equating Asian women's condition with backwardness and helplessness, as the degraded victims of uncivilized religious customs and cultural practices, pro-suffragist men provided a rationale for their intervention in women's political activity at home and for the British imperial presence in India – both justified by their gentlemanly capacity for salvation and civilizing reform. Similarly, albeit secondarily, by elevating women's political role in sustaining Britain's imperial pre-eminence, pro-suffragist men provided a political 'justification' for women's claims upon the state.

Attempts made by suffragist men to identify women with the future prosperity of an imperial nation aimed to ally their cause with a global power, a power infused with a sense of social mission. Laurence Housman in his political pamphlet 'Articles of Faith' strove to persuade other men of women's cultural loyalty as British subjects – identifying them as political agents and reassuring fellow suffragists by speaking of their shared attachment to the value systems of the dominant imperial culture.[50] Housman shared with many suffragist men a prediction that women's emancipation would herald 'a more feminine and hence more ethical kind of imperial rule',[51] their caretaking function over Indian women retaining the image of altruism and selflessness, countering anti-suffragist propaganda appertaining to the monstrous and vicious nature of the women's suffrage movement.[52]

The legitimization narratives adopted by Haslam and Housman to challenge British women's apolitical status simultaneously reinforced the subjugation of women and men within imperial demographies. Housman actually located colonized territories as the geographical political platform responsible for the contamination of anti-suffragist European countries. Referring to an African male anti-suffrage heckler in Hyde Park, he remarked that:

In the estimation of our friend from West Africa, of Lord Cromer, Lord Curzon and other Anglo-Indians whose minds through long environment have become infected with 'native prejudices' – there no doubt we have the voice of the Empire![53]

Presenting imperialism as a 'meta-narrative' rather than 'a mindset', Burton argues that it shaped the ideologies of oppositional groups as well as the practice and rationale of suffragist agency.[54] Adopted to impugn women's treatment as a race apart and their sharing the political status of 'subject races', the language of imperialism represented a double-edged sword. The discursive suppression of the heterogeneity of pro-suffragist support in favour of a monolithic racialism predisposed within anti-suffrage argument a linguistic colonizing of gender. Opponents paraded the rhetorical banner of racial superiority by comparing granting the vote to women with giving the vote to 'blacks' or 'natives' in the empire. Referencing the loss of national dignity and imperial credence of Great Britain, anti-suffragists courted fears of insurgent upheaval within demographies governed by the British Empire following women's enfranchisement.[55]

Even seemingly pragmatic pro-suffragist debate that was centred upon the women's franchise and the attendant revision to the electorate, betrayed constant apprehension concerning the social basis of imperial political power. This anxiety was displaced on to women's mothering and the uplifting effect of enfranchisement on eugenics and nurturing. Supportive tracts widely argued that the vote could rectify the 'grudging' efforts to educate daughters, not for professional ends but 'for their life-work, which is not merely the economic management of their households ... but the far more momentous duty of rearing and intelligent training of their children'.[56]

From the outbreak of war in 1914, the discursive locating of Germany as a masculine nation at war – a characterization supported by the wartime symbolic propaganda depicting the raping of Europe – presented the 'homeland' as a female body requiring its allies and citizens to unite to protect and defend its violation by a foreign enemy.[57] In parliamentary debate parallels drawn between women's suffrage and Russian socialism following the Bolshevik revolution heightened the sense of impending anarchy. The Earl of Lytton, the president of the MLWS, asked in the House of Lords: 'What is it in the example of Russia that we should not imitate? Not the fact *she* has introduced manhood and womanhood suffrage, but that *she* did not do it in time [my emphasis].' Fear of renewed militancy in the general disorder of postwar Britain coexisted with the discursive feminization of nationhood.[58]

War had arrested the mass movement activism of constitutional and militant suffragists. Parliament, preoccupied with the national war effort, had suspended debates on adult and women's suffrage. The resumption of the Commons debates in 1917 had taken place in a climate of national instability and fear of disorder in which decisions concerning democratic extension were deemed crucial to the preservation of an uneasy peace. In the absence of the male electorate, the Earl of Selborne, a Liberal Unionist, anticipated in January 1918 that if the House of Lords vetoed the women's suffrage proviso, the outcome would be chaos. He warned that

> In the climax of this war you will split the nation from top to bottom. You will have against you not only those of the women who have desired the franchise; you will have against you the men who desired the franchise, and the seamen and soldiers who are looking forward to the franchise.[59]

Women's wartime participation in munitions, industry, agriculture and administration and women's service overseas had demonstrated their capacity to fill numerous roles previously designated as masculine. Lord Hugh Cecil remarked, 'War has shown that there are an enormous number of things which before were supposed specially to appertain to men . . . which women can do almost as well as, or even sometimes better than, men.'[60] In the debates of 1917 justification for exercising political opinion had no longer resided in questioning the perceived conservatism and reasoning powers of the women concerned, but in the increasingly nebulous conceptualizations of masculinity and femininity. Lord Hugh Cecil surmised: 'What lies behind arguments is the effect on the general relation of the sexes and on the general position of man in life.'[61] Anti-suffragist oratory, which continued to emphasize the differences between men and women, lost political momentum following the blurring of sex role categorizations.

Whether votes for women were delayed or expedited by the war, the war effort provided men with a convenient political justification for conceding the vote which operated across party divisions. The prewar entanglement of women's suffrage and adult suffrage no longer obstructed reform. The formation of a coalition government in 1915 minimized previously conflicting party considerations, a

detachment reinforced by the conditions of women's enfranchisement negotiated in the Speaker's Conference in 1917.[62] When, in
1918, the Representation of the People Act granted the vote to
women over 30, it enfranchised those married to householders and
those who would have been eligible in their own right for the local
government franchise previously, had they been male.[63] This extension of the vote did not represent a transformation in the attitudes of
the majority of MPs towards women. The suffrage debate of 1917
had demonstrated that if the women's clause were defeated, the
government would proceed with the rest of the bill. At the same time,
if the amendment to enfranchise women at 21 years were carried, the
government pledged to abandon the entire measure.[64] The re-
strictions of the 1918 Act resulted in the introduction of 8,479,156
women to the electoral register, enfranchising only 39.6 per cent of
women and ensuring that the number of female electors did not
exceed the number of male electors.[65] Sylvia Pankhurst retro-
spectively surmised: 'masculine timidity entrenched itself against
the dangers of majority rule!'[66]

If, in 1918, peacetime and the homeland were perceived as
feminine, the state was unmistakably a masculine arbitrator of
welfare. The evocation of sex roles was preordained in explicitly
gendered language within social welfare programmes designed to
transform the conditions of family life. Prominent architects of the
postwar welfare state 'envisioned a manly state that actively intervened in the lives of its citizens'.[67] In 1914, Housman had
remarked that 'Woman expresses ... the communal side of things,
man the individual'.[68] Sharing with anti-suffragists a continuing
emphasis on women's natural altruism, Housman upheld an ideology
easily translated into state programmes of postwar recovery. Operat-
ing through the male heads of households, social reform policies
'perpetuated the division of labour between fatherly state and moth-
erly society'.[69] The state-instigated regimentation of sex roles
broughta resurgent emphasis on motherhood, an area in which
women could excel without competing economically with men.
Women were incorporated into the welfare state, not as individual
citizens equivalentto men, but as members of a family, a sphere
separated from civil society. Socialists in the Social Democratic
Federation and the Independent Labour Party failed to intervene in
these ascriptive political principles of sex role association and
prioritized men's wage levels in their visions of social and economic
progress. Unsurprisingly, women's right to vote rested uneasily with

a postwar criterion of welfare equated with the male family wage earner. The increasingly marginal position of women in the labour market following the war, the gendered language of welfare provision and the onus on protecting the 'family wage' would impose serious limitations on women's newly won right to citizenship.[70]

Extra-parliamentary pro-suffragist men were constrained by the ideological vocabularies available. They were understood and controlled within existing discourses they did not choose and confined within a model of political relations in which they had marginal purchase and limited effectiveness. Progressive reforms were impeded because these men lacked an accessible critique of the partiality of language – the incorporation of traditional male dominance within written and spoken language.

Attempts to broaden the linguistic dimensions of political expression were insufficient. Reverend Horne's idealistic prediction of a 'new language of political life' anticipated that the presence of women within political life would signal

> the birth of a new order, and instead of the old harsh, coarse words that have governed politics there will be newer and nobler words that will have their influences, and instead of might and instead of force and instead of strife, we shall have the words justice, humanity, liberty, peace, equality.[71]

The figure of Womanhood in the political arena did not materialize. Parliamentary suffragists, by emulating Maguire's pledge to modify the masculine gender role, proposed to bring to society and political life the benefits of the good within the feminine character. This revision, without relinquishing the power of men through the equal representation or participation of the sexes, retained men's traditional dominance within the nucleus of government, the family and public life. It minimized the hierarchy of social relations and institutions in which, and through which, men were able to dominate women. The majority of parliamentary pro-suffragists remained unable or unwilling to recognize how the administration and ritualization of political life excluded women by naturalizing their invisibility through codes of professional access, the hierarchical structure of party, and the ethos of informal and formal party management.

The language of support for women's full political representation remained entrenched within political ethnographies of masculinity. Fluid but persistently masculine definitions of eligibility for the

franchise characterized the chronology of suffrage reform, definitions cohering to industrial, imperial and socialist transformations
and the acclimatization of war. In peacetime, women's citizenship
rights remained subject to constitutional and welfare reforms
imagined in a patriarchal male community of fathers, sons and the
state. Within men's rhetoric, women, womanhood and women's
bodies were persistently signified as other than the public. The
physiological function of women, their domestic experience and
engineered altruism were transformed into proclamations of women's
natural 'political' proclivities.

The interwar discourse of liberal individualism incorporated the
language of freedom, equality and individual consent and perpetuated a linguistic disembodiment which masked the political
forms of embodiment, roles, contexts and practices constructed as
masculine. The naturalized division of labour within the home and
in child-rearing was largely accepted and the relation between the
structure of the institution of marriage and the formal equality of
citizenship was essentially disregarded. This virtually unchallenged
'sexualization' process would continue to encumber women's realization of full political rights following the Representation of the
People Act 1928 which finally extended the vote to women over 21
years of age.

NOTES

1 Hansard Commons Debates, 1 May 1872, 3rd series, vol. CCXI, col. 45.
2 D. Morgan, *Discovering Men, Critical Studies on Men and Masculinities*, London, Routledge, 1992, p. 157.
3 See M. J. Shapiro, *Language and Political Understanding: The Politics
of Discursive Practices*, New Haven, CT, Yale University Press, 1981.
4 M. Pugh, *Women's Suffrage in Britain 1867–1928*, London, The
Historical Association, 1980, p. 6.
5 See E. S. Pankhurst, *The Suffragette Movement, An Intimate Account of
Persons and Ideals* (1931), London, Virago edition, 1977.
6 See B. Harrison, *Separate Spheres: The Opposition to Women's Suffrage
in Britain*, London, Croom Helm, 1978, pp. 91–107.
7 F. Mort, *Dangerous Sexualities: Medico-moral Politics in England since
1830*, London, Routledge & Kegan Paul, 1987, pp. 112–36.
8 See L. Bland, *Banishing the Beast: English Feminism and Sexual
Morality 1885–1914*, Harmondsworth, Penguin, 1995.
9 G. Bernard Shaw, 'The Unmentionable Case for Women's Suffrage',
in *The Englishwoman* 1 (February–April, 1909), Grant Richards,
pp. 112–21.
10 H. Sussman, *Manhood and Masculine Politics in Early Victorian*

Literature and Art, Cambridge, Cambridge University Press, 1995, p. 11.

11 A. Clark, 'Gender, Class and Nation: Franchise Reform in the Long Nineteenth Century', in J. Vernon (ed.), *Re-reading the Constitution*, Cambridge, Cambridge University Press, forthcoming.

12 ibid.

13 Hansard Commons Debates, 27 April 1892, 4th series, vol. III, col. 1459.

14 ibid., col. 1502.

15 Pugh, *Women's Suffrage*, p. 14.

16 Harrison, *Separate Spheres*, p. 47.

17 D. Morgan, *Suffragists & Liberals: The Politics of Women's Suffrage*, Oxford, Basil Blackwell, 1975, p. 29.

18 S. Rowbotham, *Hidden from History: 300 Years of Women's Oppression and the Fight Against It*, London, Pluto Press, 1973, p. 90.

19 S. Rowbotham and J. Weeks, *Socialism and the New Life – The Personal and Sexual Politics of Edward Carpenter and Havelock Ellis*, London, Pluto Press, 1977, pp. 16–20.

20 J. K. Hardie, 'Women and Politics', in B.Villiers, *The Case for Women's Suffrage*, London, T. Fisher Unwin, 1907, p. 81.

21 ibid., p. 82.

22 ibid.

23 T. D. Benson, 'Socialism and Service', Tracts for the Times, No. 11, London, Independent Labour Party, 1906, p. 7.

24 ibid.

25 J. H. Levy, 'The Enfranchisement of Women', a speech delivered from the Chair at a meeting at St James's Hall, 26 April 1892, London, P. S. King & Son, 1892, pp. 5–6.

26 See J. K. Hardie, *The Citizenship of Women*, London, ILP, 1905, pp. 3–4.

27 Rev. Lloyd Thomas, *The Emancipation of Womanhood*, London, the Women's Press, 1912, p. 3.

28 See H. Guest, 'Votes for Women and the Public Health', London, the Women's Freedom League, 1913.

29 I. Zangwill, 'One and One is Two: A Tribute of Literature to the Cause of Women', in Villiers, *The Case for Women's Suffrage*, p. 206.

30 G. Gould, 'New Tracts for the Times: The Democratic Plea', London, Cassell, 1912, p. 11.

31 *Votes for Women*, 15 November 1912.

32 Villiers, *The Case for Women's Suffrage*, p. 214.

33 See G. A. Aldred, *For Communism: A Communist Manifesto Defining the Workers' Struggle and the Need of a New Communist International, with a History of the Anti-parliamentary Movement, 1860–1935*, Glasgow, Kirkwood Press, 1935, pp. 90–5.

34 ibid., p. 90.

35 ibid., p. 15.

36 Rev. R. J. Campbell, 'Women's Suffrage and the Social Evil', a speech delivered at Queen's Hall, 7 December 1907, London, Men's League for Women's Suffrage, 1909, pp. 4–5.

37 C. Pateman, *The Sexual Contract*, Cambridge, Polity Press, 1988, pp. 79–80.
38 T. J. Haslam, 'Women's Suffrage from a Masculine Standpoint': an address by Thomas Haslam in Dublin and Cork, Dublin, the Irish Women's Suffrage and Local Government Association, the Ormond Printing Company, 1906, p. 16.
39 J. Masefield, 'My Faith in Woman Suffrage', a speech delivered at Queen's Hall, 14 February 1910, London, the Woman's Press, 1913, p. 9.
40 ibid., p. 3.
41 ibid., p. 5.
42 Campbell, 'Women's Suffrage and the Social Evil', p. 4.
43 ibid.
44 I. O. Ford, *Women and Socialism*, London, Independent Labour Party, Rydal Press, 1904, p. 9.
45 Sussman, *Manhood and Masculine Politics*, p. 11.
46 A. Burton, *Burdens of History: British Feminism, Indian Women and Imperial Culture 1865–1915*, Chapel Hill, NC, University of North Carolina Press, 1994, pp. 18–19.
47 ibid., pp. 5–18.
48 T. J. Haslam, 'The Rightful Claims of Women', an address delivered by Thomas J. Haslam, Mansion House, Dublin, the Ormond Printing Company, 1906, p. 4.
49 R. Kabbani, *Imperial Fictions: Europe's Myths of the Orient*, London, Pandora, 1988, p. 78.
50 L. Housman, 'Articles of Faith in the Freedom of Women', London, A. C. Fitfield, 1910, p. 13.
51 See Burton, *Burdens of History*, pp. 41–52.
52 ibid., p. 209.
53 Housman, 'Articles of Faith', p. 13.
54 Burton, *Burdens of History*, p. 28.
55 See J. D. Rees, Hansard Commons Debates, 27 April 1908, 4th series, vol. CLXXV, col. 238.
56 Haslam, 'The Rightful Claims of Women', p. 4.
57 S. Kingsley Kent, *Making Peace: The Reconstruction of Gender in Interwar Britain*, Princeton, NJ, Princeton University Press, 1993, pp. 23–6.
58 Hansard House of Lords Debates, 19 December 1917, 5th series, vol. XXVII, col. 278.
59 Hansard House of Lords Debates, 10 January 1918, 5th series, vol. XXVII, col. 473.
60 Hansard Commons Debates, 19 June 1917, 5th series, vol. XCIV, col. 1659.
61 ibid., col. 1660.
62 Pugh, *Women's Suffrage*, pp. 32–5.
63 Kingsley Kent, *Making Peace*, pp. 91–2.
64 Pankhurst, *The Suffragette Movement*, p. 606.
65 F. W. S. Craig (ed.), *British Electoral Facts 1832–1987*, Aldershot, Parliamentary Research Services, Gower 1989, p. 78.
66 Pankhurst, *The Suffragette Movement*, pp. 606–7.

67 S. Koven in A. Parker *et al.* (eds), *Nationalisms and Sexualities*, London, Routledge, 1992, p. 383.

68 L. Housman, 'The Moving Spirit of Womanhood: Notes of a Lecture June 1914', published, with other lectures, by the Theosophical Society, in *Theosophical Ideals and the Immediate Future*, London, the Theosophical Publishing Society, 1914, p. 36.

69 Parker, *Nationalisms and Sexualities*, p. 383.

70 See J. E. Cronin, *The Politics of State Expansion: War, State and Society in Twentieth-Century Britain*, London, Routledge, 1991, p. 25.

71 Rev. C. S. Horne, 'A Speech Delivered at a Demonstration in Queen's Hall', 26 January 1909, Men's League for Women's Suffrage, 1909, p. 10.

Chapter 7

Citizens, Scotsmen, 'bairns'

Manly politics and women's suffrage in the Northern Men's Federation, 1913–20

Claire Eustance

On 18 July 1913, passers-by in Downing Street in London witnessed a demonstration in support of women's suffrage. Although hardly an unusual occurrence by this time, what made this deputation distinct from others, was that it consisted of approximately forty local government dignitaries. These men, who were mostly from Glasgow and Edinburgh, had unsuccessfully attempted to meet the Prime Minister to put their case in favour of granting women the parliamentary vote. A report in *The Globe* captured the novelty of the event:

> There was a Scottish invasion at Downing-street [*sic*] this morning. Its main feature was the unique spectacle of a couple of men being allowed to deliver speeches from the´doorstep of the Prime Minister's residence.[1]

Scores of reports were printed that contained variations on these themes, and with different degrees of support and disdain. Overwhelmingly, media interest focused on cynical references to Asquith's refusal to receive the deputation, and many reports were accompanied by photographs (Plate 7) that emphasized the visual impact of a deputation of men milling around in Downing Street.[2] Unlike so many deputations of women activists before them, no members of this deputation were arrested, and shortly afterwards they left the vicinity.

The actions of this deputation of 'Northern Men' were certainly not the first of this kind by men. In particular, the Men's League for Women's Suffrage (MLWS) had made use of petitions to ministers and lobbying since the society's formation in 1907. Nevertheless the sight of these 'elderly gentlemen', who were 'strangers to the streets of London', provoked unprecedented coverage and comment.[3]

Plate 7 The Northern Men's Federation in Downing Street, July 1913.
By permission of The British Library

Ironically, as the Men's League for Women's Suffrage *Monthly* remarked, their failure to see Asquith was 'the solitary male effort for Women's Suffrage which has received adequate notice in the Press'.[4]

One reason for the press interest lay in the heightened tensions over women's suffrage, which were manifested in the increasingly militant incidents associated with the campaign. Women – and some men – had been forcibly fed, and generally the arguments of supporters and opponents of the campaign were becoming ever more vehement. Militant women were subjected to vicious accusations of being hysterical, and unsexed, and as Holton's and Balshaw's chapters demonstrate, there had been cases of violent treatment and discrimination towards male campaigners. However, it was in this highly tense climate that public men from Scotland chose to publicize their support for the campaign for women's enfranchisement.

This chapter explores the motivation behind the decision of these men to call on the Prime Minister in July 1913, and the subsequent activities of the Northern Men's Federation for Women's Suffrage (NMF) until shortly after women over 30 first voted in 1918. The federation members' actions and arguments provide a way of understanding how these men's images of themselves as citizens and Scotsmen connected with their support of female enfranchisement. The chapter will demonstrate how their apparently straightforward emphasis on the logic and justice of equality between men and women, exposed conflicting attitudes to, and critiques of, manly behaviour towards women, and politics more generally.

The motivating force behind the July deputation of 'Northern Men' was the women's suffrage activist, and former actress, Maud Arncliffe Sennett. Born in 1862 into a well-off, Conservative family, Arncliffe Sennett's experiences as an actress and then as an owner of a manufacturing business, distinguished her from other women of her background and generation. A married woman by 1906, she was attracted to women's suffrage after hearing Millicent Garrett Fawcett speak, and joined the National Union of Women's Suffrage Societies (NUWSS). Shortly afterwards Arncliffe Sennett endorsed militancy and briefly joined the Women's Social and Political Union (WSPU). In 1908, unhappy with the autocratic attitudes in the WSPU, Arncliffe Sennett joined the Women's Freedom League (WFL), and served for two years on its National Executive Committee before once again resigning. Although Arncliffe Sennett was also a member of the Actresses' Franchise League, by 1911 she was working, in her words, as a 'free lance' campaigner.[5] Nevertheless, her aptitude for public speaking and her popularity on suffrage platforms had brought her into contact with many men and women who supported women's suffrage.

The funeral of WSPU activist Emily Wilding Davison, in Morpeth in July 1913, marked the beginning of Arncliffe Sennett's involvement with male supporters from Scotland. (Davison died from injuries sustained following her protest at the Derby.) It was here that she met Edinburgh businessman Alexander Orr and his wife, after they had travelled down to the ceremony. The profound shock following Davison's death, possibly compounded by spurious comments from some quarters of the press, had apparently convinced men like Orr that it was time to do more to press for an immediate women's suffrage measure.[6] Arncliffe Sennett was urged by Orr to visit Scotland to enlist the support of male voters for her plans to march on Parliament.[7] With characteristic decisiveness Arncliffe Sennett agreed, and with the help of two Edinburgh sisters and WFL members, Jessie and Nannie Brown, she moved swiftly through informal networks of councillors in Edinburgh, and subsequently in Glasgow, gaining pledges of support from them to join a men's deputation to London. Arncliffe Sennett's original intention to get more men to demonstrate actively both their support for women's suffrage and also their indignation at the passing of the 'Cat and Mouse' Act, found steady encouragement, and during her visit to Scotland the nucleus was formed of what was later to become the Northern Men's Federation for Women's Suffrage (NMF).[8]

The men who responded to Arncliffe Sennett's appeals constituted a formidable and impressive group, and many had a long history of public service in Scotland. There were approximately 200 members of the NMF in Glasgow and Edinburgh by July 1914, and all were in possession of at least one parliamentary vote.[9] At least forty were councillors and bailies from Edinburgh and Glasgow, while others had distinguished themselves on trades councils or as magistrates. The election of these men to public office personified a trend in larger Scottish cities towards the election of professional men, retailers and 'working-men's representatives' in place of more wealthy middle-class industrialists.[10]

The most active members of the NMF between 1913 and 1918 were drawn from Scotland's middle classes. Born and educated in Scotland, most were married or widowed businessmen or professionals, and their numbers included a tea-rooms proprietor, a solicitor, an architect, and a writer and poet.[11] Their political interests were mixed across Conservative, Liberal and Socialist parties in Scotland.[12] The incidence of such cross-party alliances reflected a tendency among many male supporters at this time not to locate women's suffrage within any one party doctrine. As Henry Harben, JP stated in his speech at one of the first NMF meetings in November 1913, 'to grant votes to women was the logical outcome of the principles of all political parties alike'.[13]

It is likely that many of those who agreed to take part in the deputation to London had formed their opinions about women's suffrage long before Arncliffe Sennett's visit in 1913. As far back as 1882, Edinburgh's town council had passed a resolution in favour of women's suffrage, and this support was re-emphasized in debates in both Glasgow's council and Edinburgh's in subsequent years.[14] Moreover, as Leah Leneman has shown, by 1913 there was vibrant and organized support for women's suffrage among Scots, and this was manifested in numerous branches of women's suffrage societies and some men's societies.[15]

Particular stress was placed by NMF members on the liberal notion that women's skills and attributes were of equal importance in society to men's, and no just reasons could be given for denying women the vote based on their character. In anticipation of the July 1913 deputation to the Prime Minister, a booklet was produced containing the speeches the men planned to make to Asquith. One member of the deputation, W. Cuthbertson, a JP from Edinburgh, made the case that women should have the vote because of their 'intelligence', 'patriotism' and 'ability'. More revealing still was the language he used in making his plea:

> we, the citizens of no mean cities, approach you with all the manliness that in us lies – manliness stirred in us by the love we bear our sisters, our daughters, and our wives – to ask you to bring forward such a measure as may make for the freedom of women.[16]

Here Cuthbertson made one of very few direct references to the manly characters of himself and his colleagues. This extract indicates how masculine identity was intrinsically bound up with citizenship. In emphasizing their status as voting citizens, Cuthbertson had drawn on a number of characteristics associated with ideals of late Victorian manliness: dignity, tenacity and independence.[17] Furthermore, his reference to the welfare and interests of female family members epitomized middle-class male chivalrous and protective attitudes towards respectable women. Cuthbertson's was not an isolated voice, and the acceptance of patriarchal family relationships was confirmed in other speeches written by deputation members.[18]

The formation of a deputation in support of women's suffrage on these terms, was an expression of their understanding of what constituted appropriate manly political conduct. However, by refusing to meet the deputation in July 1913, Asquith had rejected any acknowledgement of the 'Northern Men's' status as autonomous, influential citizens – he had also undermined their manliness. It was these slights towards the respectable councillors and bailies from Scotland that captured the interest of the press, even more than the subject of their demands. Asquith's treatment of the deputation was the focus for bailie James Alston's anger when he declared on the steps in Downing Street, 'We shall insist upon our rights . . . and urge upon our representatives in Parliament to defend our rights.'[19] However, matters were not improved by the disinterested, somewhat mocking, reception the deputation received from the majority of Scottish MPs at a subsequent meeting at the House of Commons.[20] Geo. N. Barnes MP, in an article in Glasgow's socialist paper *Forward*, went as far as to call it 'a waste of time', adding that it had 'merely irritated most who took part'.[21] Although it was their support for women's suffrage that had initially motivated the 'Northern Men', their treatment by Westminster politicians had exposed, and caused them to defend, their self-image as 'manly', dignified, voting citizens.

The depth of feeling about the great insult the deputation had been subjected to, can be located in prior developments in Scottish municipal affairs. From the 1860s, municipal corporations in Edinburgh and, particularly, Glasgow had been held in relatively high esteem by the residents of these cities. Furthermore, these comparatively representative councils contrasted with the numbers of Scottish men who held the parliamentary franchise at that time. Even after 1884, only three out of five men in Scotland could vote, compared with two out of three in England and Wales.[22] Although there was a subsequent shift towards a greater emphasis on Parliament, it is apparent that even in the twentieth century, municipal affairs still had greater relevance to many Scottish people's lives than distant Westminster, especially since a good many Scottish constituencies were held by English men.[23] The bailies and councillors on the deputation in July 1913 certainly appeared self-consciously to cherish their civic status in Scotland, yet it was this that was so summarily ignored by the politicians at Westminster.

The lack of respect implicit in the responses to the deputation also touched nerves connected to a sense of Scottish pride. Tangible threads of cultural nationalism were evident in many celebrations of Scottish culture in the early twentieth century, and one member of the deputation, the writer and poet John Wilson McLaren, was particularly sensitive to how Scottish pride had been insulted.[24] He expressed his dissatisfaction in a verse of the poem he later wrote in commemoration of the first NMF deputation to London:

> We've come from the North, and the heather's on fire,
> To fight for the women – our only desire;
> At last we've been roused thro' the treachery shown
> By knaves at Westminster – the knaves we disown![25]

In subsequent years the collective voices of men like Cuthbertson and McLaren rose in growing critiques of corrupt government from Westminster. They lamented not only its treatment of women, but also its disregard for the value of voting men's – in this case, Scottish men's – opinions. Potentially, the issue of women's suffrage had opened up an alternative, non-party avenue for these 'Northern Men' to criticize prevailing systems of government.

The 'Northern Men's' experiences in London, although frustrating and even deemed humiliating by some of their countrymen, were nevertheless invigorating. After their return to Scotland, proposals by Maud Arncliffe Sennett to form an organization of northern voting men to bring further pressure to bear on the Liberal government, were adopted. In the original proposal, Arncliffe Sennett had planned to establish branches all over the north of England and in Scotland. However, of those that were formed the strongest were in Glasgow, Edinburgh and on the Scottish borders at Berwick-on-Tweed.[26]

The principal features of the federation's constitution as drawn up by Maud Arncliffe Sennett, were comparable with a number of other suffrage societies. Clauses included a commitment to act outside of party interests, and an adherence to constitutional methods. The distinguishing criterion of membership was that all members held the parliamentary franchise in order that they could bring pressure to bear on their parliamentary representatives. A commitment to militancy was not included in the constitution, and Arncliffe Sennett justified this by stating that because members had votes, there could be no alternative to lawful actions.[27] However, this statement merely confirmed attitudes among many NMF members that militancy was neither advisable nor desirable.

Although a non-party stance was common practice in many suffrage societies, the case of the NMF may not be so straight-forward. Given that a high proportion of members would have continued to adhere to their party interests in their municipal activities, it does open up questions as to whether this commitment was merely lip service or a genuine attempt to side-line their party differences. On one level, it reflected a belief that women's suffrage was a moral issue, rather than a party political one. However, on another, the playing-down of party politics was indicative of NMF members' disillusionment with the present Liberal government. Although the nature and breadth of this criticism varied, men defining themselves as either Liberal, Conservative or Socialist found common ground in their condemnation of the government trickery and deceit over women's suffrage.

Although there were a number of similarities between the NMF and other men's societies, the NMF was distinct in terms of the degree of involvement of women. Maud Arncliffe Sennett, although based in London, acted as honorary organizer/president through the NMF's existence, and from the beginning she determinedly placed herself at the centre of decision-making processes. She later recalled in her autobiography, *The Child* (1938), that 'having had experience of committees' (a reference to her disillusionment with the WFL), she 'asked the men to do without one'.[28] The apparent willingness shown by members of the federation to subordinate themselves to undemocratic authority – particularly that of a woman – ran contrary to the 'Northern Men's' prior vigorous defence of their autonomy and manly dignity while in London.

There were a number of occasions throughout the history of the federation when members appeared to put unprecedented amounts of trust in Maud Arncliffe Sennett, and an interesting emotional rela-tionship developed between her and the male membership. In public, the proud, dignified 'Northern Men' put a great deal of emphasis on their forthright convictions and manly dignity, and yet, towards 'their founder' they displayed unstinting, even passionate devotion. Following a visit by Arncliffe Sennett to Scotland in November 1913, John Wilson McLaren composed a poem to commemorate her trip. It overflowed with admiring references to her 'Self-sacrificing, noble soul!' and one verse in particular characterized an intense leader–follower relationship:

And had nae fear, tho' ye're awa'
We'll haud till't day and nicht,
We're bonnie fechters, ilka ane,
    And that ye brawly ken,
And we're out for Votes for Women –
Your bairns – the Northern Men![29]
                    [My emphasis]

McLaren's admiration of Arncliffe Sennett was not confined to his verse. On the contrary, his correspondence, and that of other members, contained similar accolades and expressions of deference to their president, which intensified over the years.

This relationship between Arncliffe Sennett and members of the federation was mutually sustaining. On most occasions after her visit to Scotland in late 1913, Arncliffe Sennett's letters of advice and instruction to the federation membership used the address from McLaren's poem, and began, 'Dear "Bairns"'.[30] Although no direct reference was made to her motives for such a maternal form of address, it is possible that because in relationships between women and men there were no acknowledged precedents of women officially dictating political issues to men, Arncliffe Sennett attempted to mould her relation with the membership into a maternal one. As Tosh comments in Chapter 1, maternal affection, warmth and emotional openness were acceptable to constructions of manliness, as long as they were strictly demarcated from male behaviour.

Yet, the most committed men in the federation appeared to have no difficulty in reconciling their masculine identities with Arncliffe Sennett's leadership, and many used the term 'bairn' in their correspondence with her. However, their attitude towards Arncliffe Sennett was an exception, and no other women were singled out by federation members for such deference. On the contrary, a discreet silence was maintained regarding the day-to-day involvement of Nannie Brown, the Edinburgh federation secretary, in what was officially an organization of voting men.

In order to justify having a female leader, it is possible that the NMF members identified Arncliffe Sennett as a maternal figure so as to prevent any impression that the relationship could be of a sexual nature. Consequently, their acceptance and use of the title 'bairns' could be construed as a sentimental, even poignant expression of respect and deference. However, given the ambivalence towards Edinburgh-based, Nannie Brown, it is apparent that the NMF members' deference to Arncliffe Sennett was possible only because she lived in London and was therefore not in a position to influence their daily lives. Another crucial counterpoint to NMF members' attitudes towards Arncliffe Sennett, and any potential undermining of their masculine self-image, was their knowledge that she was still ultimately an unenfranchised woman, and in no official or profound position of power over them. Their acceptance of her position was voluntary, and as such she represented no threat to either their status or their manly autonomy. Moreover, far more significant in validating masculine self-image was the respect and acknowledgement of other men.[31] Arncliffe Sennett's position was in direct contrast to Herbert Asquith, who as one of the most powerful men in Britain, *was* able to undermine their status, something that was clearly demonstrated in Westminster in July 1913.

Evidence that gender roles were not profoundly subverted by those involved in the NMF was apparent in the type and range of activities undertaken. These reflected a telling gendered division of labour as Arncliffe Sennett and Nannie Brown were responsible for a great deal, although not all, of the mundane work of organizing and correspondence. While some men, notably Edinburgh member Andrew Sloan and Robert Gaul from Berwick-on-Tweed, occupied their time writing letters of protest, particularly about the treatment of suffrage prisoners, others were content simply to add their names to letters written to ministers and government departments by Arncliffe Sennett.[32] Although their involvement certainly extended beyond symbolic gestures of support, the federation's distinguished members generally preferred to direct their energies into making speeches at public meetings, or intervening in other political campaigns, notably the Leigh Burghs by-election in February 1914.[33]

Nevertheless, the willingness of so many of Scotland's influential public citizens to support women's suffrage publicly was unprecedented, and drew various responses from fellow campaigners, opponents and sections of the press. Whilst other suffrage campaigners were on the whole very supportive, the apparent contradictions between the members' activities in support of what had become an immensely controversial issue, and their civic status, elicited criticism, even among sections of the press relatively sympathetic to women's demands. This led to a number of attacks on the federation, particularly in the period following the NMF London Convention and second attempt to meet with the Prime Minister in February 1914.

On this occasion more than 100 members of the federation in Scotland travelled down to London, including among their number the Lord Provost and Senior Magistrate of Glasgow.[34] Once again Asquith refused to meet them, and instead offered them an interview with his private secretary. The deputation refused, and in their subsequent speeches criticism of government ministers and MPs was unequivocal. James Alston emphasized the discourtesy to which they had once again been subjected. It was, he argued, a slight to the 'whole electorate of Glasgow'.[35] Edinburgh Labour councillor Gerald Crawford went further and poured scorn on those men who claimed to represent voters, calling members of the Cabinet 'puny piffling pigmies', and MPs 'creeping, crawling catchpennies'.[36] Crawford's choice of words directly challenged two fundamental tenets of the manliness of Britain's elected politicians, namely their independence and their integrity.

In Scotland, scathing reactions in the press to Crawford's comments highlighted the ways male supporters of women's suffrage were undermined and marginalized. One correspondent signing him/herself only as 'Variety', commented that Crawford's '*magnum opus*' might have 'been dubbed "quite smart" by the proud parents had it been invented by a boy of ten, but the newspaper-reading public in general and the writer in particular are . . . "fed up" with it'. The anonymous correspondent then offered his/her own scathing characterization of the male supporters in the federation as 'Trashy, travesting triflers' or alternatively 'Ranting, roaring rascals', and 'Petty, pattering prattlers'.[37]

Other attempts to undermine the actions of the members of the federation focused on their public positions, as well as their supposedly mild natures. A report in the *Edinburgh Evening Dispatch* picked up on another press report describing the members of the deputation as 'Scottish minor public men':

> These men at home are quiet, unassuming, inoffensive folk, never known to use an angry word, but always ready to turn the other cheek to the smiter. . . . It would be well that we enquire of these gentlemen on their return what strange afflatus descends upon them when in the Metropolis. . . . It is a great pity to see our townsmen like that. The subject appears too much for them. They should leave it to the 'major' public men.[38]

The language used was a barely disguised attempt to belittle the standing of the deputation, and to cast aspersions on its members' manliness. Other critics of the NMF's actions applied frameworks more usually associated with politically defined men, and blamed their actions on their party allegiances. Another anonymous correspondent to the *Edinburgh Evening Dispatch* accused the federation of consisting mostly of members of the Independent Labour Party and other socialist societies. These claims were hastily denied by Edinburgh secretary Nannie Brown, who in reply stressed the mixture of party interests among the membership, and how their conviction that women's suffrage was a just cause made them 'determined to work, even at the sacrifice of their party politics'.[39] Lastly, the furore included the often aired claim that male supporters advocated militant methods. It was left to Mabel McLaren, wife of Edinburgh member John Wilson McLaren, to proclaim their 'courage', and to assert that there 'are thousands of women to-day who feel proud of the Northern Men'.[40]

NMF members were not silent observers of the challenges to their intelligence, independence and dignity. On the contrary, Gerald Crawford had defended them by attacking the lack of such manly traits among women's suffrage opponents in Westminster. Another thrust of attack came in the form of accusations that the Liberal government was acting with contempt for democracy. This was translated into practical actions, and by March 1914 John Wilson McLaren claimed that he had received more than 150 pledges from Liberals that they would not in future support their anti-suffrage Liberal MP, Charles Lyell.[41] In the same year at a meeting organized under the auspices of the NMF, a resolution was passed which urged members to refuse any support to the Liberal Party, because it had not 'shown a sufficiently developed sense of honour' and was 'opposed to the interests of the Nation and clean government'.[42]

NMF members' disillusionments with the attitude of the Liberal Party towards women's suffrage had become inextricably linked with their anxieties about democracy in Britain. Because their consciousness of their masculinity was so closely linked to their investments in democracy, it is possible to see how attacks by NMF members on the Liberal government amounted to a critique of their manliness. As they saw it, those men who refused to endorse women's suffrage, particularly politicians in Westminster, were not upholding manly values and so deserved to be castigated and their positions of power challenged.

However, the federation members' critique of the system of

government only went so far. For these men, women's enfranchisement symbolized the right for men *and* women democratically
to alter conditions in society – it did not constitute any desire
radically to reappraise gendered relations of power. The members of
the federation confined their attacks to anti-suffrage ministers and
MPs, and remained remarkably lacking in self-reflection about the
deeper ramifications of male-defined political and social dominance.
Because of this, the possibilities of alliances with those women's
suffrage societies like the Women's Freedom League (WFL) that had
begun to explore the potential for broader, explicitly feminist
campaigns were ultimately to be severely limited.[43]

The outbreak of the hostilities in August 1914 marked the beginning of a decline in the numbers of federation members actively
engaged in the suffrage cause. However, along with leaders of a
number of other suffrage societies, Maud Arncliffe Sennett pressed
supporters to continue the campaign.[44] In Edinburgh, the federation
responded by backing the work of the WFL and the newly established
Women's Emergency Corps. A meeting organized in November
1914 apparently signalled a new direction in federation members'
interests, when resolutions were passed demanding a weekly pension
for widows of men killed in the war. Additional calls to raise funds
in order to provide work for women made unemployed during the
war, connected broadly with other fund-raising efforts to alleviate
unemployment in the early stages of the fighting.[45] Stirred into action
after some months spent adjusting to the war, the Glasgow federation
passed similar resolutions at a meeting convened in the city in the
following January.[46]

Although members of the NMF endorsed these women-related
initiatives, it was Maud Arncliffe Sennett who was primarily responsible for drawing attention to them. Overwhelmingly, the resolutions and letters issued in the name of the NMF during the war were
written by her, often without direct reference to the membership,
although usually with their tacit agreement. The meetings that were
organized by the NMF members in Scotland after August 1914,
demonstrated how their anxieties about the war had affected their
work for women's suffrage. At an Edinburgh NMF meeting in July
1915 that was held to discuss the war, it was announced that the event
was 'non-contentious', and merely intended to 'demonstrate the near
relation of war to women and the need of unity between men and
women to avert war in the future'.[47]

During these early years of the war, the resolutions passed, and the speeches made, by NMF members were continuations of a chivalrous desire to protect the interests of women, while at the same time continuing to justify demands for their enfranchisement. Edinburgh federation member Councillor Graham made this clear in his speech to the July 1915 meeting, arguing that because of the 'sacrifices' women were required to make through the war, and their entry into industries, they were entitled to 'equality in affairs in the future'.[48] However, what now concerned them more was the practical impact of the war on the lives of all Glasgow's and Edinburgh's citizens. In particular, NMF councillors in Glasgow faced a volatile situation, produced partly by the vast movement of munitions workers into the poorer working-class districts of the city, which culminated in the rent strikes first undertaken in May 1915.[49] James Alston, a stalwart member of the NMF since its formation, gave a great deal of support to the Glasgow rent strikers. His death from pneumonia in November 1915 was a sad loss to this campaign and a blow to the somewhat beleaguered NMF in the city.[50] Although middle-class businessman Robert Ferguson continued to co-ordinate the NMF, the number of NMF activities in Glasgow did not again reach the levels known before August 1914.

What was absent from the speeches and actions of the NMF membership, was the previous attacks on corrupt government. It is possible that the war against Germany had placed these criticisms in a new light, given the powerful messages put across that the war was being fought in order to defend British democracy. Certainly the conflict had a profound effect across Scotland, and there was a widespread response to calls to enlist, including from members of the NMF.[51] Even in the case of those who were above the required age limit, some had sons who went off to fight, and among the war casualties was the son of Glasgow secretary Robert Ferguson, and NMF member James Campbell, who was killed in action.[52]

Federation member and Edinburgh councillor Gerald Crawford was among the millions who volunteered for service before the introduction of conscription in 1916. Crawford, who had previously been opposed to war, was bitterly criticized by his constituents for his change of attitude. In an open letter to his electors he explained his belief that he had to act to bring the war closer to an end. It would, he stated, 'be a blow struck in the cause of humanity'.[53] Crawford's letter to Maud Arncliffe Sennett from an army training camp near York demonstrated that he continued to believe in women's suffrage, but also that his priorities had changed: 'I do not think the Suffrage Cause can ever go back now, but it is difficult to determine what may happen when the very foundation of society is in the melting pot.'[54]

John Wilson McLaren made his own tribute to Crawford in a lengthy poem printed in the *Leith Observer* in November 1915, which abounded with anti-German sentiments in what was the epitome of the patriotic fervour evident across much of Britain (at least in the early stages of the fighting). Moreover, McLaren's attitude towards Crawford's 'bravery' was indicative of the image, so ingrained in public consciousness, of the heroic fighting man, ready to defend his country, and, if necessary, to die.[55] At the other end of the spectrum of attitudes, there is no evidence of any organized federation opposition to the war among Edinburgh and Glasgow NMF members, although before his death James Alston had voiced his abhorrence of conscription.[56] Nevertheless, over the ensuing years, even the patriotic fervour of McLaren dulled into regret as the destruction continued and casualties increased.

Robert Gaul, a NMF member from Berwick-on-Tweed, was one of very few in the federation who was known to be a conscientious objector. There is no evidence to suggest that Gaul's pacifist views were publicly criticized by any other members of the federation, and he continued to work under the auspices of the NMF. Judging from a sharp increase in his correspondence with Maud Arncliffe Sennett, Gaul intensified his work for women's suffrage during the war, and he spent time corresponding on the subject in a local newspaper.[57] Interestingly, what emerged in the letters published on the subject in the *Berwick Advertiser*, were underlying changes in attitudes towards women's suffrage demands. Gaul was the focus of attacks from members of his own community, not because of his support for women's suffrage, but because of his failure to enter military service.[58] Such changes in attitude were apparent across Scotland, and by 1916 cautious but supportive comments in the press, in addition to women's suffrage 'conversions' like that of the Scottish MP Charles Lyell, marked the end of widespread attacks on the characters of both female and male supporters.[59]

By mid-1916, the impact of the war, and Maud Arncliffe Sennett's continued presence in London, had served to impair communication between the members in Scotland and their president. Particularly in Edinburgh, members had begun to show a belated interest in the democratic organization of the federation, and had proposed that they form an Executive Committee (an earlier attempt in 1914 had been abandoned). Arncliffe Sennett responded cautiously but positively. However, shortly afterwards she tendered her resignation as president.[60] If any proof were required by Arncliffe Sennett of her continued exalted status among the members, the letters she subsequently received provided this. Nannie Brown's telegram following a meeting in Edinburgh telling Arncliffe Sennett that the 'Bairns refused to consider her resignation', culminated in her decision to remain.[61] Although this incident demonstrated continuing devotion to their president, it nevertheless prevented the membership from developing more of their own initiatives. Instead, Arncliffe Sennett continued to write letters on behalf of the federation, and Robert Ferguson signed fifty blank sheets of paper in order to enable her to do so. Although an Edinburgh-based Executive Committee was formed, its members continued to endorse Arncliffe Sennett's correspondence campaigns, and it was not until 1917 that the committee drew up an agreement stipulating the conditions Arncliffe Sennett was required to adhere to when writing on their behalf.[62]

The year 1916 was of crucial importance to the resolution of the women's suffrage issue. In spite of continuing unease between Arncliffe Sennett and some members, rapid progress in Westminster brought NMF members back into touch with the campaign. In August 1916 a final deputation of 'Northern Men' attempted once more to meet the Prime Minister. Once again this was denied but, in a more conciliatory tone, the NMF was invited to express its views by letter. Undeterred, ten members of the federation and Arncliffe Sennett travelled to London, and on 18 August managed to enter No. 10 Downing Street where they were eventually met by the Chief Whip.[63] The deputation's speeches conveyed the same demands for justice and democracy, previously expressed, but on this occasion party political interests also emerged. For example, Labour bailie Mr Hamilton Brown raised the issue of equal pay and Mr Campbell, president of the Edinburgh Trades Council, emphasized the interests of women newly entering industry.[64]

With far fewer members, and a smaller proportion of councillors and bailies, Arncliffe Sennett's subsequent claims that this deputation had been the most successful, were rather overstated – except perhaps in the sense that the men who had made the journey from Scotland were at last given a degree of the respect they had demanded from Westminster. The promised concessions on women's suffrage that followed later that year, owed more to changes in attitudes brought about by the war and the campaigns of other women's suffrage societies, than to the impact of the federation.[65] Moreover, the absence of any representative of the NMF in the much larger women's suffrage deputation to the Prime Minister high-lighted the marginality of the federation to the women's suffrage movement in these crucial years.

The difficulties inherent in the federation's finding a role in women-oriented campaigns and reforms emerged clearly during the remainder of 1916. During this time Arncliffe Sennett, with the support of federation members, focused her attentions more fully on challenging the clauses in the Defence of the Realm Act (DORA) which amounted to regulated legalized prostitution.[66] Towards the end of 1916, Arncliffe Sennett presented her 'Manifesto on Venereal Disease' to the membership. In it she proposed that all brothels should be raided and the names of all the women and their male customers exposed. Arncliffe Sennett also moved that the 'Rubber Stores' where men could obtain contraceptives, should be closed by Act of Parliament.[67] As it later emerged, although NMF members had agreed to endorse the 'Manifesto' out of loyalty to their president, many were profoundly unhappy about its content. For the first time Arncliffe Sennett did not receive a rapturous reception when she subsequently visited Scotland.[68] It was left to the wife of one of the members to convey delicately to Arncliffe Sennett the NMF's objections to the appearance that they were attempting to censor other men's behaviour, and the implication that they 'were not as other men'.[69] The responses to the 'Manifesto' were an indication of the limit of NMF men's support both for their presid-ent's views and to measures affecting women generally. This was a crucial juncture where the members had shown their failure to contemplate any fundamental gendered evaluation of male behaviour and men's culpability in women's subordination.

Furthermore, their responses to the limited measure granting the vote to women over 30 demonstrated that for the men in the NMF, democracy overrode any other issue. Although the legislation was generally welcomed, member Hamilton Brown's harsh words to-wards the 'jelly fish ladies' who had agreed to the partial measure were echoed by other members.[70] Offended at being isolated from the final negotiations between a joint committee of suffrage societies and the government, Arncliffe Sennett and the federation members took some comfort in seeing themselves as one of the few suffrage organizations that had remained committed to the principle of equal suffrage.

Similarly cut adrift from the joint 'suffrage victory' celebrations, the NMF staged its own commemoration of the suffrage measure. At a dinner in Edinburgh in March 1918, which was attended by Arncliffe Sennett and members of her family, her achievements and dedication were celebrated by her most consistent and faithful supporters.[71] As she later remarked, 'What care I about the snubs of the London leaders who leave me out of all their "celebrations". Have I not my "Bairns" and the generous devotion of each other and of me and my little efforts.'[72]

However, the celebrations and demonstrations of 'devotion' were soon to be eclipsed by the impact of the franchise reforms and the broader ramifications of the devastating war. Reflecting on the need to reform society, Edinburgh NMF member John McMichael had commented to Arncliffe Sennett, 'Don't imagine for one moment that "Votes for Women" is going to save the world from wickedness and folly. No – it needs something greater and better and deeper than that.'[73] The response of members to the pressure to bring about changes in society was to reinvest in the political programmes and philosophies of the political parties, something that had been apparent during the final NMF deputation to London in 1916. In fact, the 1918 Representation of the People Act, in creating a mass working-class electorate for the first time, had galvanized all the political parties. In Scotland in particular, which had seen a proportionately greater rise in the number of electors, none of the political parties could ignore the need to secure men's votes and those of women over 30.[74] Amid such domination of party interests and concerns, the non-party constitution of the NMF must have seemed relatively unimportant by comparison.

Nevertheless, the comradeship among members and their commitment to the NMF that had developed during the preceding four years were not dismissed lightly. Some members seriously explored the possibilities of maintaining the federation as a campaigning body, although, significantly, the focus was no longer exclusively on women's disabilities. First, prolonged discussions took place concerning Arncliffe Sennett's proposals to transform the federation into the Northern Men's Political Federation to work for 'social reform' on non-party lines.[75] Second, Arncliffe Sennett drafted a 'Land Charter' devoted to reforming laws relating to inheritance, mortgages and leasehold, and sent it up to the members for their approval.[76] However, the responses to both of these proposals highlighted profound political divisions among the now depleted membership, and Gerald Crawford, who had returned from active service, was not alone in his call for the federation to follow socialism. This in turn drew the response from John Wilson McLaren that 'several of the "bairns" seemed to have got side-tracked' because they were not *free* men but tied to some Party', yet his comments barely disguised his own preferences for Liberalism.[77]

The plethora of letters Arncliffe Sennett received from federation members in 1918 was testimony to the lack of a common political agenda among the membership. Mutual beliefs in women's suffrage had kept the federation united, but the resolution of this issue in the destructive climate of war, had exposed the limitations of the non-party objectives first adopted in 1913. By the end of the war in November 1918, the federation had stopped holding meetings, and the balance of funds was finally passed over to the WFL's treasurer, Elizabeth Knight, in September 1919.[78] The rapid changes that had taken place during these months not only confirmed the party political differences among NMF members, but also exposed the ideological gulf between NMF members and those non-party women's organizations that continued to campaign for female equality after 1918. Certainly no NMF members acted on Knight's suggestion that they join the non-party WFL and adopt its reforming feminist programme.[79]

Many ex-members of the NMF instead devoted themselves to what was deemed more conventional male political activity. In December 1918, NMF member William Graham had been elected to Parliament as a Labour member for Central Edinburgh. Graham was one of those who continued to advocate equal suffrage rights for women, and in appreciation of this, gained a place on the Six Point Group's 'White List' of supportive MPs.[80] Another NMF member, Adam Millar, stood unsuccessfully as a Labour candidate for the Edinburgh Town Council in 1919, although he was subsequently elected and served throughout the 1920s.[81] John Wilson McLaren, who had helped Millar's opponent to victory in 1919, rejoined the Liberal Party and was himself elected as a 'progressive Liberal' to the Edinburgh Council in 1920.[82] Gerald Crawford left Edinburgh to work as an election agent for the Labour Party in Manchester, although he subsequently returned and also won a seat on the Edinburgh Town Council in 1926.[83]

During the 1920s, there was no recurrence of the concerted non-party campaigns on behalf of women on a par with those undertaken by the NMF between 1913 and 1918. On the contrary, during the decade, those NMF campaigners who now served on the town councils in Edinburgh and Glasgow became embroiled in municipal power struggles between the Liberal and the Socialist factions. Although some maintained a correspondence with Arncliffe Sennett, this was limited to reflections on past work. Edinburgh councillor Adam Millar was one NMF member who did continue to devote some attention to the social and economic concerns of women in municipal affairs. However, his comment to a Women's Co-operative Guild meeting in 1926 that 'there was great scope for women's activities in public life' was indicative of prevailing views that women no longer laboured under any fundamental gender inequality.[84] The reasons for this lack of awareness of the barriers women continued to experience, can be located in NMF members' attitudes towards women's suffrage in preceding years. Women's suffrage had been a matter of principle, of democracy and of justice, and supporting it was an expression of their chivalrous attitudes towards the female sex. The fulfilment of women's suffrage was envisaged not as the beginning of a transformation of gender relations in society, but as its culmination.

Nevertheless, the actions of the NMF in supporting women's suffrage, and the real questions raised about party interests, democracy, and the accountability of politicians and leaders in Westminster, do illuminate previously unacknowledged concerns within the male political establishment in the heated climate of British politics before and during the First World War. The crisis over women's political status produced related anxieties about men's political status and 'manly' political behaviour. However, when the focus of this crisis was deemed resolved following the 1918 franchise reforms, so connected anxieties about 'manly politics' were silenced.

A final comment belongs to John Wilson McLaren, who wrote to Maud Arncliffe Sennett shortly after his election success in August 1920. McLaren remarked that he often saw the 'Bailie and Town Councillor "Bairns"' while on council business. He wrote, 'We are a happy family and in the smoke room, often speak of the guid old days!'[85] The irony of these men discussing their experiences of the suffrage campaign in an environment that continued to be closed to women, exemplifies what was both exceptional – and conventional – about the Northern Men's Federation for Women's Suffrage.

NOTES

1 *The Globe*, 18 July 1913, Maud Arncliffe Sennett Collection of Press Cuttings, Pamphlets, Leaflets and Letters on Women's Suffrage (hereafter referred to as MAS), British Library, vol. 25, p. 17.
2 See MAS, vol. 25, pp. 14–19.
3 Unknown press cutting, MAS, vol. 25, p. 19.
4 Men's League for Women's Suffrage, *Monthly*, August–September 1913, p. 215.
5 M. Arncliffe Sennett, *The Child. Autobiographical Reminiscences*, London, published privately by C. W. Daniel Co., 1938, pp. 17–18, 53–66. By the time Arncliffe Sennett wrote her autobiography, she defined herself as a Liberal.
6 See *Forward*, 14 June 1913, p. 4 for comments on coverage of Davison's accident in the *Glasgow Herald*.
7 Arncliffe Sennett, *The Child*, pp. 85–6.
8 ibid., pp. 85–90.
9 No exact membership figures are available. *The Haddington Advertiser*, 31 July 1914, noted that the Edinburgh Federation had 160 members, and *Forward*, 20 September 1913, p. 6, reported that at the inaugural meeting of the Glasgow Federation, 40 members enrolled. See MAS, vol. 26, p. 45, and vol. 25, pp. 40–1.
10 N. Morgan and R. Trainor, 'The Dominant Classes', in W. H. Fraser and R. J. Morris (eds), *People and Society in Scotland Vol. II, 1830–1914*, Edinburgh, John Donald Publishers, 1990, pp. 128–9.
11 For biographies of John William Chesser, John Cowan Drummond, Edward Rosslyn Mitchell, John Rusk, James Stewart, John Wilson McLaren and James Wilson, see George Eyre-Todd, *Who's Who in Glasgow in 1909*, Glasgow and London, Gowans & Gray, 1909; *Scottish Biographies, 1938*, Glasgow, E. J. Thurston, 1938; A. Eddington, *Edinburgh and the Lothians at the Opening of the Twentieth Century* (1904), Edinburgh, Peter Bell, 1984.
12 N. Brown, *Edinburgh Evening Dispatch*, 17 March 1914, p. 4.
13 *Forward*, 6 November 1913, p. 6. For Harben, see our Introduction.
14 L. Leneman, *A Guid Cause. The Women's Suffrage Movement in Scotland*, Aberdeen, Aberdeen University Press, 1991, pp. 19, 25–6.
15 ibid., *passim*.
16 *For Women's Suffrage. Scotchmen at Downing Street, Speeches by the Delegates, July 18th 1913*, p. 10, MAS, vol. 25, pp. 18/19.
17 For further discussion about masculinity, and late Victorian manliness, see John Tosh, 'What should Historians do with Masculinity? Reflections on Nineteenth-century Britain', *History Workshop Journal* 38 (Autumn 1994), p. 183 (pp. 179–201), and *passim*.
18 *For Women's Suffrage*, pp. 11–13.
19 Reported in *Edinburgh Evening News*, 18 July 1913, MAS, vol. 25, p. 15.
20 Letter from A. Barrow to M. Arncliffe Sennett, 8 September 1913, MAS, vol. 25, pp. 40–1.
21 *Forward*, 26 July 1913, p. 1.
22 M. Lynch, *Scotland. A New History*, London, Century, 1991, p. 416.

23 C. Harvie, *Scotland and Nationalism. Scottish Society and Politics, 1707–1994* (1977), London, Routledge, 1994, p. 18.

24 See comments of Morgan and Trainor, 'The Dominant Classes', in Fraser and Morris (eds), *People and Society*, p. 124. J. Wilson McLaren was the author of a number of books and plays on Scottish life and culture: see *Scottish Biographies*, p. 497.

25 'Justice For Ever! War Song' by J. Wilson McLaren, MAS, vol. 26, pp. 4–5.

26 Leneman suggests that a sense of Scottish national solidarity was responsible for the strength of the NMF branches in Scotland. See, L. Leneman, 'Northern Men and Votes for Women', *History Today* 41 (December 1991), p. 41.

27 Policy of the Northern Men's Federation for Women's Suffrage, MAS, vol. 25, pp. 14–15.

28 Arncliffe Sennett, *The Child*, p. 97.

29 'To Mrs Arncliffe Sennett', MAS, vol. 25, pp. 78–9. Also published in *Votes for Women*, 12 December 1913.

30 For example, see MAS, vol. 27, pp. 12–13, 14–15. See also MAS, vols 25–8. In this record of the NMF campaign, Arncliffe Sennett often made notes referring to the devotion and 'faith' of her 'bairns'.

31 See J. Tosh, Chapter 1 of this collection.

32 Andrew Sloan to McKinnon Wood, MP, 23 July 1914, MAS, vol. 26, p. 87.

33 See, *Edinburgh Evening Dispatch*, 14 February 1914, p. 4, and James Alston to Arncliffe Sennett, 24 June 1914, MAS, vol. 26, pp. 38–9.

34 *Edinburgh Evening Dispatch*, 10 February 1914, p. 2, and 16 February 1914, p. 4. For details of Convention and deputation, see Arncliffe Sennett, *The Child*, pp. 100–5, and *The Scotsman*, 16 February 1914, MAS, vol. 26, p. 19.

35 *Edinburgh Evening Dispatch*, 16 February 1914, p. 4.

36 ibid.

37 ibid., 17 February 1914, p. 4, and 19 February 1914, p. 4.

38 ibid., 17 February 1914, p. 4.

39 ibid., 17 March 1914, p. 4. Brown also gave her estimate of the party allegiance of the membership in Edinburgh: Liberals 43, Unionists 27, ILP 16, other Socialists 6, Labour 22.

40 ibid., 13 March 1914, p. 4.

41 ibid., 19 March 1914, p. 2.

42 Resolution passed at meeting of Executive of NMF, 11 July 1914, MAS, vol. 26, pp. 44–5.

43 See C. Eustance, '"Daring To Be Free": the Evolution of Women's Political Identities in the Women's Freedom League, 1907–1930', University of York, DPhil, 1993, Chs 4–7.

44 M. Arncliffe Sennett, Pamphlet issued to the Northern Men on the outbreak of war, 14 August 1914, MAS, vol. 26, pp. 50–1.

45 *Edinburgh Evening News*, 23 November 1914, MAS, vol. 26, p. 48, and see C. Harvie, *No Gods and Precious Few Heroes, Scotland 1914–1980*, London, Edward Arnold, 1981, p. 11.

46 Passed at meeting, 13 January 1915, MAS, vol. 26, pp. 54–5.

47 *Edinburgh Evening Dispatch*, 12 July 1915, MAS, vol. 26, p. 66.
48 *Christian Science Monitor*, 24 August 1915, *ibid.*
49 Lynch, *Scotland. A New History*, pp. 424–5.
50 *Glasgow Herald*, 23 November 1915, MAS, vol. 26, p. 75.
51 Lynch, *Scotland. A New History*, pp. 422–3, and see Arncliffe Sennett's comments in MAS, vol. 26, p. 54
52 R. Ferguson to M. Arncliffe Sennett, 6 July 1918, MAS, vol. 28, pp. 126–7, and *Stirling Observer*, 24 July 1917, MAS, vol. 26, p. 50.
53 *Evening News*, 10 January 1916, MAS, vol. 26, p. 51.
54 G. Crawford to M. Arncliffe Sennett, n.d., MAS, vol. 26, p. 50–1.
55 *Leith Observer*, November 1915, MAS, vol. 26, p. 74. See also G. Dawson, *Soldier Heroes. British Adventure, Empire and the Imagining of Masculinities*, London and New York, Routledge, 1994, pp. 1, 56, and *passim*.
56 *Forward*, 27 November 1915, MAS, vol. 26, p. 77.
57 See MAS, vol. 27 [misc.], pp. 80, 86–7.
58 *Berwick Advertiser*, 30 March 1917, 5 April 1917, 12 April 1917, MAS, vol. 27 [misc.], p. 80.
59 *Edinburgh Evening Dispatch*, 8 August 1916, and J. Wilson McLaren, letter to *Evening News*, 8 November 1916, MAS, vol. 27, pp. 28–9, and p. 50.
60 M. Arncliffe Sennett to 'Bairns', 1 July 1916, MAS, vol. 27, pp. 12–13. See comments by Arncliffe Sennett, ibid., p. 13.
61 Letter to M. Arncliffe Sennett from NMF members, MAS, vol. 27, pp. 14–15.
62 MAS, vol. 27, pp. 44–5, and NMF statement, 22 January 1917, vol. 27 [misc.], p. 71.
63   MAS, vol. 27, pp. 29, 33–6.
64 *Manchester Guardian* [London edn], 19 August 1916, MAS, vol. 27, p. 40.
65 See S. S. Holton, *Feminism and Democracy. Women's Suffrage and Reform Politics in Britain, 1900–1918*, Cambridge, Cambridge University Press, 1988, pp. 116–50, for an account of women's suffrage activists' campaigns, 1914–17.
66 MAS, vol. 27, p. 46.
67 MAS, vol. 28, p. 34.
68 Report of Year July 1916–July 1917, MAS, vol. 27 [misc.], pp. 132–3, and Robert Ferguson to M. Arncliffe Sennett, 14 December 1916, MAS, vol. 27, n.p.
69 Arncliffe Sennett, *The Child*, p. 129.
70 Hamilton Brown to M. Arncliffe Sennett, 7 April 1917, MAS, vol. 27 [misc.], pp. 92–3.
71 MAS, vol. 28, pp. 16–19.
72 MAS, vol. 28, p. 16.
73 J. McMichael to M. Arncliffe Sennett, n.d., MAS, vol. 27, pp. 14–15.
74 Lynch, *Scotland. A New History*, p. 428.
75 M. Arncliffe Sennett to 'Bairns', n.d., MAS, vol. 28, pp. 70–1.
76 MAS, vol. 28, p. 18.

77 J. Wilson McLaren to M. Arncliffe Sennett, 21 July 1918, MAS, vol. 28, p. 26.
78 R. Ferguson to E. Knight, 25 September 1919, MAS, vol. 28, p. 125. (Balance £5s 4s 2d.)
79 E. Knight to R. Ferguson, 27 September 1919, MAS, vol. 28, pp. 124–5.
80 *Time and Tide*, 8 November 1922, reprinted in D. Spender, *Time and Tide Wait For No Man*, London, Pandora Press, 1984, p. 136. See also for details of Six Point Group.
81 J. Wilson McLaren to M. Arncliffe Sennett, 28 November 1919, MAS, vol. 28, pp. 128–9. Reports of the Edinburgh Council elections in the *Edinburgh Evening News*, 22 October–2 November 1926. Millar's wife, Mrs Eltringham Millar, was also elected as a Labour councillor in the 1920s.
82 J. Wilson McLaren to M. Arncliffe Sennett, 28 November 1919 and 10 August 1920, N. Brown to M. Arncliffe Sennett, 11 April 1920, MAS, vol. 28, pp. 128–9, 130–1.
83 McLaren to Arncliffe Sennett, 10 August 1920, ibid., and *Edinburgh Evening News*, 2 November 1926, p. 9.
84 *Edinburgh Evening News*, 22 October 1926, p. 9.
85 McLaren to Arncliffe Sennett, 10 August 1920, MAS, vol. 28, pp. 128–9.

Appendix 1
Key events 1890–1928

1884	Third Reform Act; 59 per cent of adult men registered to vote.
1889–94	*The Workman's Times* published.
1893	Independent Labour Party formed.
1897	National Union of Women's Suffrage Societies founded.
1900	Formation of Labour Representation Committee
1903	Women's Social and Political Union founded.
1905	WSPU endorses militant tactics.
1906	Liberal Party wins the general election.
1906	Emmeline Pethick Lawrence joins the WSPU as treasurer. Frederick Pethick Lawrence also supports the militant campaign of the WSPU.
1907	Men's League for Women's Suffrage founded.
1907	Women's Freedom League founded.
1908	Anti-suffragist Herbert Asquith becomes Prime Minister.
1908	Men's League for Opposing Women's Suffrage founded.
1909	People's Suffrage Federation founded.
1910	Men's Political Union for Women's Enfranchisement founded (anti-government).
1910	All-party Conciliation Committee formed. Militant truce declared.

1910	(July) First Conciliation bill passes second reading – government intervention prevents further progress.
1910	(September) Men's League adopts an anti-government stance.
1911	(May) Second Conciliation bill passes second reading – government intervention prevents further progress.
1911	(November) WSPU resumes active militancy.
1912	Frederick Pethick Lawrence writes 'The Man's Share'.
1912	(March) Third Conciliation bill defeated at second reading.
1912	(July) Government 'Franchise and Registration' bill passed second reading (manhood suffrage bill, with promised allowances for women's suffrage amendment).
1912	Frederick and Emmeline Pethick Lawrence expelled from WSPU.
1913	(January) Government 'Franchise and Registration' bill withdrawn. Women's Suffrage amendments ruled out of order by the Speaker.
1913	(January) WFL resumes active militancy.
1913	(April) Prisoners' Temporary Discharge for Ill Health bill ('Cat and Mouse Act') passed.
1913	(July) Deputation of 'Northern Men' travels to London in attempt to meet Prime Minister. Shortly afterwards, the Northern Men's Federation for Women's Suffrage founded.
1914	United Suffragists founded.
1914	(February) NMF second deputation to Prime Minister
1914	Outbreak of First World War
1915	Formation of Coalition government
1916	(August) NMF final deputation to Prime Minister
1916–17	(October) Speaker's Conference on electoral reform meets (includes measure on women's suffrage).

1918	(February) Royal Assent given to the Representation of the People Act. Full manhood suffrage, and women over 30 enfranchised.
1918	(November) Armistice signed.
1918	(December) General Election; women over 30 vote.
1919	Sex Disqualification (Removal) Act passed.
1923	Frederick Pethick Lawrence elected as Labour MP for Leicester West.
1926	Emmeline Pethick Lawrence becomes president of the Women's Freedom League.
1928	Representation of the People Act: full, equal adult suffrage for women.

Appendix 2
Men's pro-suffrage societies 1890–1920

KNOWN MEN-ONLY OR PREDOMINANTLY MALE SOCIETIES FOR WOMEN'S SUFFRAGE

(English) Men's Committee for Justice to Women
Liberal Men's Association for Women's Suffrage
Male Electors' League for Women's Suffrage
Men's Federation for Women's Suffrage (also occasionally described as the Men's Federation for Women's Enfranchisement)
Men's International Alliance for Woman Suffrage
Men's Liberal Society for the Parliamentary Enfranchisement of Women
Men's Liberal Suffrage Society
Men's Political Union for Women's Enfranchisement (numerous local branches)
Men's Society for Women's Rights
(National) Men's League for Women's Suffrage (had numerous branches and there were also independent Men's Leagues formed, e.g Sussex Men's League, West of Scotland Men's League)
Northern Men's Federation for Women's Suffrage

MIXED SOCIETIES FOR WOMEN'S SUFFRAGE WITH RELIGIOUS AFFILIATIONS, ACTIVELY SUPPORTED BY MEN

Church League for Women's Suffrage
Free Church League for Women's Suffrage
Jewish League for Women's Suffrage
Scottish Churches' League for Women's Suffrage

KEY SOCIETIES WITH KNOWN MALE INVOLVEMENT

Conservative and Unionist Women's Franchise Association

Cymric Suffrage Union / Forward Cymric Suffrage Union

Irish Women's Suffrage and Local Government Association

London Graduates' Union for Women's Suffrage

London Society for Women's Suffrage

National Political League for Men and Women

National Union of Women's Suffrage Societies (umbrella organization with numerous local suffrage societies)

New Constitutional Society for Women's Suffrage

People's Suffrage Federation (Adult Suffrage)

Spiritual Militancy League

Suffrage Service League

Union of Ethical Societies

United Suffragists

Women's Emancipation Union

Women's Franchise League (begun in 1889)

Women's Freedom League (numerous local branches; men could not be members before 1918)

Women's Social and Political Union (numerous local branches; strictly female membership)

Women's Tax Resistance League

Index